The Zeta Message

CONNECTING ALL BEINGS IN ONENESS

by
Judy Carroll
and
Helene Kaye

Wild Flower Press
P.O. Box 1429
Columbus, NC 28722

Library of Congress Cataloging-in-Publication Data

Carroll, Judy, 1952-
The Zeta message : connecting all beings in oneness / by Judy Carroll and Helene Kaye.
p. cm. -- (The Zeta series ; v. 2)
Includes bibliographical references.
ISBN 978-0-926524-70-5
1. Human-alien encounters. 2. Grays (Extraterrestrial beings) 3. Carroll, Judy, 1952- 4. Kaye, Helene, 1960- I. Kaye, Helene, 1960- II. Title.
BF2055.G73C37 2010
001.942--dc22
2010030154

Cover Photograph: Brett Parrott
Manuscript Editors: Brian L. Crissey and Pamela Meyer
Cover & Interior Design: Pamela Meyer

Printed in the United States of America
Address all Inquiries
Wild Flower Press
P.O. Box 1429
Columbus, NC 28722

Info@granitepublishing.com

Dedication

We dedicate this book to our Zeta family
– our beloved Guides and Teachers –
for your Lessons, Love and Light,
as well as your endless
Patience, Compassion and Encouragement.

Thank you for helping us to learn and to grow,
which in turn is enabling us to help our fellow humans.
Love does indeed conquer all!

ACKNOWLEDGEMENTS

First and foremost we acknowledge Helene's family – her husband Gary for his endless patience, support, love and understanding through some very challenging times, and their two children, Kira and Ben, for the amazing contacts, teaching and messages they have been instrumental in bringing through for the betterment of all.

We would also acknowledge Dr. Janet Colli, Ph.D., a clinical psychologist based in Washington, D.C., and an associate of the late and highly respected psychiatrist, Dr. John Mack, M.D., and author of *Sacred Encounters*. Our heartfelt thanks go to Dr. Colli for her support, advice and understanding, and most especially for her belief in and acknowledgement of the reality of ET contact, and the fact that it is not something to be feared, but rather an important and significant step in our evolution as human beings.

Dr. Colli's research as a professional in the field of human consciousness fully confirms the understanding we have come to from many years of ongoing and at times fully conscious contact with our Zeta friends. This contact is *all* to do with expansion of consciousness, which is exactly what evolution in the Human Kingdom is all about.

TABLE OF CONTENTS

FOREWORD

Janet Elizabeth Colli, Ph.D.

Interspecies communication is alive and ongoing on Earth, especially in the land down under. Just beneath the crust of consciousness, its ingredients — a homegrown mixture of communication between humans and so-called aliens — are being chemically and energetically changed, like leavened dough. This interspecies communication is at last breaking through to the surface through the daily activities of young Kira and her brother Ben's night terrors. Kira's off-planet workplace is the Mothership, known affectionately as the "Workshop." Her devoted companion and spiritual guide is Oris, one of those beings commonly called Greys, or Zetas. His black cloak is set off by a wide-brimmed Cordobes-style hat trimmed with ribbons, whose various colors denote his teaching specialties. Kira writes in verse,

I board the Ship
As I do every night,
To help the people in their plight.

Interspecies communication is difficult to verify. Substantiating interspecies communication is an enterprise in which we all engage with much trepidation. No one wants to be fooled or branded a "true believer" — in short, to be overwhelmed by the desire to believe. Nor do the principals in this story want to be labeled "cranks."

But what makes *The Zeta Message* such a special story is that its authors have undertaken a practical, empirical approach to verify their claims. As such, this book and its docudrama companion volume *Human by Day, Zeta by Night,* are superb examples of the deeply human quest to reach outside of our limited sensory perception to fathom what lies beyond. To read these remarkable books is a unique opportunity to see ourselves, as if for the first time, through the objective eyes of wise, non-human life forms.

Judy Carroll advises common-sense caution because the teachings Oris gave to Kira have been interpreted and filtered through a teenage mind, which is a minefield in the best of situations. Judy is savvy about the "screen memories" that human minds create so as to interpret, simplify, or fill in missing details. She asks that we take Kira's strange and rather fantastic story with a grain of salt. Her cautiousness stands us in good stead to continue reading with an open — yet not gullible — mind. As a clinician of the mind, I trust her call for caution.

But why believe that young Kira imparts anything from a non-human, intelligent species? Judy admits that "the Zetas are not the easiest folk to communicate with.... You have to be on the correct brain wavelength." What does that really mean to a psychotherapist like me? Yet when we read the parallel life stories of Judy and Kira's mother Helene, we feel their honesty and want to follow them down the rabbit hole, to more fully explore this alternate reality. Judy and Helene report decades of burgeoning contact experiences. Their meticulously documented life stories include Judy's first memories of how the Greys began to make themselves known to her, weaving in and out of her explorations and past-life recollections. Her pioneering path is quite tangible, and we easily follow her trail as she describes how she honed her awareness and her skill at interpreting their "very profound telepathically communicated imagery." We are privy to her internal process as she analyzes, scrutinizes and evaluates. In short, it is the authors' ability to meta-communicate, to write clearly about their inner processes, which gives a degree of validity to Judy's claim that "I was 30 years old when the Zeta family [finally, in full consciousness] contacted me." By that time, we are savoring her contact, too.

It is said that psychotics differ from mystics in that the latter know not to talk to psychiatrists about their visionary experiences. Judy has the power of discrimination, good judgment and exquisite sensitivity needed to avoid upsetting others. She secures our trust when she fully admits the workings of her "limited human brain," as she describes how she processes and filters through words the Greys' imagery.

It is only natural that claims of interspecies communication undergo a verification process. Does it matter that Judy's "clear recall of carrying out work alongside, and as one of" the Zetas — is corroborated by Helene and others? Absolutely. The authors document just such corroboration. A third party verifies that Judy appeared in her Grey form in her bedroom in the middle of the night, and her own level-headed husband reports receiving "the shock of his life" when on several occasions he also saw a different, "strange-looking" face superimposed over Judy's features. The plot thickens. Teenage Kira now becomes part of the verification process, as her information and recall is checked and balanced against Judy's and Helene's. Is it significant that Kira backs up Judy's "half-buried but still partly conscious memories" of carrying out procedures on humans on board the disc, or that obscure details regarding who was on board the craft tally exactly with Judy's memory? Absolutely. And what about "the excellent proof" that Oris is around them all the time, virtually a family member?

Well, Helene first found Judy through a mutually known Reiki instructor, and eventually this family of humans ingeniously devised a system of multi-level, sensory channels of communication to verify their interspecies communication with their family of Greys. It is an interesting experiment, indeed, to which Oris himself, directed them. With Kira using her clairvoyant sight to guide them, while listening to Oris, she conveyed his words to Helene, who, apart from one stunning event, could not hear him herself. Helene has to work through feeling (clairsentience); Kira through seeing (clairvoyance), while Judy works through hearing (clairaudience). Helene tested her clairsentient ability by having Oris touch particular parts of her body — the top of her head or her right shoulder — then seeking Kira's confirmation through her clairvoyant ability. Did Kira "see" Oris with one hand on her head and the other on her shoulder? Read on. For such experiments are repeated more than once.

The Zeta Message documents an impressive display of cooperation among humans to verify their interactions with non-human beings, who act primarily within an immaterial, other-dimensional realm.

Interspecies communication, as anyone acquainted with the research within ufology knows, is no mere walk-in-the-park. The fear engendered by the physical body upon the approach of an ET often shatters the ego — whether from the sudden collapse of our collective belief system ("We are alone in the universe."), or from encountering the wholly unfamiliar energy field of a very different kind of being. I liken our panic to the response of a wild animal encountering a human in the woods (here, humans are the "wild ones," with untamed limbic systems). Instinctively, we are wildly fearful until our limbic response is tamed and mediated by our higher-order, frontal cortex.

Such fear is not unknown to Judy, who refers to it as "a seemingly unavoidable reflex response that gradually dissipates with understanding." She likens it to the shamanic "dark night of the soul" (while Oris is said to agree). Again, Judy sparks trust (even if Oris as yet may not). Yet Judy claims to have dealt with her fear. If that is true, then we all stand to learn a lot from her, for we may all stand on the threshold of an era of conscious interaction.

"I was 48 when Helene's family first contacted me," writes Judy, "so I had a lifetime of contact experiences behind me, including a number of clearly remembered and positively uplifting ones to fall back on, along with a deep familiarity with the Zetas and their way of working.... What I had to fall back on was... that in all my contacts with the Zetas, I'd never been hurt, and I felt comfortable with them. To me they were family and had been for years."

Reading this book, we follow Judy's facilitation of Helene's family, who had no such conscious recall of their own connection with the Greys. *The Zeta Message* may well serve as a how-to guidebook on dissipating or transforming the fear that often arises upon encountering so-called aliens. While Judy fully believes that the Greys' influence on her — through their guidance and teachings — was overwhelmingly positive, Helene's family knows absolutely nothing about ETs. Yet ultimately, the extreme terror and confusion experienced by Helene's family is effectively transformed. How this transpires makes for a riveting tale.

Enter seven-year-old Ben, Helene's son. For anyone who has dealt with "night terrors," a sleep disorder entailing dissociative states of extreme fear, or sleepwalking — *The Zeta Message* is essential reading. Whether or not other-dimensional realms are at the root, Helene's support for Ben forged a conscious link to her son's reality, and created a shared three-dimensional reality. As we extend our limited conscious awareness, Helene's careful work with her son models how to rely on our senses, in this case, proprioception or touch, to cautiously proceed to multi-dimensional awareness. Such a process is what any of us face when we extend our limited awareness to encompass the beyond — whether near-death experience (NDE), out-of-body experience (OBE), or after-death communication

(ADC). Ultimately, Helene effects a radical change in her son's sleep disorder. In an era when psychiatrists rush to treat sleep disorders with psychotropic drugs, and trance states are seen as evidence of pathology, I shudder to think how Ben might have been treated by unsympathetic professionals who cannot step outside their box of readily diagnosable maladies to entertain the possibility that a non-ordinary state is evidence of a larger reality knocking on their door.

But the person who demonstrated the most radical change was Judy, who readily shifts between her soul-identity as a Grey and her body-oriented, Earthling consciousness—which do not, she tells us, always coincide. Surprisingly, "the fleeting sensation of fear" that she experiences as Judy-the-human shifts as well when she dons her Zeta identity. But with customary candor, she shares with us her very real confusion over her dueling identities. "At times I feel totally Zeta; at other times very Earth human, so where do I fit in, and what am I really?" she writes.

Indeed, according to Judy and Helene, most ufology investigators and researchers perceive only the tip of the iceberg, from which it is nearly impossible to reach meaningful understanding of the new multidimensional reality. According to Judy and Helene, all will have to radically expand our perceptions of reality. We all will have to thoroughly shift our paradigms. Otherwise, we cannot begin to understand these two Aussie women as they delineate everything from the Great Chain of Being and the vibrational placement of Zetas and angels relative to humans, to the past-life personalities or "karmic baggage" of their "upstairs" helpers. It is a tall order.

Ultimately, overcoming the fear and egotism that separates one human from another appears to be the key to interspecies communication and humanity's spiritual growth. At least we are told as much by Oris. No matter if you believe Oris to be merely an aspect of Judy's personality, or a fully fledged, objectively real ET, her story goes a long way towards helping us all feel "perfectly comfortable and familiar in his presence." No matter Oris's true identity, the wisdom of his words is self-evident:

> It is only when fear and egotism are overcome that real spiritual progress can be made, and the only way to overcome fear and egotism (which is simply a facet of fear) is to face it head-on. People need to be pushed out of and beyond their

"comfort-zones" if they are to achieve real growth and evolution on the soul level.

Did Oris really wander off into the lounge room to sit with Kira to watch the soccer playoffs on TV? The very prospect turns ufology on its head. After all, writes our guileless guide, Judy, "Who really cares about 'lights in the sky' when you have Zetas visiting your home on a regular basis!"

INTRODUCTION

In the skeptical and highly controversial field of serious research into contact between humans of Earth and other extraterrestrial and/or interdimensional beings, people want facts. They want to hear real accounts of experiences that have happened to real people. As a participator in ET contact since early childhood, I've been given the opportunity to speak out about my ongoing experiences at several conferences and groups and in the process have come to the realization that there is a real need at this time for ones like myself to come forward openly and speak out — not from a place of fear but rather from understanding. People long for the opportunity to meet, speak with, question and be reassured by somebody who has had first-hand experience of otherworldly contact.

Many folks I've spoken to have their own fascinating stories to tell — stories they've been able to validate by talking with me and reading my books. By connecting in this way, they have experienced a deep sense of relief because they too have heard similar messages from and had contact with similar beings to those I write and speak about in such familiar terms. As I found out myself when I first began to inquire and read up on the subject of ET/human contact, there is just *so much* fear, speculation and misunderstanding out there, and not near enough love.

A common complaint from researchers and experiencers alike has been that the ETs, particularly those known down here as "Greys" or "Zeta Reticulans," will not communicate. There's been a huge amount of anger and fear expressed over this issue, with a number of people believing that these beings are cruel, evil and even demonic abductors of innocent human victims. Then there are those who insist that the so-called Greys are simply an emotionless "army" of robots in the employ of an "evil alien group out to conquer Earth." Again and again the accusation of a refusal to communicate, and of having no real understanding of human emotion and fear has been aimed at the Zetas.

This, I can assure you, is not the case, and in fact is the very reason why these books have been written. More about that shortly.

The Zeta Message is a detailed account of my own human life-journey and subsequent awakening to Zeta consciousness, as well as that of a family I assisted through a series of amazing and at times fully conscious ET contact experiences. The family's awakening process happened very suddenly and quite spontaneously after their attunement to Reiki, whereas mine has taken place through a series of gradual upgrades of my human consciousness to a higher "megabyte capacity" of Zeta awareness over a lifetime, thus enabling downloading of the relevant information.

The understanding that people on Earth now have of computer technology makes this process so much easier to explain. My first upgrade took place at the end of 1967, which was 15 years after my birth at the very end of 1952. It began taking effect immediately with conscious recall of a past life lived in Spain in the early 1800s. The reason for this recall was to heal and release major karmic issues from that life that had been brought through to the present.

The second upgrade occurred in 1983, and was followed by a number of years of intense study to fully ground the Zeta knowledge and understanding of energy into my Earth human consciousness so that it could then be passed on to others through avenues such as Tai Chi and Reiki, which I was instructed to teach.

The third upgrade in June 1995 included detailed instructions on the writing of these books for the purpose of relaying information on ET/human contact from the Zeta perspective — to present *their* side of the story, but also my side as a life-long experiencer/participator, and my subsequent journey of awakening.

By 2000, with the "zero hour" of 2012 fast approaching, quicker downloading of information was required. This necessitated the awakening of others to help out, thus contact was made with this family via a mutual friend. The family's mother is my co-author.

One of the first Zeta memories that began coming to the surface after the 1995 upgrade was of my death as a result of the crash of one of our discs. Part of this memory included a close friend/co-worker who died along with me. The relationship we shared was what could be described in Earth human terms as a twin soul. In other words, we were the same soul essence manifesting through two physical bodies or "containers," to use the Zeta term. From the very first moment I spoke with Helene on the phone in June 2000, I recognized her as being this co-worker. The recognition was not physical but rather at soul level. When her awakening process took place sometime later, it turned out that she too had felt this instant sense of recognition.

After our "physical death" and subsequent return to the Zeta soul group, a discussion followed that resulted in a mutual decision to return here in Earth human containers to continue our work of awakening others. The timing and circumstances of this return were all carefully planned beforehand. Once the two of us made that first contact by phone down here, fully conscious contact was then able to be re-established with three Elder teachers to whom we are also intrinsically linked on the soul level. Hopefully by reading our story you will come to understand that the Zetas do understand — what it is to be human, what it is to experience fear, pain and emotion, and most of all, that they also understand and experience love, which truly is the driving force, not just on Planet Earth, but of *every* sentient being in the whole universe.

I would like to begin by introducing my dear friend and co-worker Helene Kaye, to say a few words of introduction:

Hello, my name is Helene, and I was introduced to Judy at the turn of the new millennium when my whole family started to experience weird and strange happenings in our home. These happenings were so weird in fact that we really didn't know who to turn to for help and advice. We knew very well that other people — doctors, psychologists, etc. — would at best think we had great imaginations, and at worst think that we were all crazy and in need of psychiatric care if we'd tried to approach them with our experiences of mysterious flashing lights, terrified children who were "seeing people" in their bedrooms, scary dreams, strange noises, etc. My husband Gary and I kept hoping that it would all eventually stop and go away, but it never did — it just kept getting worse.

My only reason for allowing our personal information to be put forward and made public in this book is to help other experiencers of ET visitation. Even to this day many of our friends and family have no idea of what we went through, and I'm sure there are many others out there who can relate to that. My family's names have been changed to protect their privacy, but they have all given Judy and me permission to speak out on their behalf.

Without Judy's help, knowledge and love, God only knows where we all would have ended up. With this in mind, as well as with a deep sense of compassion and understanding towards others in such a position, came my decision to reach out to those out there who are going through similar experiences, to help them to move forward from a place of fear, and into the arms of love and Oneness.

1
Family in Crisis

June 2000.

It was a cool, sunny afternoon when the phone rang: "Hi, Judy?" the slightly nervous-sounding voice responded down the line. "I'm Helene. Did Ian contact you about our problem? Can we please talk? I just don't know what the heck is going on here, and he said you might be able to help us. He told me you've had similar stuff happening around you for ages, and that there's nothing to be scared of, but it's all so weird. Please help me to understand what is going on in our house." She then proceeded to give me a harrowing but very familiar account of the strange and disturbing "activity" that was taking place in their normally quiet and peaceful suburban family home. I'd been expecting this call since the day before, when my close friend and Reiki teacher, Ian, had phoned for assistance on a rather worrying matter that had arisen in connection with the family of one of his students — the woman with whom I was now speaking.

Helene had learned level-one Reiki with Ian in 1996, in order to help her two children with their asthma. It had proven very successful and enjoyable for the whole family, and after she went on to do level two at the end of 1999, Gary, her 12-year-old daughter Kira, and her 7-year-old son Ben decided that they too would like to learn. It was a week or so after the family's attunements were carried out in early June 2000 that the disturbing "activity" in their home began.

As Ian explained to me over the phone, the first hint of what lay ahead for the family started with young Ben waking one night screaming in terror. When his mom went in to him, he was almost hysterical, tearfully describing a man whom he had seen standing in the corner of his bedroom. The man was dressed all in black, with a long cape over his shoulders and a broad-brimmed hat pulled down low over his face. Other activity then followed in the form of strange "beeping" noises being heard, lights flashing through the kitchen skylight at night, and a large dog suddenly appearing in the lounge room then going through to Ben's room, where it mysteriously disappeared. No doors or windows were open at the time, and the family's own dog, a large black Labrador, was locked outside. Other human-like figures had also been seen around the house.

Helene and Gary knew that Ben's experience with the mysterious "Man in Black"* was more than a simple night terror or vivid imagination, for Gary himself almost walked into a similar figure in the hallway when he went to calm his son's terrified screams late one night. The activity surrounding the family then stepped up to another level of concern when young Ben began experiencing strange "trance-states" in which he was almost completely oblivious to everything going on around him, including his mother's reassuring voice. During these states he became totally caught up in a world of fear.

Ian assured me over the phone that the whole family was very well grounded — ordinary, average folk not at all into dabbling in anything remotely occult or even slightly New Age beyond using Reiki to relieve Ben's asthma. Ian had tried to assist the family by visiting their home to carry out a Reiki cleanse. We've both done this on occasions, as Reiki is a wonderful tool for neutralizing negative energy. It's a totally positive and loving energy that cannot be used in a harmful way, and we both knew that it would be impossible for the Reiki itself to have caused anything negative to be drawn into the home.

The Reiki cleanse didn't work. In fact, after it was carried out, the "activity" increased, and to add to the situation, Ian was due to leave on an overseas holiday the very next day, hence his desperate phone call to me for help. He was puzzled and concerned, because Reiki had always worked in the past to clear away negative energies in the form of ghosts, poltergeists, etc. As he said to me: "What in the name of heaven is going on? *Why* hasn't the Reiki helped? This has never *ever* happened before, and I just don't know what to do!"

---

*The "Men in Black" who menace people that have undergone encounter experiences are an Earth human-created caricature of the Zeta Teachers. They are specifically designed to cause fear and distrust of the real Zeta Teachers who also dress in black, as do priests and nuns. The difference is in the energy field surrounding them. The real Zeta Teachers have loving, gentle energy; the "Men in Black" do not.

But his description of the black-clad figure, the mysterious dog and other happenings in the family home were ringing loud and clear bells with me, and I guessed the reason: Reiki wasn't getting rid of the disturbances and in fact was serving to draw them in more strongly since Reiki shifted the energy to a higher place, making the ETs more comfortable.

The "Man in Black" also seemed very familiar to me. I even thought I knew his name, and I did know that he *loved* Reiki. On a deeper level of consciousness I'd also been expecting this contact since Christmas 1998, when a psychic friend made a prediction that in June an even closer relationship was going to be established with my ET friends. I'd also been told that my contact dealt with the "spiritual" side of things, and another person would be brought in to access the "physical" aspect. If my guess was correct, then this black-clad being was the same one responsible for initiating my own journey of spiritual growth and transformation, which began in 1983 with what is commonly known as an "ET encounter experience."

This highly significant and life-changing contact in 1983, in which two perfectly solid, three-dimensional Zeta beings appeared beside me in full daylight on an otherwise completely normal Sunday afternoon, was the culmination of a lifetime of ongoing ET contact. It's only now, looking back through a more expanded conscious awareness, that I'm able to fully comprehend and appreciate the vast amount of preparation that led up to this momentous event and to subsequent happenings that have taken place since.

My story begins with an early, first-remembered episode somewhere around the age of three — an episode which, 50 some years later, is still quite clear in my mind. It took place in and around our very ordinary suburban home in South East Queensland, Australia, where I lived with my parents, older brother and grandmother. I must guess the specific time frame of such an early encounter, but it helps to remember that the Zetas give great significance to the number three, as it represents Creation and Balance, and multiples of three are also important. Experiencers of contact with them often hear three, six or nine knocks as a prelude to a contact experience, and many of my remembered contacts have taken place on such dates and at such ages. Even in our human realm, many people believe things happen in threes.

My memory is of being taken by the hand of a tall, very thin female person with whom I felt deep familiarity. This woman took me to a railway station somewhere up near the top end of our street, where we boarded a train. It was a pleasant and exciting experience, and I can still recall what it felt like to my child's mind — the excitement, wonder and anticipation of the journey to come. The woman, whom I thought of as a "grandmother figure," held my hand tightly and protectively, just as an adult would with any three-year-old.

So familiar and at ease was I with her that afterwards, recalling the adventure, I thought it was my real-life grandmother who'd taken me. She was living with us at the time, and on several occasions I asked her about our trip on the train. Of course she had no idea of what I was talking about, and when I insisted with all the stubbornness of a three-year-old that: "Yes, Nana, we *did*! We walked up the street to the station. *Please* take me again — it was *fun*!" The fact was pointed out to me repeatedly that there *was* no station at the top end of our street. The nearest railway station was miles away, too far for poor old Nana to have walked, and therefore it must have been only a *dream*.

But even at that age I knew that it was different. I knew what dreams were like, and this was not one. It was a strange sensation, being so sure there was a station at the top of our street but then eventually coming to realize that there wasn't. Every time I thought about it my mind seemed to split in two. Even now this memory is still clear to me, along with the knowledge that I was taken somewhere wonderful and magical. I now understand that it took place in an altered state of consciousness, as most (but not all) ET contact experiences do. In many cases it's only the astral (spirit) form that is taken, leaving the physical body or "container" as the Zetas call it, safely tucked up in bed.

This is the reason why some people undergoing an encounter experience mistakenly believe that their soul is being taken and so become very fearful. They're aware of an "essence" being drawn out of their body, which in fact is only their astral form. This astral aspect of our being leaves the physical body every night during our sleep state, which is a perfectly normal occurrence and nothing to be afraid of. I assume that this is what happened in my case, although the fact that I woke upside down in my cot and totally disoriented a number of times may indicate otherwise. On these occasions the whole household was awakened by my terrified screams.

As well as not knowing whether I was taken physically or astrally, the other aspect of this incident I'm not sure of is the exact location. The street in which we lived was a cul-de-sac, with homes occupying every block, whereas around the corner and a little further on was a vacant block of land and fewer houses. If the "railway station" and "train" was really a disc, which I assume it was, this other location would have been a more suitable landing site. To reach this place we would certainly have headed up our street towards the dead-end, but then turned right into a side street and then left into another street. As is very typical with this sort of partial recall, I clearly remember some section while others are a complete blank.

The Zetas often use this partial memory block and screen-memory technique (and sometimes we do it to ourselves) to assist us in dealing with the potential shock of such an incident and to make it seem more normal and closer to our limited understanding of what we perceive reality to be. In those days my child's mind could accept being taken by a familiar grandmother figure to board a train much more easily than it could have accepted being taken by an ET to board a disc.

The fact that I had so much underlying fear as a child tells me that this was not an isolated incident but rather a regular happening, and that probably the screen memory was only put in place that one time when I retained a partial conscious memory of being taken. Perhaps on other occasions where there was no conscious recall of events, a part of my child's mind experienced subconscious fear as a result. I now understand that this fear was simply a reflex response from the human part of my psyche, which had forgotten what was really going on. It gradually dissipated as I matured and came to understand things more clearly and consciously, but unfortunately for some experiencers of ET contact this deeper understanding doesn't seem to happen, and so the fear is carried through to adulthood.

On the surface my childhood world seemed happy and secure, with loving parents and an older brother who always looked out for me, but deep disquiet lurked not far beneath. The difficulty was that this sense of disquiet and unease was intangible, not something that could be seen openly and explained in physical terms like family problems or financial insecurity. My home life was happy and loving, and although financial troubles did arise from a failed family business venture when I was 10, my parents coped with it and never allowed our family closeness or my childhood security to suffer. However, every night as darkness descended, so did my sense of fear and dread.

This even carried over into my waking hours up to a point, with inexplicable feelings of anxiety and depression sometimes coming over me. I hated school, which didn't help matters, and I had awful trouble fitting in. I felt "different" somehow, and it was as if on some deeper level my classmates sensed this, and treated me accordingly. I sometimes wondered if they were picking up on my nighttime fears, but how could they? I kept them very much to myself and never spoke of them at school.

Many children fear the dark, but for me it went beyond that, to a point I couldn't begin to explain to anyone, not even myself; and this intangible terror continued right through into my early teens. I thank God to this day that my parents were patient and understanding, and that my mother was willing to stay beside me every night until I fell asleep. This went on, I'm embarrassed to say, right up until I was 10 or 11, when it reached a point where I forced myself to go to bed on my own, but still with an open door between the bedroom and the lounge room where my parents sat watching TV.

I carried a sense of shame about this until just a few years ago when information began to emerge on the subject of ET contact and the so-called Star Children and Star Seeds — children and adults who carry a certain amount of ET genetics in their makeup and have ongoing contact with their ET family right from the time of their birth. This contact can potentially involve quite a lot of fear until deeper understanding emerges.

As these people were described, with some of them speaking out about their strangely inexplicable fears, phobias and abilities, things finally began to fall into place. For those like me whose contact has been with the Zetas (the ones with large heads, huge dark eyes and very thin bodies) the fear is often of eyes, puppets, dolls and clowns. This is because some of the Zetas, who have evolved past the need for physical biological bodies, instead use partially artificial ones when they need to interact in our physical world. This gives them a rather doll or puppet-like appearance and way of moving. It was the subconscious memory of these bodies that triggered my childhood terrors.

My fear of eyes forced my mother to go so far as to black out a picture in one of my storybooks of a cat hiding in a bush with only its eyes showing. I was terrified of this illustration, and would not look at that page. The lighted windows of houses at night also caused a sense of disquiet within me. I referred to them as "window eyes." A picture in another book, of a puppet with stick-thin, jointed limbs also had to be blacked out, and even now, I still dislike clowns intensely. Funnily enough, my fear of eyes turned into a fascination with them in my early teens. I used to draw them all over my exercise books at high school, and they were always the almond-shaped eyes of the Zetas.

The childhood fear that affected me most deeply was of someone, or some*thing* coming into the house at night and attacking me or taking me away. In an attempt to calm this fear, my parents ended up placing my bed in the big sleep-out where my brother had his, and right outside the open door of their bedroom. In this way I was virtually surrounded by family and should have felt very safe and secure, but no, there was still a large, dark veranda behind me, and a hallway of shadows in which I could always sense presences.

And so the fear continued unabated, with many mornings finding me sleeping in bed with my long-suffering parents — the only place where I felt safe. This sense of fear was inexplicable at the time, because apart from a couple of consciously remembered experiences, and only one of these that happened later on in my teens was actually frightening, I had no definite recall of anything out of the ordinary.

Like many who've had ongoing encounters with the Zetas, owls have featured in my life on two occasions that I can consciously recall. My first owl encounter occurred one night when my parents left me alone in the house (asleep in bed) to go outside in order to investigate a strange sound in the garden. The next morning my mother described it to me as sounding like a Morse code signal. After an extensive search of the grounds they eventually traced the sound to a huge owl perched on the roof of our house.

When told about it the following morning, I was uneasy that my parents had been lured outside, leaving me alone and vulnerable inside the house. The mere thought of this owl perched up above me on the roof with its huge eyes gleaming in the dark filled me with unspeakable dread.

My second owl encounter occurred many years later when I was married and living in the country. This encounter involved being "haunted" by an owl for three days. Every time I stepped outside the house to attend to the horses or dogs, this owl was sitting on the nearest fence staring at me intently. Nothing frightened it away, not even our three Labradors and cat playing boisterously around the yard, and I went so far as to wonder if it were someone's pet, although that would not have been likely. A very distinct feeling of wanting to connect with me emanated from it — a need to communicate — and I felt that if I'd sat quietly on the lawn it would have come to me, but being scared of birds, I wasn't game to try, just in case.

On the third day of its visit, I sat under the house to read. Ours was a high-set "Queensland-style" home built up on stumps but completely enclosed underneath so the pets could be locked up securely at night and the horses couldn't get in to help themselves to the hay and grain that was stored there. The only way in was through two narrow doorways, but this was not going to stop an owl on a mission. As I sat reading my book, it flew straight in through the side doorway and perched boldly on a rafter directly above my head.

Brave soul that I am, I ran for my life out the other doorway, book held open over my head for protection, to take up a position where both doorways could be seen so I'd know when the owl flew out — but it didn't. Eventually I summoned the courage to go back in to look for it, but it had disappeared, never to be seen again.

It wasn't until I thought about this incident later that it occurred to me what extraordinary behavior it was for a wild bird to act in this way, and for an owl to even be out and about sitting on fences in broad daylight. Then I questioned whether or not it really was an owl or maybe some other type of bird of prey, but what other large bird would fly in through a narrow doorway to perch itself on a rafter above somebody's head? The whole incident just didn't add up, which is very typical of many such ET encounter experiences.

Along with these (then) inexplicable fears that haunted my life, several past-life memories impinged upon my consciousness as well, making life rather disturbing to say the least. Like my first contact experience, the first one of these began making its presence felt at around age three, with a close identification with Russia. At an age when I was still grappling with the concept of "overseas," foreign countries and other cultures, I suddenly developed a strange fascination with Russia and its people. As far as I know there are no Russian links in my family, so this couldn't be explained in physical genetic terms.

This past-life link was eventually confirmed during the eight years I took part in a weekly meditation/psychic development group in which past-life recall was considered perfectly legitimate and part and parcel of our training. In fact I needed to do quite a lot of healing work on this past Russian life, which was that of a Gypsy who died in a concentration camp not very long before my present-life birth. Once this life came through to a conscious level where it could be more easily dealt with, worked through and let go of, a huge burden was lifted from my psyche. Other past lives have also impacted strongly upon the present — one lived in Japan that began surfacing at nine, and another in Spain that started coming through when I was 15.

Behind the façade of these partially remembered human lives, a parallel Zeta life has also flowed, often mirroring experiences that were taking place down here, as if the soul needed to view events from both perspectives in order to understand the bigger picture.

2
Childhood Earth Life

Although many younger folk are now starting to awaken to deeper awareness at an earlier age, it usually isn't until you reach middle or old age that you're able to look back over your life and see a pattern, a grand plan as it were. As with many situations, when you're right in the middle of it and caught up in day-to-day living, even though certain happenings and coincidences will stop you in your tracks with a loudly exclaimed "Wow, isn't that just *amazing*!" you still usually aren't consciously aware of aid, guidance and even quite active intervention from behind the scenes.

When we do notice it, some of us think of this assistance and guidance coming directly from God, while others think in terms of guardian angels, saints, our own higher self, Spirit Guides, deceased ancestors and perhaps even ETs. My personal belief is that it's all of the above, with Source (God) energy as the common denominator manifesting into our lives on the Earth plane through whatever channel fits our personal belief system or our needs at the time.

After 50 years or more of ongoing contact with what I like to refer to as "upstairs" or "the family," the one thing I've been told over and over again is that love is the creative and nurturing energy force behind everything in our universe. It permeates all of Creation, not just Planet Earth but *everywhere*, and could be thought of as a cosmic "super-glue" that binds us all together in Oneness — angels, spirits, ETs and Earthlings — no matter which culture, planet or dimensional frequency band we happen to be inhabiting in any particular lifespan. This is what is meant by *the greater reality*.

The household in which I grew up was not particularly religious, but a lot of my childhood revolved around churches and religion. My brother sang in a choir and served on the altar at church for a number of years, and I attended a convent school run by the Sisters of Mercy up until I was 12, when I left primary school for our local state high school. In this way religion did play a major role in my upbringing despite the fact that our parents were not regular churchgoers, except to ferry us back and forth to our various activities.

People tend to confuse religion and spirituality, believing that they're the same thing, but they're not. Religion deals with belief,

whereas spirituality is more a state of consciousness. The two may go hand in hand but not necessarily, and this understanding describes my parents very succinctly. They were highly spiritual but not particularly religious.

Between the combined effects of ET contact experiences and quite profound past-life recall throughout my childhood, I sincerely thank the "Powers That Be" that my every-day home life was happy, secure and serene with a close, loving family. With only one of my parents born in Australia, I didn't have the extended family contact that many of my peer group enjoyed, except for a grandmother who lived with us until she passed away when I was five.

My mother's family had migrated to Australia in the 1800s from a small country in Europe that no longer exists. She was an only child, her younger brother having died of peritonitis at an early age, but her mother, the Nana I knew, was of a traditionally large middle-European family. There were several second cousins around somewhere that I never met but who sounded rather madcap and fun, and I do wonder if perhaps it was the drop or three of Romany (Gypsy) blood in the family that was responsible for their somewhat "different" and colorful approach to life. This of course would have been kept very quiet in those days. In an old wedding photo I have of them, their cultural roots are quite evident in their unusually dark coloring and black, flashing eyes.

My mom loved dancing more than anything else in life, and I believe in her youth she was very good at it. She was particularly fond of Latin American styles — tango, rumba, etc., which would have suited her fiery temperament and dark good looks. Right up until the time of her death she adored brightly colored clothes and lots of jewelry.

My father's side of the family was an interesting mixture of English, Creole (Spanish/South American), and French. His grandmother was a flamenco dancer of Spanish Gypsy descent living in Chile prior to her marriage to an Englishman. This thumbnail sketch of my family background illustrates how we select our family before we are born, for better or for worse. As a human/ET down here with a future job to do, growing up in such a family environment nurtured and encouraged my natural-born inclination to explore spiritual matters from a deeper and more open perspective. The last thing I needed would have been a family atmosphere of repressive and rigid dogma.

As I now understand, everything was carefully planned beforehand so that as I matured into adulthood, the diverse cultural background of this family began to resonate with a natural trait born out of the astrological makeup specifically chosen before birth. This resulted in a fascination with and a reaching out to other cultures, along with an urge to unite people in Oneness through deeper understanding and mutual respect. This inner urge towards bringing people together started out initially on an international level, but eventually progressed to interplanetary.

Up until the age of 12 I'd been perfectly happy and satisfied with what the nuns at school taught us, along with the concept of God as a larger-than-life bearded male figure emerging from a thundercloud. It wasn't until my early teens that burning questions began arising in my now-maturing mind, such as: How could God possibly be like that? What is He really? Where is He? My young mind pondered deeply upon the fact that millions of people worldwide believe in the existence of this "God," including mature and well-educated ones, and the staggeringly huge organization that comprises the Church is built on and totally dependent upon this concept and assumed reality and existence of "God," so there had to be something to it — surely — but what was God, really?

On top of this there were other puzzles, other unanswered questions in my mind — the presences that I was aware of around me, the strangely clear memories of other existences that at times almost overwhelmed me. Were there such things as ghosts? Had I lived somewhere before? What happens when we die? And what about the deep connection I felt with nature? The messages I picked up from trees, flowers and animals and the strange "something" I could discern in the very atmosphere itself when I lay back relaxed and with my eyes half-closed on a clear, sunny day? Overriding all of this was a longing, a yearning, and a sense of "homesickness" for the stars. To go out into the garden at night and look up to the stars stirred feelings in me beyond words. Why did this always make me feel like crying?

No one else around me seemed to be affected in this way, or even to contemplate asking these myriad questions. And what was this overwhelming sense of "mission" that had been with me since quite early childhood? I knew I was here to *do* something — but what was it? As long as I live I'll never forget the inexplicable and totally conflicting emotions that filled my heart and mind on the

occasion of the Russian satellite "Sputnik" passing overhead. Of course we all trooped outside to see and marvel at it, but this tiny pinpoint of light traversing the night sky made me want to cry. It also stirred fear, yearning, loneliness — and a sense of love way beyond anything that I could physically express.

By age 12 I was ready to start high school and was really feeling dissatisfied with what was being taught by the nuns about God and religion. I was questioning the rigid dogmas of the traditional Church, and what especially put me off was the belief force-fed to us by the nuns on a regular basis that one *must* be Catholic in order to be accepted into heaven.

My parents rarely attended church, and didn't even seem to follow any particular religion, but within our family unit the Golden Rule, "Do unto others as you would have them do unto you," always applied, and there was nothing but gentleness, compassion and love. Some other homes of school friends that I visited however, whose families were considered by the nuns to be pillars of the Church, did not always feel so good, with drunkenness, bad language and other negative goings-on. As a child I was very sensitive to energy, and didn't feel comfortable at all in the presence of these people.

Because of this dissatisfaction with Catholicism, I opted to go to a state high school, which was more convenient and closer to home anyway. This was fine for a while, but then I began to miss the devotional aspect — the comfort of the daily group prayers and the highly meditative act of reciting the rosary in the peace and quiet of the church. Time spent in that beautiful old building, with the ever-present scent of flowers and pungent aroma of incense, stirred something within me way beyond anything that words could express. "Connectedness" is the only word I can think of to describe it.

I'd always loved this time out, which was such an intrinsic part of convent life, and I had learned at an early age to sink gently into an altered, meditative state. Even at eight or nine I knew how to slip quietly into alpha mode and experience the incomparable sensation that occurs during meditation when the energetic frequency steps up to a higher wavelength and your spirit touches the Divine. Back then I had no conscious understanding of the science behind it. All I knew was that something important and profound was now missing from my life, and still there were those unanswered questions.

I decided to explore some other religions, spending about a year or so singing in an Anglican choir, attending a service at the local

Methodist church, questioning my Russian Orthodox and Jewish friends — but all to no avail. My many questions were still unanswered, and I couldn't find the meditative aspect that so appealed to me in Catholicism. I had a feeling the Orthodox and Jewish may have had something along these lines, but both of these belief systems are intrinsically linked to their cultural roots, so one really needs to be born into them to be able to integrate to that extent.

Some of the other ones I attended even went so far as to teach that meditation is evil, but why? As I've since come to understand, prayer is talking to God and meditation is listening to Him — so how can listening to God be evil? It seems to me that this is a major problem on this planet — people not listening to God enough! Surely if we really want to get by in life then we must allow God the time and space to speak to us! Eventually I returned to the fold of Catholicism, feeling very broad-minded and ecumenical, but no wiser as far as deeper issues were concerned. The strange thing was — nobody else around me really seemed interested one way or the other. My friends at school only cared about clothes, boyfriends and the latest pop music.

Like many children educated in convent schools in the 1960s, I'd toyed with the idea of becoming a nun, but this wouldn't have suited my temperament at all. I loved my freedom far too much, and could never have coped with the restrictions and unquestioning obedience of convent life. My problem was that I had *too many* questions, and burning away inside me was an ever-present awareness of a connection back to something intangible but profoundly sacred, something that I yearned for on the very deepest level of my being. Even as a child I knew that there was much more to the concept of "religion" than was generally taught in the traditional churches, and it was this that I hungered for.

Many people down here, particularly those of a more religious persuasion, believe that the human race of Earth is the ultimate form of Creation. After all, it was only a few hundred years ago that the unquestionable "truth" taught by the all-powerful Church ruled that the sun revolved around the Earth and that Earth was the center of the universe. Anyone who had the temerity to claim otherwise was in danger of being put to death for their "sinful and heretical way of thinking." Although this totally erroneous assumption has since been set aside, a great number of people here still believe that Earth humans are unique and special in the eyes of God, alone created in

"His" image and therefore the most intelligent and spiritual life-form in the cosmos.

When full-on open contact with ET and interdimensional humans does eventually occur on this planet, one of the hardest revelations for many Earth folk to accept will be the fact that these so-called "aliens" are more advanced spiritually, and have a far deeper connection to and understanding of Source (God) than is generally experienced down here. The sad truth is that in reality, Earth humans are one of the most *dis*connected of all human species in the cosmos.

For other ET cultures, connection to Source is not a matter of faith and belief as it is down here, but rather pure, conscious knowing. This connection and knowing, which is an intrinsic part of Zeta consciousness, is what I yearned and searched for as a child. I felt the loss of it profoundly, like a deep, aching void within, which I tried unsuccessfully to fill with Earth-plane religion.

This is not to say that there was no comfort to be found in religion. I did find it to a limited extent, which for many folk is quite sufficient, but on some deeper level of my being I knew there was more, but this could only be found by tapping into the Zeta part of my consciousness. In order to do this it was necessary to embark upon a spiritual quest — a personal journey home, which would entail the gradual opening up of this hidden aspect, which until then had remained buried on deeper levels of the psyche.

This state of unconsciousness had been chosen on purpose, to enable me to experience a more profound understanding of actually *being* an Earth human, but then came a point when the waking-up process had to begin. Because of this enforced state of unconsciousness that I'd been living in throughout childhood, it was unavoidable that the first contact with home that occurred just prior to my fifteenth birthday would involve fear. A number of lives down here in Earth human form had been undertaken as part of an ongoing learning experience, with the inevitable "karmic baggage" being collected along the way. This now had to be dealt with and cleared in preparation for the work that lay ahead.

My contact experience at 15 was the first of a series carried out through my life in order to gradually upgrade my consciousness to a higher "megabyte capacity" of deeper conscious awareness. By this time I was sleeping alone on the back veranda of the flat where my parents were then living. My brother, who is seven years older than me, had moved out by then, so there was only the three of us.

One night I woke up to find myself totally paralyzed from head to toe and feeling very strange. I now understand that I was in an altered brain-wave state, but back then my conscious knowledge of such things was non-existent. Suddenly the doorknob began to turn, and I knew that someone outside was trying to get in. Absolutely terrified, I struggled with every ounce of my being to pull myself out of this weird state and to call to my parents, but I couldn't do either. I was yelling at the top of my voice, but nothing was coming out of my mouth. Then I lost consciousness only to wake as normal the next morning.

For years I put this experience down to a prowler trying the back door of our flat in an attempted break-in, but certain things didn't quite add up. Why hadn't I woken normally with something like that going on, and called my parents? How could I suddenly just go back to sleep when I knew somebody was trying to break in? And how could I have seen the doorknob turning so clearly? It wasn't being rattled or wrenched hard, but rather turned slowly and gently, and this room was at the back of the flat, so there were no streetlights to illuminate my vision. It was quite dark once the kitchen and lounge room lights were switched off, as of course they were in the middle of the night. I was also very aware of being in an altered state, with God knows how many hours of missing time involved, thus allowing plenty of opportunity for the first downloading of Zeta information to begin.

At the end of 1967 the long-awaited final term of tenth grade dragged slowly by, with the infamous junior exam looming ahead. I still loathed school with a vengeance, and didn't intend to continue with formal education, but I had no idea of what I wanted to do with my life. "Upstairs" did however, and the upgrade I'd been subjected to only a short time before was due to start taking effect. A tiny corner of Zeta consciousness was ready to be opened.

It began when our high school music teacher decided to play a piece called "Rhapsody España" for our class. As I sat listening to this wonderfully evocative music, something switched on inside me in the way of a very vivid past-life memory. I found myself no longer sitting in a hot, boring classroom in South East Queensland, but rather dancing to the pulsating rhythm of flamenco in a smoky tavern in the south of Spain. The sensation stirred my senses so strongly that it was all I could do to sit still. I clearly felt the dress swirling around my bare legs, the cold hardness of the stone floor under my feet, and the presence of someone dancing with me.

As with the early childhood experience of being taken by the tall, thin woman to "board the train," for those few moments it was as if I were experiencing two different realities at the same time. I knew very well that I was sitting in class listening to a piece of music, but I knew equally well that I was dancing flamenco in a tavern in Spain. But how could this be? I was no dancer by any stretch of the imagination. Unlike some of my school friends, I'd never had the slightest desire to learn ballet, tap or dance of any sort, but all of a sudden this incredible and all-encompassing passion for Spain and flamenco dance came over me like a tidal wave. As the weeks passed, this passion didn't abate. My one and only burning desire in life was to learn to dance flamenco, but in mid-1960s Queensland, Australia, this was easier said than done.

My parents were surprised but at the same time really pleased that finally I was linking in to their European roots, and so they encouraged me all they could, but repeated attempts to find a teacher of such an exotic art form as flamenco were unsuccessful. Rumor had it that there'd been someone around once, offering classes in what the locals referred to as "flamingo dancing," but by then she'd given it up as not viable in our town and moved on to other pursuits. Dance schools too were not as diverse in those days as they are now, only offering ballet, tap and jazz. It was therefore time for "upstairs" to intervene once again on my behalf.

Over the years I've come to understand that a person's birthday is often a spiritual turning point or at least a window of opportunity through which new possibilities can be presented. Only a week or so after my fifteenth birthday an article appeared in the newspaper featuring a local girl who'd been working for several years with a dance company in Spain. She'd decided it was now time to return to her hometown to start up a Spanish dance school. This was the first of many such "amazing coincidences" that have manifested in my life over the years, and which served to consolidate my deeply held conviction that other more powerful and very intelligent forces were at work behind the scenes. And the timing was amazing, coming at a point in my life when I'd just finished my formal schooling but had not embarked on anything else in the way of work or studies.

Many people are aware of these forces, and over time I've learned to respect them, to go with the flow as it were. Of course as humans we have free will, but at the same time you'll often notice that when you go to do something, to start a new project, to change your job, change your residence or whatever, sometimes things flow easily and sometimes they don't. The trick is to learn to tune in and listen to the subtle messages. If your way keeps getting blocked by difficulties then it's time to reassess the situation and ask yourself, "Am I really doing the right thing here? Am I following God's will or is it purely self-will that I'm indulging?" Difficulties and obstacles put continually in our path usually means the universe is telling us: "No, hold on, wait!" The problem is, sometimes our Earth-bound human free will is not necessarily God's will, and instead of listening and taking note of the Cosmic Message Service, we fight it, determined as the feistiest two- year-old to get our own way — and then we grumble, complain and blame God when things go awry.

I was on the teacher's doorstep the very next day to sign up, and I started classes the following week. The tuition fee for one term of 12 weeks was $12 — a bit of money in those days with only Dad working and our family not well off by any means, but he was happy to pay because he knew this opportunity would be good for me in many ways. Mom too was really pleased, being so fond of dancing herself she encouraged me all the way, relieved to see that her only daughter was not quite as tom-boyish and elephantine as previously thought, and perhaps even potentially graceful and ladylike given a bit of training and dedication.

At the end of the first term I was still extremely keen and looking forward to continuing, but the teacher, realizing she was on to a good thing with more students than she could comfortably handle, decided to double the tuition fee. There was no way my parents could afford that, so in stepped "upstairs" again with their timely aid.

Although I'd never danced a step in my life prior to taking these classes, the flamenco came so naturally to me that the teacher offered to give me free *daily* instruction in exchange for my assistance in helping her to teach. This amazing offer came right out of the blue before I'd even had a chance to tell her that I couldn't afford the higher fee. Needless to say I was absolutely stunned and unable to believe my incredible "luck."

She was a strict and demanding teacher and a trained ballet dancer, and she coached me rigorously and to the point of painful exhaustion on posture and the discipline of dance movement, for which I thank her to this day. Trying to coordinate intricate footwork while playing equally intricate counter-rhythms on a pair of castanets taught me the value of practice, practice and more practice, along with a good lacing of dedication, discipline and determination. It was also great for assisting in the balance of left and right hemispheres of the brain as preparation for certain aspects of work I was to undertake later in life. By the time she decided to return overseas to pursue her own career, I was ready to teach and perform myself.

3

DANCING WITH SPIRIT

Once my feet had been guided onto the right path through that first contact at 15, it was time for a more conscious connection to be established with the Teachers "upstairs." This connection, however, had to be made at a level of consciousness that I could comfortably access. At that stage I'd only undergone one upgrade, and therefore my "hard-drive" was still operating on a lower "megabyte capacity," so only a limited amount of information could be downloaded. Modern-day Star Children born since the 1980s have much higher capacity "hard-drives" built into their Earth human containers, so more data can be accessed at an earlier age.

The Zetas are very knowledgeable when it comes to working with life-force energy, which is the creative energy of the universe. They are able to link in to the deepest recesses of the human mind in order to create an appropriate scenario/situation to fill a particular need or to provide a lesson that is required for growth on the soul level. In those days, ETs were simply not a part of my Earth human reality. The 1969 Moon landing had taken place, but nobody around me knew about or discussed such topics as UFOs, ETs, or contact experiences. Perhaps in places such as Roswell, NM, there was more awareness of these possibilities, but certainly not in my hometown, or at least not among those with whom I associated. It was for this reason that "upstairs" had to resort to more subtle means to achieve the required link-up.

Reality for me back then was my dancing, so if I was to eventually go all the way back to tapping in to my Zeta family roots, it had to start through my human family roots, specifically the Spanish Gypsy ones. This suited "upstairs" perfectly, and it was no accident that I'd initially been born into such a family and then guided into flamenco, the dance of the Spanish Gypsies.

The Zetas have strong links with tribal societies down here. The Native American people for example honor, love and respect the Star Nations, as do others, including the Romanies. These tribal societies on Earth are the very ones who, through their simpler and more natural lifestyles, have managed to retain a deeper and closer link with the finer and subtler realms beyond the limited third-dimensional "reality" of more "civilized" cultures.

I'll never forget being approached at a UFO conference by a Native American man. I'd been on an experiencers' panel, and I had been the only one to speak out positively about contact with the Zetas — all the others had nothing but fear and negativity to offer. This man was waiting at the door when I came out. He made his way straight to me and took both my hands in his, and tears glistened in his eyes as he spoke of the love and respect his people have for the Zeta folk. He said how hurtful it was to hear all the negative comments made by Westerners who just don't understand, and he thanked me warmly for my positive words. Around his neck he wore a beautifully crafted pendant in the shape of a triangular Zeta head, complete with the huge eyes. We gave each other a hug and he disappeared into the crowd, leaving me standing there close to tears.

South America, where flamenco is very popular, is also a major center of UFO activity and ET contact, where the streams of ET and Earth human consciousness flow together strongly. Even the flamenco dance itself provided excellent preparation for the work that lay ahead, for the most important component of flamenco is an underlying and intangible "something" the Gypsies call *Duende*.

The word *duende* translates as soul/spirit/essence, and it is a state of mind — a level of consciousness that one aspires to reach through the driving rhythm of the music. It is not something that can be learned and not all performers manage to achieve it, for it is an elusive point where left-brain "technology" switches to right-brain "soul." *Duende* is the essence of authentic flamenco — a state of mind that descends upon a performer as a spiritually transcending experience similar in effect to the trance inducing drumbeat of other types of tribal music. This is not surprising, as flamenco owes some of its roots to Shamanism.

Looking back, I now understand that the combination of this family background and my early training was all orchestrated very carefully and precisely by "upstairs" as a means to an end. Once at an ET encounter group I was asked by someone how I manage to place myself in a deep enough right-brain altered state to connect with the Zeta teachers, but still retain enough left-brain connection to write down what they're telling me. This person had been a long-time meditator, so she knew about altered states, but she could not comprehend how I could operate in both realms at the same time.

The answer is that I've been trained to do this since childhood. To begin with, my Gypsy roots provided a natural-born genetic ability to be able to link in to these other realms. This natural ability was enhanced through dancing flamenco, which entailed performing quite intricate physical movements while allowing my mind to shift into a trance-like state. This was then taken to an even deeper level after another upgrade at 30, when I was directed to learn Tai Chi, which is known as "moving meditation." The dancing requires the ability to retain physical and mental discipline while operating in an altered state, thus my diplomatic role down here on Earth as a spokesperson for the Zetas is something I've prepared for since before birth.

In 1969 I was invited to represent Spain in an All Nations Variety Show with an expected audience of hundreds. This was my first major public dance performance, and I was extremely nervous — in fact petrified, but equally determined to do it well.

Waiting backstage for our turn, my sense of unease grew and grew. I really wished that I could forget the whole thing and just *go home*. What in the name of heaven was I doing here? I was no performer, and *hated* being the center of attention. Others milled around me, talking loudly and excitedly, all professionally polished "show biz" types right down to the last carefully permed hair on their heads. The feeling that I was in the wrong place and just not part of this scene became stronger with every passing moment.

In the end it became obvious to me that if I was going to go out there and perform, then a few minutes of peace and quiet were sorely needed. This was as good an excuse as any to give the guitarist anyway. The truth was I headed for the nearest toilet with the firm intention of either being quietly but thoroughly sick or else locking myself in for the night.

As it turned out, I didn't do either, but rather for the first time in my life I decided consciously to try to meditate. I didn't quite realize what I was doing or why, but what triggered my attempt was an old memory that came to me of the peace and serenity I'd experienced as a child in church saying the Rosary and listening to the monotonous cadence of the Latin chants. At that time I had no idea that this *was* meditation, but I did clearly recall the state of deep tranquility and heightened perception that I'd often managed to tap into so easily, which was exactly what was needed now. I instinctively began with some concentrated deep breathing to ease the sickness in my stomach, and then I started repeating what I now know is called a mantra. It was simply the words of a much-loved Latin hymn, but they served very well to calm and divert my mind from the discomfort and fear that was threatening to engulf me.

Sitting there in a toilet cubicle at the back of the dressing rooms I recaptured the sense of utter peace, love and protection that always came when I consciously opened my mind to God? Spirit? Whatever! It was at that moment, while my vibrational frequency was heightened and receptive, that "upstairs" was able to draw close to offer much-needed help. I emerged a while later feeling different — quite "electric" and slightly out of myself but perfectly calm, and as I stepped onto the stage and began to dance, something extraordinary took place.

At that time in my life I'd never heard of mediumship or spirit channeling, but as our performance began, my vibrational frequency was raised to a higher octave, and I'd quite consciously put a message out asking for help, which in turn allowed "upstairs" to step in and take over the controls. I didn't know what was happening, but someone seemed to be there with me, gently merging their body and mind into mine, and the feeling was of upliftment, joy and love. The rhythm of the music carried me along effortlessly, as a different personality took over, and the *duende* came upon me. At the end of the performance we took our bows to loud applause, and I walked off stage feeling strange and slightly dazed.

My career as a dancer took off that night, and at every performance the "Teacher" took over, with a different-feeling personality. Sometimes he danced "in" me and other times he danced with me as an invisible partner. On these occasions I felt overshadowed by a gentler, smaller female presence. Even though I'd never been to Spain, let alone danced or studied there, I was often told how authentic my flamenco was and asked how I'd ever learned like that here in Queensland. These comments were put to me by Spanish people, some of whom were *aficionados* who understood flamenco and who'd been among the Gypsies in Spain and seen them dance. A Spanish Gypsy friend even sent his daughters to me for lessons, one of whom ended up going back to Spain to perform professionally.

During the following years my Teacher in spirit was always there in the background, opening doors for me and providing opportunities. Often it seemed that I "just happened" to be in the right place at the right time. If I was ever out of work, a sudden inexplicable urge to go somewhere or contact someone would always lead to more work being offered. I soon came to realize that my invisible Teacher was a real softy, and, like a loving parent, a few well-timed tears when things weren't going right quickly brought a response of help from him, and I'm ashamed to admit to exploiting this on a couple of occasions.

Spanish dancing certainly wasn't the easiest profession to provide permanent work, but my Teacher always saw to it that I didn't have too many nights off. When I wasn't performing I was teaching, which kept me almost too busy, and in a constant state of amazement at the strange coincidences that were always happening to me — coincidences that other people noticed and commented upon as well. Another comment made to me on several occasions was how much my aura changed when I danced.

Knowing absolutely nothing about spirit contact, I never even thought to ask this Teacher's name, but one was given anyway, with the Spanish name "*Manolo*" coming into my mind whenever he was around. I knew this name from somewhere and felt strangely drawn to it but had no idea why. In those days I had no real understanding of past lives and reincarnation, and it wasn't until years later that I found out where it came from. The ET connection wasn't understood until long after, when the Zeta Teacher Oris introduced himself to young Kira and kept referring to a life he'd lived on Earth as a human in Spain. It was then that the realization dawned that "*Manolo*" was none other than Oris.

He was always there when needed, *providing* I relaxed enough to let him come through. I knew something strange was going on but didn't comprehend it. All I knew was that when I danced I felt so different that I was a little scared, but the feeling that came with it was always of happiness and elation, never anything negative or unpleasant, and instinctively I felt safe and secure.

Neither had I any idea of the depth and breadth of my lessons, for there was far more to "*Manolo's*" teaching than Spanish dance. While he was with me I was still well aware of what was going on around me, always in control of the situation and able to stop at any time I chose. Because of the state of Oneness that we shared as an intrinsic part of Zeta consciousness, no deep trance-state was needed. This Teacher was so much a part of my own higher consciousness that it was possible for me to remain almost totally present. All I had to do was open my mind sufficiently to allow the required information/knowledge to be downloaded from the group mind, rather like sending an email from one computer to another, or downloading information from the Internet. The "Internet" in this case being the Zeta soul consciousness.

Other lessons involved patience, compassion, and how to relate to the needs of others. They ignited an urge within me to bring people of different cultural backgrounds together in Oneness. Through this came an understanding that racism is most often based in ignorance, and that mutual understanding and education is the solution to it. *This does not only apply between cultures and nations, but will in times to come apply on an inter-planetary level as well.*

Working in a field such as flamenco, I continually came into contact with newly arrived migrants who often couldn't speak much English. There was an influx of Spanish migrants at that time because of the repressive Franco regime, which caused many to flee the country. This sad situation continued until the time of his death in November 1975. The Migrant Services here did what they could to provide basic accommodation and food for these people until they could get work and eventually a home of their own, but lack of English made it hard for them at first.

I often spent hours at the Migrant Center just sitting with them and talking, trying to offer what little help and comfort I could, feeling very young and inadequate with my far from perfect Spanish. Sometimes they needed help shopping, looking for work or carrying out business at the bank. The simplest transaction or interview can be a major worry when you can't speak the language. Most business people were friendly and helpful, but occasionally we'd come across one who wasn't so kind. Experiencing what it is to be on the receiving end of this impatience taught me never to be like that myself. During this period of my life I wasn't only learning from *Manolo*, but from these friends as well, who taught me much in the way of courage, hard work, sheer determination and tolerance.

Once at a private home where we were hired to entertain guests for a fund-raising function, an altering experience occurred regarding the other female personality who sometimes stepped into my physical body while I danced. Just as I was about to step out into the room where we were to perform, I happened to glance in a mirror to check my costume and makeup, and could hardly recognize myself. The face that looked back at me was not mine.

At that moment there was no time to stop and think about it as the show was due to start, but later on in an attempt to explain it to myself I put it down to lighting, makeup or whatever — after all, what else could it be! But it still amazed me how different I looked, not just in the structure and shape of the face, but the expression as well. What had looked back at me from the mirror was a small, sharply pointed and rather triangular face with very large, dark eyes that slanted upwards at the corners, and Indian-dark skin. This experience would stay with me.

Like many who work in show business, I tended to socialize with like-minded folk. Some may think the world of flamenco is very romantic, but performing four nights a week, including Fridays and Saturdays, as well as rehearsing and teaching, was plain hard work. Despite enjoying a little help from "upstairs" I still had to practice daily and keep myself fit, so with practically no social life outside of work it was inevitable that I would end up marrying my partner, a guitarist with whom I'd worked for several years. We were both fond of animals — I owned a couple of dogs and he loved horses, so we decided to settle in the country. It was on this property that my second owl experience occurred, when one of these strange birds flew under the house to perch on a rafter above my head.

It was around this point in my life that "upstairs" also took a hand in another way. Despite all the searching I'd done in my early teens to find answers to my deeper questions on spirituality, I'd come out none the wiser and ended up returning to the fold of Catholicism. With high school to contend with, then a busy career as a professional dancer, my mind was far too caught up with physical life to put much thought into spiritual matters. However, once married and settled into a quieter life in the country, I had more time on my hands.

One day, searching in the bookcase for something different to read, I came across two books belonging to my husband. They'd been written by a Buddhist teacher, but in easily understood Western style. Even for these two books to have come into my possession was a miracle in itself, because my husband was not into reading much, but had been given them years before by a cousin. He'd read and quite enjoyed them but then put them aside. When we married and moved to our first home he didn't bring any other books with him — only these two.

In them I found a gold mine of information on subjects such as reincarnation, life after death, spirits, auras, healing and clairvoyance, and as I devoured them, all sorts of previously inexplicable things began falling into place, and a very familiar chord deep in my subconscious mind started to reverberate. I was remembering all of this from somewhere before in some time past. It was *so* familiar, and it was the knowledge I'd sought without success in all the churches I'd visited in my early teens. These books stirred up other memories as well, because of all Earth's religions, Buddhism comes closest to Zeta spirituality. In fact the whole Zeta lifestyle is akin to Zen Buddhism.

All my life I've experienced certain recurring themes through dreams. Some of these I thought of as my "Gypsy" dreams, which were sometimes pleasant in that they revolved around dancing, but at other times they were frightening, such as one in which I was a Gypsy man trying to catch a horse out in a field. Just as the animal was safely secured, a squadron of large, black warplanes came roaring across the treetops towards us. The horse began to panic and rear in fright, causing me to despair of being able to get both of us into the safety and shelter of the trees. I woke from this one shaking in fear and almost in tears of frustration.

Another recurring dream always found me trapped at the base of a high, steep cliff with the ocean tide coming in. A sense of terrible panic would arise as I searched and searched for a path up the cliff to escape the fast-approaching water.

The third type of dream involved a search for a particular priest-figure that I knew I needed to connect with. Although not realizing it consciously at the time, this had spilled over into my waking life, causing me to always be on the lookout for this person at the various churches I'd visited. There was precognition involved as well as a past-life memory, because I did eventually meet up with this person from the past. Strangely enough, he too had been a regular attendant at the one church that I was particularly drawn to, but he arrived on the scene a year or so after I'd moved on — obviously the timing wasn't right back then.

4
VISITATIONS

One night in early 1983, several weeks after my thirtieth birthday, I experienced a most wonderful and uplifting dream. In it I found myself sitting on the bank of a stream talking to somebody very special, and on waking the following morning clearly remembered that it was the Teacher. I associated him with *Manolo*, but at the same time I knew that he was somehow much more. This is very hard to explain in three-dimensional terms. It was as if *Manolo* were part of him, but only one facet, with me being another facet, but he was more than just the two of us.

I couldn't quite recall what he looked like, but the impression was of a mature and highly respected Elder, with dark skin and very large black eyes. At the time, with flamenco still a big part of my life, I thought of him as a Romany Elder, but there was something else about him that I couldn't quite recall. It was something different, not quite human — devic maybe — that I felt with him.

His physical appearance however was not an issue. It was the love and sense of connection that left a lasting impression that remained with me for days afterwards. The depth of love that flowed between us was beyond words, leaving me feeling lonely and "homesick" whenever it came to mind in the days that followed. And I knew him *so* well from somewhere — he was totally familiar to me. Time ceased as we sat together in gentle and easy communion on the bank of the stream, speaking at length on matters of great importance which only now, more than 20 years later, I understand on a conscious level.

Others came by while we were there, and I was left with the impression of being in the company of a highly respected Teacher, but that night his main focus was on me. It was as if these others knew not to interrupt for too long and quickly moved on, leaving us alone to speak of matters in private — matters which I could not recall on waking. What I did recall however was the sense of intimacy, trust and complete openness, and the love — deep, profound love beyond description in Earthly terms.

It was as if we knew, understood and were connected to each other right at the very core of our being. Nothing was hidden, no barriers stood between us on any level. It was a feeling of profound vulnerability but at the same time total acceptance, trust and unconditional love of a depth that one would have to experience personally to be able to fully comprehend. Although I didn't consciously realize it at the time, this was a preliminary discussion and a preparation for what was to come.

It was a warm afternoon a week or so later when my husband's family — mother, father and older sister were visiting us as they often did for a Sunday outing in the country. His parents had arrived in Australia before the Second World War, and settled in North Queensland where his dad worked in the sugar cane industry. Moving to the city in the 1960s, they missed the rural lifestyle of their former home, with its lush tropical rainforests and fields of cane stretching to the horizon, and so they enjoyed coming to visit our property. They were always happy to lend a hand with the endless chores that come with having animals to care for. In the middle of the afternoon I started feeling a little off-color, as if I were coming down with the flu, and so I excused myself to go upstairs to lie down for a while in the back bedroom, which was quiet and private. By then we'd moved into a new home, a modern, Spanish-style two-story house with living areas downstairs and bedrooms upstairs.

Relaxing but not asleep on the bed I suddenly found myself in what I now know was a trance state, paralyzed from head to foot and with a loud roaring/buzzing sound ringing in my ears giving me a headache. It actually felt like the top of my head was coming off or being opened up. Although my eyes were closed, I could "see" two small, slender figures standing on the left-hand side of the bed about level with my arm. They were watching me closely and seemed to be communicating with each other as well as with me on a deeper level of my awareness, although all I could physically hear was the loud buzzing sound. I believe there may have been a third entity behind me.

The two I could see stood between the bed and the window and were perfectly solid, three-dimensional beings that blocked my view out of the window. My thought was that they were family members — my mother-in-law is a small, dark, slightly built woman, and I thought one of them was her by the similarity of build, large dark eyes, and also the feeling of close familiarity. Their presence actually reassured me and removed all the fear I'd first experienced on finding myself paralyzed.

When I returned to conscious awareness a little later — missing time was involved — it occurred to me that I'd been in a deeply altered state and that my Visitors could not have been physical family members. My mother-in-law would never dream of coming into a room like that to watch me sleeping, and anyway, there were two that I could see, and my sister and father-in-law were bigger, taller people, as is my husband. The family had in fact spent all afternoon working together outside. Thinking about it later, I realized that one of the beings was the Teacher I'd spent time with in the dream, which had occurred only a week or two before. No wonder my fear had dissipated at the familiar sight of him.

Although not consciously aware of it at the time, these two contact experiences involved the next significant upgrade to my "hard-drive," which served to open up a much stronger link back to Zeta consciousness. This link was to enable me to access deeper knowledge and understanding, which was to change my life completely.

In the first contact, during the "dream," this process was discussed fully with the Zeta Elder with whom I share a soul connection. No wonder on waking that I was aware of something extremely profound having taken place, along with a sense of great excitement and anticipation. At last we were getting down to the business of why I came here in the first place — it was time to "get on with the job!"

The second contact a week or so later was when the actual upgrading process was carried out. For this to take place, my whole energy system had to be "opened up" to allow the necessary adjustments to be made, just as a computer can be upgraded to increase its megabyte capacity so that more information may be downloaded into the system. It was this temporary "opening up" that enabled me to hear the strange roaring/buzzing noise, like someone who has been profoundly deaf since birth who suddenly can hear. In Earth human terms this process might be akin to a "walk-in experience," because the upgrade to my energy system allowed a much greater volume of Zeta consciousness to be accessed or expressed through my consciousness.

As in a walk-in experience, not very long after this episode subtle but profound changes began to manifest within me, along with a strong urge to return to city life. This was totally out of character, because up until then I'd deeply valued the quietness and isolation of country living, and nothing would have induced me to move back to town. However, after this encounter changes began taking place, and it was as if I were being told: "Okay, you've had enough time out. There's work to get on with and you can't do it by hiding yourself away out here." Another driving urge that arose within was to learn Tai Chi and meditation.

I tried meditating using a yoga nidra tape, but being a dancer by profession I was an active, physically oriented person, and I found meditating this way very difficult. Little did I realize at the time that this was the very reason why the Zetas had also recommended Tai Chi, which also provided good proof of their presence in my life, because back then I hardly even knew what this was. Here in Queensland in the early 1980s such things as meditation and Tai Chi were generally looked upon as being very much "out there" and decidedly New Age, but the urge to learn these disciplines was as strong as the urge that had come upon me as a 15-year-old to learn flamenco. Little did I know consciously the amazing future that the Zeta family had planned for me.

Apart from an ongoing fascination with the night sky and stars, any conscious understanding of ET contact was also right out of my field back then. I'd really never given such contact much thought. Greys or Zetas I'd simply never heard of, let alone read books or seen pictures, and as for the beings I'd encountered previously, I never could properly recall what they looked like. I was aware of small thin bodies, darkish skin color and large black eyes, but I now believe they may have been using a light-screening process, as they often do, for those first couple of encounters that I could consciously remember afterwards.

It wasn't until about 1989 that I read my first book on the subject, and in one way it was reassuring to read of somebody else having the same weird encounters as I'd experienced, but on another level it was difficult and unpleasant, because by then I felt totally comfortable and at home with my "family," and in this book the relentless fear-factor was offensive and hard to relate to.

At first I put any idea of moving firmly out of my mind because it simply wasn't practical. We'd sold our horses by then, but we still had two dogs and a cat, and I knew very well that my husband wouldn't want to move back to town, having put so much work into this property. I also was torn in two, still loving the country living, but always feeling this ever-present nagging awareness of something big that needed doing in my life, and a return to the city was necessary for it to be carried out, but what it was that I needed to do, I really had no idea. I did know that it involved teaching of some sort, and it wasn't dancing, but what else could it possibly be?

Over the next year however things changed dramatically. Our 12-year-old dog Sara contracted heartworm disease, despite my having medicated all the dogs regularly. In those days it was considered incurable, so we had her put to sleep, leaving us with only one dog and the cat. Then my father-in-law passed away at 84, causing my husband to decide for himself that perhaps it would be better for us to move back to town so his mom could come to live with us. She couldn't drive, and she really valued her independence. Leaving her daughter and her many close friends in the city to move to the isolation of our property would have been hard for her.

I too have never liked driving, not learning until my late twenties. I'd had no need or desire to do so in my teens, as we lived in an inner-city suburb with excellent public transport right at our door. We could even walk into the city if we were feeling energetic, which Dad and I often did, he continuing on to his place of work and I to my dance classes.

A move closer to city, shops and transport suited me as well from this aspect, not to mention the other more intangible urgings I'd been experiencing since the strange encounter experience. We were a bit concerned because a house with a granny flat close to shops and transport and for the right price was not going to be easy to find, but again "the family" stepped in to provide exactly the right place for us in 1986, three years after my two contacts.

5
SPIRITUALISM

It was only a week or so after we'd settled into our new neighborhood that I happened to notice a poster in a window at the local shops advertising Tai Chi classes due to start in the area. The cost was reasonable; they were to be held within walking distance of home; and the teacher sounded pleasant and friendly over the phone when I rang to enquire, so what more could be asked!

Ten of us turned up for the first lesson, in which we were given a talk on the benefits of Tai Chi and a little of its history, then the teacher did a demonstration of what we'd be learning. After that he proceeded to guide us through our first tentative steps. Right from the very start I loved it, and with a strong desire still lingering in the back of my mind to learn meditation, and the trouble I'd had up until this point trying to do it, I saw the potential straight away.

What I hadn't realized previously is that Tai Chi is known as moving meditation, and in many ways resembles a dance in that it's a series of flowing physical movements set in a pattern that's designed specifically to promote balance and harmony within the underlying energy system of the body. As these movements are very precise and complex, being based on energy flow and self-defense, the mind must remain totally focused and calm, not allowing any outside distraction to impinge upon the concentration. In fact to perform Tai Chi properly, a very deep level of concentrated mind control is required, making it a most effective form of meditation. In other words, this was an absolutely ideal way for a physically oriented dancer to learn the art of meditation, which would never have occurred to me without help and guidance from "upstairs." At the end of the first term I received a certificate to say I'd completed the course to the satisfaction of the instructor, and out of a class of ten, only two of us decided to continue. I felt as if I'd come home.

After living in the country for 10 years, the idea of moving back into suburbia with lots of other people living close by was a bit daunting. We were relieved therefore to find that ours was a quiet street, with pleasant neighbors all around us. An elderly retired couple lived at the back; to our left was a family with two young daughters, and on our right a rented house with two people sharing, both of whom soon moved on.

We were both very busy at the time and out most weekends, so when the new neighbors moved in we hardly saw them at first, finally catching up one afternoon over the back fence. They were a working couple who, like us, had a large dog and no children, and on that first meeting they kindly invited us over for dinner that evening. I felt a bit guilty because after all, they were the newcomers, so it was really our place to extend an invitation, but I'd been so busy that I'd hardly had time to prepare meals for us, let alone for guests.

We'd made a reasonably good sale on our property, and with the money left over from buying a house, we'd managed to acquire a second property — an older-style, fairly run-down place that we were renovating with a view to either renting out or re-selling. This was what was keeping us so busy, with weekends devoted to sanding, scraping, painting and cleaning. On top of this, we owned and operated a cleaning business that took up several nights a week, and my husband also worked during the day, so our lives were very full.

Our new neighbors' invitation caught us unexpectedly, without so much as a bottle of wine to take with us as an offering. Thinking quickly, I pulled some herbs out of the garden and stuck them into a pot to take over as a thank-you and a house-warming gift all in one, hoping they'd appreciate such a thing.

Jenny's eyes lit up when I handed them over. She went on to explain that she was fascinated with herbs and herbal remedies and asked whether I knew much about them. She asked if I'd ever heard of the Bach Flower Essences, which I hadn't, and as we talked, things began falling into place. Jenny was a Spiritualist and a practicing psychic healer. Recently arrived from Tasmania with her husband and dog, she'd been developing her abilities through meditation for about 10 years.

Jenny then went on to tell me of her good friend and teacher Irene who had also recently relocated to Queensland. Irene, a Spiritualist minister, trance medium, healer and clairvoyant, was planning to start up a small meditation and psychic development group nearby, and Jenny was planning to attend. She extended me an invitation to accompany them to a Spiritualist service so I could meet Irene.

This visit was a most interesting experience, as such things as clairvoyance, spirit channeling and healing were quite new to me, as I had never witnessed them in action. Little did I realize that channeling is exactly what I'd been doing for many years through my dancing. Irene wasn't conducting the service that evening, so she and her daughter Katrina sat with us in the congregation. Small, fair and slightly built, Irene was friendly, bubbly and very down-to-earth with a great sense of humor. I liked her immediately. Afterwards we spent some time talking and getting to know each other over a cup of coffee. Obviously concerned that I hadn't been one of the members of the congregation to receive a short psychic message during my first Spiritualist service, she kindly offered me one on the spot.

This prediction, made in early 1987, was that someday I would be travelling overseas to "find my roots." Eight years later it happened exactly as Irene had foretold, when an opportunity came for me to travel to the UK for a family reunion. Thus I certainly found my human roots, meeting up for the first time with many relatives from all over the world. I found much deeper spiritual roots as well on this incredible trip — but more on that later.

Irene must have been checking me out that evening, because a couple of days later she invited me to join the development circle she planned to start up. It was a hard decision for me to make because I was so busy at the time with house renovation, part-time work and Tai Chi classes, but I also knew that it was a golden opportunity, presented to me on a platter, so to speak. It was to be a closed rather than an open circle, which meant that it was not open to anyone who came along but rather open only by invitation to a small number of sitters. We planned to meet weekly in order to develop our latent psychic, clairvoyant and healing abilities through meditation.

Never having done anything like this previously, I felt honored to have been invited. Jenny was also going to be taking part, but she'd been meditating for 10 years, so I understandably felt a little nervous, but Irene assured me that Katrina, who'd never meditated in her life, would also be there and therefore I wouldn't be the only raw beginner. I decided to give it a go.

As I've come to understand over the years, everybody is born with natural psychic abilities, but if you want to take it further, you really need to do training of some sort. This does take quite a lot of time, dedication and plain hard work, plus much patience, and it really needs to be done under the guidance of a trusted and qualified teacher, as there are certain dangers involved in playing around with such things on your own. A closed circle is the way to go if it's at all possible, because this enables the same group of sitters to come together week after week, gradually building up the necessary energy with no outside interference. You soon learn to relax and feel comfortable working together, which is most important, as self-confidence is the key to this type of development. Irene proved to be an excellent teacher — caring, patient and very grounded, not ego-centered at all, but genuinely dedicated to bringing out the best in her students.

Like my "upstairs" Teacher, one of the main things Irene taught us was control, that it is *our* body, so no matter what spirit person is working with us, *we* are the boss, and this must be respected. She had no time for mediums who did not practice such control. I clearly recall her answer to a woman attending one of her public talks, who complained about being woken at all hours of the night by a Spirit Guide wanting her to do channeled writing. Irene told her in no uncertain terms to be firm and to tell them to go away and come back at a more reasonable hour.

Ego too was something Irene had no time for. She herself had been blocked and held back by such a teacher who became threatened by her blossoming abilities. Such things as channeling so-called Ascended Masters or even angels was not encouraged in our group, because there's simply too much potential for ego to creep in.

As Irene used to tell us — if a medium has developed long and hard enough to have raised her vibrational frequency to a level through which such exalted beings can *genuinely* communicate, then neither channel nor spirit needs any longer to claim such titles. Genuine spiritual masters or angels are unlikely to proclaim themselves as such.

Unfortunately there are many inflated egos in this field, and with like attracting like as happens when you work with spirit energy, lower astral plane entities are drawn to these channels like flies to honey. Such entities can very easily disguise themselves as "highly evolved spiritual masters" and can cause many problems with their channeled messages. Just being psychic or clairvoyant seems to tempt some people to set themselves up on a pedestal and to charge megabucks for their "special gifts," which is a great pity, because everyone possesses these perfectly natural abilities, not just certain privileged folk. Some may have a greater natural ability than others, but we all have the potential, given a bit of practice.

The main key to working safely in this field is to take the time to work on yourself, first and foremost, in order to raise your energy frequency to the highest possible level. This can only be done by balancing and harmonizing your energy system through spiritual practice of some sort, for example Reiki, meditation, yoga, etc. It cannot be done overnight — it takes time, patience and a great deal of dedication and discipline, but this is all part of the training anyway.

The Buddhist aspiration of right mindedness is also most important, because when you're working with spirit, like attracts like, so you only get back what you put in. In other words, if the medium is motivated by greed, ego or the need to manipulate and control others, then that is exactly the sort of spirit they will attract into their energy field. It is for this reason that great care must be taken.

6
PAST LIVES

We began sitting in Irene's meditation/development group in early 1987, and for Katrina and I, both first-timers, it was an interesting experience to say the least. In a closed circle the aim is to get the same small group of sitters working together on a regular basis in order to build the energy levels as much as possible without interruption. This has the effect of assisting the sitters in reaching deeper levels of awareness and by so doing bringing forth latent psychic and clairvoyant abilities more easily, quickly and safely.

Strict guidelines need to be set down, and deep commitment is necessary to ensure that the group energy builds up consistently over weeks, months and years, because if one member's attendance is irregular, or new members keep arriving on the scene, the energy is disrupted. In other words, you cannot just come and go as you please. Irene laid this on the line with us right from the start. Our group met every week, year in year out, and if anyone missed a session we had to have a good excuse. Discipline of the mind is very important in this type of work, and it begins with the dedication required for regular attendance at group meetings.

I also started Tai Chi instructor training during this period, which meant heavy and demanding practice sessions, often at 7:00 a.m. at our center in town. Once I began teaching fulltime I had a morning and an afternoon class on the other side of town on the following day, then I had to show up at the local church hall for an evening class. Everyone else in our group was in the same position, working fulltime with the usual mandatory early morning start, but we rarely missed a meditation session. And as for not being able to make it because of another engagement — no way! Our Monday evening circle was sacred.

A closed circle operates along the same lines as the sacred circle or pentagram drawn on the floor in Wiccan ceremonies in that it's a protection device. Once you're all seated and the circle has been opened, usually through a short prayer and the joining of hands, you cannot leave your seat without permission from the group leader. If you really must get up, for example to visit the toilet, the person running the group must cover your place until you return.

On the very first meeting of our group, Irene led us through a short meditation session to ease us all into it, but after that the sessions always went on for at least an hour and sometimes longer, quite a long time to sit still if you're not used to it.

Such an extended time period is most necessary, particularly for beginners, to allow the mind to settle into a deep enough state for interdimensional communication to take place. The brain must at least come down to alpha state if genuine psychic communication is to manifest, and true meditation is deeper still. Spirit contact generally happens at the astral level, and can actually be a block to deeper states if you get too caught up in it. Buddhist nun Tensin Palmo, author of *A Cave in the Snow*, says: "The whole point (of spiritual practice) is not to get visions but to get realizations. A realization is the white transparent light at the center of the prism — not the rainbow colors around it." The truth of the matter is, if you get too caught up in seeing and hearing at the astral level, these "rainbow colors" often hide the center light from your vision. As we sat quietly through the hour or so, Irene remained awake and vigilant, watching over us clairvoyantly to observe what was happening, which would then be discussed afterwards.

The first few sessions were a real eye opener for me, as I had never done anything like this before. The more experienced sitters would speak of different sensations they'd felt during the session, various Spirit Guides and teachers that had come to them with messages, what they'd sensed about objects such as a book or flower being placed in their hands. Listening to their descriptions of the sensation of being overshadowed by a spirit entity, I began to understand a little more clearly the process that had been happening to me when I danced.

Early on I received proof of Irene's ability as a clairvoyant when one evening she informed me that my recently deceased dad was present, standing behind me. Although she'd never met him nor seen a photograph of him, she proceeded to describe him exactly, right down to the aroma of his favorite pipe tobacco. He was a fairly distinctive-looking man, so I had no doubt she could really see him.

It was in those early days of training that I became more familiar with my old friends from my time as a dancer. Week after week Irene used to comment upon a male spirit person who stood ever watchful behind my chair as I meditated. Several other clairvoyants also saw him with me on different occasions, and the description given always tallied exactly with someone who'd appeared to me once in a dream. He was a very dark man with black hair, strong features and dark eyes, who always brought a feeling of warmth and protection with him.

Every time Irene saw him with me I was overshadowed by a small, slender woman with large almond eyes that slanted upwards, high cheek bones, a narrow, rather pointed face, and a plait of black hair that fell forward over her left shoulder. As she stepped into my body I could clearly feel the change of facial structure coming over my features. This was the same one who'd once looked back at me from the mirror as I was about to begin a performance.

There was another one too who sometimes overshadowed me, dark also with upward-slanting, large eyes. He was rough looking, thin and unshaven, and wore a strange little cloth bag around his neck. He sometimes brought a feeling of deep distress, causing me to push him away as we were instructed to do under such circumstances. Not long after this, the Zeta family had an interesting experience in store for me — a further "adjustment" needed for the work that lay ahead.

Waking early one Monday morning I checked the bed-side clock to find it showing 5:30, and so I allowed myself to drift off for another hour. My next awareness was that of sitting in the meditation circle, as I would be that evening. I was aware of being in an altered state but at the same time being fully conscious of what was going on, while "somebody" was vigorously rubbing a finger all around the outside of my mouth, as if I were being given a facial massage. I thought to myself: "Wow, this is great! I'm actually feeling a spirit person touching me, and it's definitely *not* imagination!"

I mentally asked why it was my mouth being worked on rather than the brow chakra, which Irene was always telling us to massage in order to stimulate the third eye. The answer was given that they wanted me to speak, but I was too tense around the mouth and jaw, so this area needed loosening up and relaxing. A very warm and strong finger was then inserted deep into my mouth as the massage continued around my teeth and gums.

It occurred to me that perhaps healing was being done as well, but that was unlikely, as I've never suffered dental problems. In fact I'm a little unusual in this respect, as I have only one filling and only

28 teeth rather than the normal human count of 32. I'm lucky that the ones I've got all work okay! The answer came that they were still working on loosening the muscles, and I thought to myself: "Whoa — don't loosen any teeth in the process, mate!" A ripple of amusement emanated from my Visitor, and a telepathic message of: "Don't worry — just relax and enjoy it." I'd forgotten how easily they could pick up on my thoughts.

It was rather like being in a dentist's chair, only much more nurturing and comforting. Sometimes my head was resting back against the front of my Visitor's body, other times he moved to the front of me. On waking I couldn't quite recall what he looked like, but his presence felt familiar, his breath warm and pleasant on my face and his fingers strong and sure, as if he knew exactly what he was doing.

I say "he" because I knew it was the Teacher. His long, thin fingers were reaching way down into places where no human dentist could have reached. At times I felt them inserted deep into my throat and pressing very hard, but it was still enjoyable and relaxing, with no sensation of choking or discomfort whatsoever. It was many years later that Helene's daughter Kira commented on how hard Oris, the Zeta Teacher, sometimes pressed down with his fingers when he did healing on her, but also how it still felt pleasant and never painful. This is actually a form of acupressure that they utilize.

All of a sudden the bedside alarm clock went off, and I must have nearly taken his arm off at the elbow as I clamped my mouth shut in fright, jumping off the bed and launching a peacefully sleeping cat in the process. But even stranger things were to follow. That evening during our usual discussion after the meditation session, and before I'd had a chance to mention a word about my early-morning experience, Irene informed me that while I'd been meditating somebody had been with me, and she was really amused because they'd been busy *massaging my face all around the mouth area.*

Irene is a very talented psychic artist, and a few weeks later she presented me with a portrait of the girl who always overshadowed me when this other one was present. I was immediately struck by her unearthly, fairy-like quality. She was attractive but rather strange-looking, with a narrow triangular face and large, dark, slanted eyes. I'd never seen an illustration of the ETs known as the Greys, or

Zetas, and it wasn't until years later when I happened to place a recently acquired copy of Whitley Strieber's *Communion* near this portrait that I was quite shocked to discover an uncanny resemblance to the ET on the cover. The face in my portrait is more human looking, and in fact it looks like the hybrids often seen on the discs in company with the Zetas.

During our next meeting Irene managed to get some information through on this girl. First she was told that the girl was one of my own past-life personalities. Up until this point all the clairvoyants in our group had described her as "Indian-looking" — not Native American but rather from India, but Irene was "told" (by "upstairs") that she was a Spanish Gypsy. The Gypsies originated in India, so this fitted. She then tried to pick up on a name, but not knowing the Spanish language at all, had trouble understanding what she was being given and could only get as far as Con.... It was then explained to her that the name meant "Little Shell" in English, which she conveyed to me. I was then able, from my knowledge of Spanish, to pick up on the name as "Conchita."

This was amazing evidence, both of Irene's ability as a medium, and also of the authenticity of the message being given, because she had no knowledge of Spanish whatsoever, but was given the accurate translation in English. Exactly the same thing happened again years later in a message sent through via Irene containing a very obscure Romany (Gypsy) word in connection with the past Russian Gypsy life. Once the name was in place, some clear past-life recall began surfacing for me, which in turn explained the sensation of two spirit people, a male and a female, being with me when I danced. Conchita was half of a set of twins — a "split soul" in other words. The twin brother was Manolo, who would soon make himself known to me on a more conscious level. The human/Zeta family from Spain was starting to come together again after 200 years. Many years later Kira mentioned to Helene that Oris often spoke to her in Spanish.

A funny incident happened once in connection with *Manolo* when another clairvoyant friend who was not such a talented artist as Irene tried to draw a picture of him for me. She got quite annoyed because she couldn't get him right, and she finally blurted out, "Damn, I just don't get it. He looks like an *alien*!" She tried adding more hair to make him appear human, but instead he looked like *Conchita*, which made sense, as they were twins. A "5:00 shadow" was then added, which really didn't help matters at all, with poor *Manolo* ending up resembling a Zeta hybrid in need of a shave.

The recall of *Conchita's* life in Spain served to resolve the dreams in which I'd experienced being trapped at the base of a cliff among rocks, with the tide coming in, for that is how I believe she died. It also helped explain a further message given to Irene, who was only able to pick up the words "whispering sea," which I think may also have been in connection with her death. I also once had a dream about her in which she turned into a dolphin to whom I gave healing. As I later found out, there's a close connection between the Zetas and dolphins.

Manolo and *Conchita* were both dancers in the past life, which has been carried through to the present life. This also fits with the Zetas, who are very much into dance. Whitley Strieber raises this point in *The Secret School**, when he speaks of the children's circles conducted by Zeta Teachers, where human children are taken to learn about such things as energy, time and space — knowledge that will be most necessary in the future of Planet Earth. Dancing is an important part of the curriculum, and graduates of the "Secret School" are, according to Strieber, known as "Dancers."

Dancing is one of the best ways to harmonize and balance a person's energy system, which underlies all of the physical aspects of the body such as the circulatory, respiratory, nervous and glandular systems. This balancing and harmonizing of the energy system is the secret behind the healing powers of such modalities as Tai Chi, acupuncture, yoga and Reiki, so no wonder the Zeta family encouraged me to look at these techniques with a view to eventually teaching them. This process of balancing and harmonizing the energy system has the effect of raising and refining our vibrational frequency, which is what spiritual growth/evolution is all about.

The dance aspect also ties in with a link between the Zeta folk and the Romanies. A number of years later I was in touch with a Romany elder who was very knowledgeable on the spiritual heritage of the culture. I once asked him if he knew who or what these so-called Greys were that I'd had contact with all my life and to whom I felt such a deep connection. I even drew a picture of one to show him. His answer was: "Oh yes! That is how we appear after physical death, when we leave the human body behind."

---

*Strieber, Whitley: *The Secret School: Preparation for Contact.* New York, NY: HarperCollins , 1997.

There are many misunderstandings and misconceptions about the Romanies (Gypsies) on Planet Earth, just as there are about the Zetas. For example, there are some who claim to be Gypsy but are not (generally these are the very ones who give real Romanies a bad name), and there are also faked and very unpleasant "alien abductions" that in reality are carried out by certain ones down here in order to deliberately spread fear and mistrust of the real Zetas, so there are certainly parallels between the two.

One evening as we sat meditating in circle, three loud knocks suddenly rang out in the room, causing everybody to jump. The next moment found me in a deeply altered state that came over me so quickly that my ears rang and I went slightly deaf, as can occur in an airplane with the change of atmospheric pressure. I then distinctly felt a spirit presence moving into my body from the right-hand side, very gently but firmly pushing me sideways. For a moment it felt as if I were going to land in the lap of the person sitting on my left.

Next I found myself in a very tall body standing up on a raised stage and looking down into an audience. My hands held castanets, and I felt slightly disoriented, because when I closed my fingers on them there was no sound, when there should have been, but I also knew that there couldn't be any sound because the castanets weren't really physically there. It was as if there were two separate brains in my head, both functioning at the same time, and each with its own perception of reality.

As the Teacher moved into me more fully, and I knew it was he, I felt much taller than my normal height, with a longer, thinner face, dark skin, high cheek bones, and eyes slanting upwards at the outer corners. The hair was so black that it had a blue sheen to it, and it was longish, oiled and pulled back into a braid. These changes were quite tangible. Through all of this I was also still aware of the fact that I was sitting in circle in Irene's lounge room. The two scenarios were being played out simultaneously. Years later I was to hear this description from Helene and her son Ben, of the sensation he felt when one of the Zeta Teachers was present in the room and he was in a deep trance state. It's just as if two separate brains are occupying the same body — a *really* weird sensation!

Back then I knew nothing of the three knocks, which are a common phenomenon in connection with visitation by the Zetas. I also knew nothing of the very tall Zetas, with whom I was to be intimately acquainted in years to come. Thinking back on the sensation I felt on that occasion, the realization is now clear that the two human aspects of the Zeta consciousness — the shared past life of Conchita and *Manolo*, were both present on that occasion, coming together as one through their present-life incarnation.

At the time I was feeling very confused with these different ones who were making their presence felt, and so one night as I lay in bed, a tall female being entered the room and sat down beside me. She explained that she was a part of me — a very psychic part with total knowledge of the past, present and future. I now realize that she, like the dark-eyed Teacher who'd connected with me in 1983, was part of the same soul consciousness. A similar sensation emanated from her, as I'd felt in his presence, of being completely loved, nurtured and understood, right to the very core of my being. She went on to say that she had important information to impart on other lives that was extremely significant to the present life — information that I would need in order to continue with my work.

She then showed two Gypsy lives to me — one in Spain and one in Russia, but there seemed to be a third life that somehow overlapped. It was all rather confusing because of this superimposed image. One life was lived in the early 1800s (the Spanish one I think), and there was a death in one of them that involved an overdose of drugs. My answer to that was: "Oh yes, that's why now I hate even taking an aspirin!"

It wasn't so much that I was given a lot of detail on these lives. At one point only a simple image was shown of an old-style Gypsy caravan with a group of people standing in front of it. The overall impression was more that this was the soul path I have followed over a long period of time, and that this path has always involved shamanic-type healing and magic. It's what my present life journey is also about, shamanic magic being simply working with natural life-force energy to heal self and others.

The understanding I have is that many people who are drawn to natural healing and spiritual development have followed certain tribal traditions over a number of lives, and my particular path in some of my past Earth human lives has been the Gypsy path, which is a very shamanically oriented tribal system. It's only by tapping into our past that we're able to bring certain skills and knowledge through to the present, thus I was given this information.

There was another aspect passed on that night as well, when my Visitor told me of two parallel lives. One "half" involved the man with the little cloth bag around his neck whose presence sometimes brought a feeling of deep distress. The name *Ferenc* had been given in connection with him, and I believe he died in a Nazi concentration camp. However, there was another name linked in here too that felt even more familiar — that name was Maris, and it was as if they were the same soul but manifesting as two physical beings at the same time, one a human and the other a Zeta. Also confusing was the fact that both Spanish and Russian lives involved twins — *Manolo* and *Conchita*, and *Ferenc* and his female twin, who was yet to make herself known.

7

Understanding Spiritual Contact

Not too long after I started sitting in Irene's group, words in the form of spiritual teachings began coming into my mind. They would start filtering through during meditation with just a line or two or perhaps simply an idea, then as soon as the opportunity presented itself, I'd sit down with pen and paper in hand and allow the whole teaching to come through. This happened nearly every week without fail, and soon there was a large folder full of these messages, some short but most were a page or two in length.

Other extremely interesting things were also going on in our circle. One evening a little light appeared in our midst, plainly visible to everyone present as it danced around the room. Taking the correct procedure we checked it out thoroughly to make sure it wasn't simply a reflection off somebody's watch or jewelry, or a light from outside. Finally satisfied that no mundane explanation applied, we sat back to enjoy its antics as it played around the room and across each person's face in turn. To top off the performance, a picture hanging on the wall above my head started moving from side to side and emitting a soft blue glow.

Once when *Manolo* was with me in circle, I found myself holding a large smoky-quartz crystal ball. It was rapidly becoming charged with energy, and a great amount of heat was building within it, glowing hot on my face and almost burning my palms. When we came out of meditation Irene asked me to close the circle by reading out one of the teachings I'd been receiving from "upstairs." Switching on a small torch to enable me to see in the still-darkened room, everyone jumped with fright when the torch beam flared up suddenly and unnaturally bright, as if from a massive surge of power, then the bulb blew. For the remainder of the evening I kept getting electric shocks each time I touched anything metallic.

On another occasion he had me up on my feet giving healing to various members of the group. As he worked through me, the temperature in the room started dropping until everyone present was reaching for coats and scarves. Years later Helene and Kira commented on this coldness in Oris's presence, which took them many months to become accustomed to.

A valuable lesson was given on this occasion, and more evidence for the reality of it all, when my index finger started hurting afterwards. One of the others in the group was highly amused by this, and went on to explain how he'd hit his finger that very day with a hammer, and now the pain was *all gone*! This incident was a major contributing factor in my decision to eventually learn Reiki, which was exactly what the Zeta family wanted me to do anyway. It was certainly a good way of convincing me.

Once the negative past-life experiences of *Ferenc* were brought to conscious awareness and cleared, the parallel Zeta aspect began to emerge through the teachings I was receiving. There was difficulty at first in getting this one to speak out, and I could clearly feel that for this being, physical human-type speech was neither easy nor familiar.

One evening in circle I became clearly aware of a most peculiar sensation on both sides of my face where the lower jaw is hinged to the upper jaw. Gentle but very strong and insistent fingers started pressing and manipulating these two points, rather like somebody operating the hinged mouth of a glove puppet. Up until this point, some doubt always played on my mind as to whether I was really channeling a spirit or that it was nothing more than an over-active imagination, hence I'd only ever managed to speak out a word or two, but this left no question — it was *real*.

Following this very tangible proof, the presence introduced itself to the circle — the name given was *Maris*, and we were told the teachings were coming from a group mind. As I was still working with the Gypsy theme back then, I thought of this mind as a Romany *Kris* — a tribal council.

Meanwhile, another member of our circle also started being overshadowed by a Gypsy spirit — a female who appeared to be closely linked to both Ferenc and Maris (who seemed to be the same soul anyway, one a higher aspect of the other). This spirit was desperately trying to communicate, but like me her channel too was having problems with self-doubt and couldn't trust enough to let her through.

Irene did everything possible to help the woman relax enough to allow channeling to take place, including picking up a name — *Jezebaba* — which proved as difficult for her to get right as *Conchita*. She also did a lovely portrait of this female spirit, whose uncanny resemblance to a drawing she'd done previously of *Ferenc*/Maris struck us all immediately. Like *Manolo* and *Conchita* they were obviously twins, except that *Ferenc's* eyes were dark and *Jezebaba's* very blue, which is unusual but certainly not unknown among the Romany folk.

It was a beautiful portrait, looking almost alive with the head held proudly, and a vibrancy and love of life shining out through the eyes. She always came into the circle when *Ferenc* or Maris were present with me, and I could feel the excitement and deep disappointment that *Jezebaba's* channel couldn't relax quite enough to allow them to converse with each other.

A truly amazing revelation occurred to provide confirmation on her name. Just as with *Conchita's* name, Irene had difficulty in getting it accurately and also had trouble with the exact pronunciation, so she jokingly referred to her as "*Jezebel.*" Coming up to Christmas and my birthday that year, one of the other members of our group, knowing of my connection with the "Gypsy Council," found a book in a second-hand shop that she felt I'd appreciate as a gift. It was a wonderful and most unusual book of Gypsy folk stories set in Czechoslovakia.

Reading through it during the holidays, I was totally amazed to come across the word "*Jezebaba*" in at least two of the stories. It turned out to be a quite obscure title given to the wise woman — the seer and healer of the tribe, who is respectfully referred to as the "*Jezebaba*," with the accent on the second syllable (the second "e'), so it was not a name but rather a title. As far as I understand, this is not a common term, even in the Romany language, which admittedly has a number of different dialects. The more common title is *Phuri Dai*, which translates as "Old Mother." *Jezebaba* must, however, have been the term used by *Ferenc's* tribe.

As time passed and I became better acquainted with these Teachers, the difficulties experienced by the other circle member in channeling Jezebaba wasn't surprising, for I came to realize how different they were, and not quite human in the Earth-sense of the word. This was eventually confirmed for me in a Tarot reading in which I was told of the non-human energy surrounding them, and that they were definitely of another planet, or even galaxy.

In the early days of our circle no one spoke of the ETs known as the Greys/Zetas. Whitley Strieber's *Communion* was, I believe, the first to introduce them in 1987. Whether it was available straight away in Australia I don't know. Back then the only ET type I'd heard of was the so-called Space Brothers — the tall, blonde, blue-eyed "Nordics" with whom I felt no particular affinity. I'd neither seen nor had anything to do with these ones, and so I assumed my Teachers were not ETs — but what were they?

The only way around this difficulty was to think of them as being "devic," the term I adopted when speaking of them in circle, but even this didn't feel right by what Westerners generally think of as devic, which is fairies, elves, etc. This was still not quite accurate in relationship to my Visitors, who I believe are the devas spoken of in the Indian Vedas. I sensed that they were closely connected to Planet Earth, because their love and caring for the planet and nature came through very strongly, but what this connection was I had no idea. At that time the concept of ETs assisting in the evolutionary and spiritual awakening process of humans on Earth was unheard of.

This confusion on the identity of my Visitors caused all sorts of problems for me that couldn't be shared with anyone. One of the greatest difficulties was that some of these "upstairs" helpers seemed to be past-life personalities of my own, but with no conscious awareness at that time of my Zeta link, I couldn't work out how the non-human aspect fitted in on a personal level. The understanding finally arrived at is that the Teacher I later came to know as Oris experienced physical life in Earth human form as the twin pairs *Manolo-Conchita* and *Ferenc-Jezebaba.* The one known as Maris is a higher aspect of Oris, and a third Teacher, Serapis, revealed to me some years later, is a higher aspect of Maris. The Zetas do work together in these multi-dimensional groups of three, and this was shown to me symbolically one evening in meditation, at the time when I was just getting to know them all.

When I did finally acquire my first book on the Zetas, I was quite shocked to discover that the picture on the front cover resembled *Conchita,* but what caused major problems for me was the way they were portrayed in the book as being rather negative, and there was so much fear on the part of the author. If there really was an aspect of me that was connected to these strange and seemingly cruel beings, then what did that say about me? The experiences described by the author tallied closely with my own lifelong experiences, and there was no doubt in my mind that his Visitors were the same as mine, but why did he experience so much fear?

By that stage I was having much more conscious recall of being taken onto discs and into clinic-like rooms where medical-type procedures were carried out on my body. I even have a scar as physical proof of this. This was unsettling at first, but the beings reassured me, telling me to just relax and it wouldn't hurt, which proved to be correct. In fact on one occasion when the time came for me to leave, I burst into tears, wanting more than anything to stay with them. That's the main reason why this book confused me so much. The author's difficulty in communicating with his Visitors didn't make sense to me because my perception of them was so very different. For me they were like family, with no communication difficulties whatsoever.

In other books I've read over the years some researchers have come up with a theory that the Zetas are robots. To the contrary, in the many dealings I've had with them over the years they've proven themselves to be very human, particularly the tall ones. They actually possess a well-developed and rather dry sense of humor, which I've seen demonstrated on many occasions. Having had personal and clearly remembered experiences of being up on the disc myself in Zeta form, all I can say is that Zetas are not robots — the same spiritual essence that motivates humans motivates them as well, and they can feel and totally understand human emotions. *In fact, up there I really don't feel very different to how I feel down here.*

A classic example of Zeta humor once came up in circle. On one occasion a member of our group experienced a sudden and desperate need to visit the toilet during our hour-long meditation session. She finally managed to attract Irene's attention to cover her place in the circle so she could leave the room. This woman was a bit of a character, and at the end of our session she apologized for any disturbance she may have caused and explained that just prior to her emergency call of nature the image of a giant chamber pot had appeared in her meditation. Immediately and with no warning whatsoever, a highly amused Zeta message telepathed clearly in my head: "Ah yes — the seat of the soul!" I, of course, burst out laughing, and it took several attempts before I was able to control myself enough to relay this uplifting little message to the others.

It has also saddened me deeply for years how some investigators of ET/human contact believe unquestionably that the Greys/Zetas are negative or evil. Having been involved in spirit contact for many years, I know what real negative energy feels like, and the Zetas are definitely not evil. If anyone should know about such things it would have to be the late Monsignor Corrado Balducci, an experienced demonologist and official Exorcist at the Vatican. He spoke openly about the ET presence here on Earth, stating categorically that they are not demonic. He also confirmed information that Oris has given us on Earth humans' place in the universe.

During an interview with Balducci in Paola Harris's *Connecting the Dots: Making Sense of the UFO Phenomenon,*[*] Harris asked him, "Why, as a Vatican spokesman do you come forward publicly in favor of the existence of extraterrestrial life?"

His reply: "Because there must be something between us and the angels. If there are other beings, they are surely more evolved than we are. We are at the bottom of the evolutionary ladder because of our ability to "see good but do evil." Man possesses a certain duality and is capable of both good and evil. It is illogical and a bit arrogant to believe that we are the only intelligent beings in God's creation. Perhaps if these other beings do not possess physical bodies, they are not subjected to our same temptations."

One of the Zeta teachers once came to my rescue when I found myself confronted by a very nasty negative entity. I tried to stand up to it, but it came at me full of aggression, attempting to kick me viciously. The next moment it wasn't me that it was up against but rather one of the tall Zetas who'd stepped quickly into my body. The entity's foot had no chance of making contact, for the Teacher, agile as a cat, spun me around out of the way and turned the attack back on the negative one in a comical way by "kicking butt" literally. This proved effective, as the tall Zetas have very large feet. Next thing I knew, the negative entity was rolling head over heels into a

* Harris, Paola. *Connecting the Dots: Making Sense of the UFO Phenomenon.* Columbus, NC. Wild Flower Press, 2003, republished by AuthorHouse 2008.

flowerbed (of all things), and the teacher was standing back, hands on hips, laughing.

This was an excellent lesson for me, because in a situation like this, if you allow yourself to be drawn into the fear, you feed and strengthen the negativity, whereas if you can laugh at it, this is your protection.

The poor old ETs usually get the blame for the negative interference that quite often occurs with those experiencing contact with ETs, but in actual fact it's astral-plane interference. I've had this happen myself on a couple of occasions, and have also witnessed it with others.

The following passage explaining exactly what is going on is from Eileen Buckle and Norman Oliver's *The Scoriton Mystery*. It's a non-fiction account of a group of people in the UK who were involved in investigating a series of ET contacts. Some were supposedly receiving messages from the ETs that seemed rather questionable. They were also hearing nasty and sometimes quite threatening voices in their heads, which worried them greatly and caused them to assume that the ETs they were in contact with were negative. A more knowledgeable person named Colin, who had dealt with such things before, eventually explained what was really going on:

> "This is astral," said Colin. "By the way, this is quite common. These voices you hear are not space visitors or anything like that. They're astral entities. I think you may find that your auric radiations have changed by the mere fact that the space visitors have contacted you. It's changed your polarity. Unknown to you they've taken away certain negative factors in your aura, in your subconscious, which you don't know anything about as yet but you'll find out about later. They've removed these, and by doing this, they've opened up a channel. Now unfortunately, whenever a channel like this is opened, the personality becomes an immediate target for all sorts of entities. The reason for this is it's a test and a trial, usually.
>
> "The great yogis of India, for instance, when they've attained certain initiations have to actually undergo a trial by lower astral entities and they're locked in a darkened room and literally plagued to death by these things. They have to

> overcome them — this is part of the initiation ceremony. All that's happening to you is that your mind is attracting these entities. They sense a positive polarity. They're like leeches. Whenever there is a high degree of psychic energy they feed off this and they're probably trying you out …"†

In my experience, when you get someone saying of the ETs: "They're telling me to do this or do that" — it's usually astral-plane interference rather than genuine ET contact. I've seen this happen a lot, and many ET contact investigators have no idea of this, focusing as they do on only the physical aspect of encounter experiences and UFOs and completely ignoring the paranormal aspects. The genuine ETs never interfere in this way. All they ever do is drop an idea or image into your mind, and then leave you to take it up or not. They don't give orders, put you down or force themselves upon you — this is astral interference — the Zetas are far more respectful than that.

This negative astral-plane interference is being force-fed to humans on a regular basis, but on deeper levels where you aren't consciously aware of it. Contact with genuine ETs has the effect of "waking you up" from this state of unconsciousness, and it is done for the purpose of bringing this previously hidden but nonetheless insidious negative interference up to the conscious level where you can deal with it more effectively. Being aware and "awake" is the key to getting back your own empowerment.

The concept of people having other parallel aspects of themselves living out lives as members of other ET or interdimensional cultures is very real. We are all multidimensional beings, with other parts of our soul essence existing in different times and different places. This is why some folk down here are strongly drawn to or experience a strong connection with one or more ET cultures, as I have with the Zetas.

When the teachings began coming through to me from "upstairs," they seemed to be from a group mind that back then I thought of as a Romany tribal council. In actual fact it was the group mind of the Zeta culture. The so-called Greys do operate in this way, but they're also capable of individual thought. They are, however,

† Buckle, Eileen and Norman Oliver: *The Scoriton Mystery*, London: Neville Spearman, 1967, pp. 210-211.

much more attuned to Oneness than are Earth humans, who prefer to do their own thing, sometimes regardless of everyone else around them.

Also for the Zetas, time is not a barrier — they can quite easily travel, exist and operate across time. In this way their past-life personalities, present-life personalities and even future-life personalities can potentially co-exist together. I know all of this sounds terribly complicated, but there we have it! There is a lot about the Zetas that is quite complex by Earth human standards, because of their ability to traverse time, space and dimensions.

One night many years ago I experienced a "dream" in which I was shown a book that seemed to be a sort of ship's log recording a very long journey, and Maris's name was mentioned in it several times. Next I found myself waiting on the edge of a forest clearing. A large, glowing orange ball of light appeared, coming towards me through the trees. It floated straight into my out-stretched arms, and I was immediately enveloped in a feeling of the most incredible love. My conscious mind noted the strangeness of the situation — to experience such boundless love coming from a ball of light.

Suddenly I found myself enclosed within a warm and loving embrace, and realized it was a Zeta Teacher holding me, with his long black cape totally enfolding my body. I leaned against his shoulder and cried, not with sadness but rather in relief, joy and welcome. The tears I shed were a complete letting go and a release of all uncertainty, fear and doubt. Just as in the 1983 encounter, the feeling of mutual love, trust and understanding was way beyond words. It was a total merging into Oneness. Seizing the moment, we held each other tightly, not wanting to let go.

As this being held me, I heard words inside my head that conveyed information about him. I was told that he is a very ancient Teacher who has manifested on Earth a number of times in protective roles towards those considered "outsiders" in the community, thus *Ferenc's* role in the Nazi Holocaust of helping Jewish people, and a life in Spain during the Inquisition, helping others through *Manolo*.

As the dream continued, I found myself sitting in the back seat of a car with three "newcomers" who'd just arrived, and it was my job to make them feel welcome, and to show them around. I was aware that they'd come a very long way. I feel that on one level this is representative of the Zeta Teachers working with and through me.

Perhaps on another level it may also be a glimpse into future work in an interplanetary sense, helping newcomers from elsewhere to integrate into the Earth community and to teach the Earth community to accept these newcomers without prejudice or fear, just as I did all those years ago with the Spanish migrants who arrived here in a new country unable to speak English.

8

REINCARNATION

One evening in circle I experienced a meditation in which I found myself in a cave with a roof covered in glow-worms. It looked strangely like a night sky ablaze with stars. Stalactites descended from the roof and stalagmites grew from the floor, reminding me of a joke my dad once told to help me remember which was which — "When the 'mites' go up, the 'tites' (tights) come down." As I studied these glistening formations, the slowly monotonous drips of water that were gradually building them could be heard in the stillness. The thought came that if I could sit there and meditate upon one of them for long enough, I'd be able to observe its slow growth. In the timelessness of the meditation state this idea seemed quite plausible. Placing my hand on the wall and feeling the soft dampness of moss, and smelling the cool earthy moisture all around, I became aware of the fact that the cave was quite chilly. As I moved along, the atmosphere became colder and more uncomfortable, and the ground underfoot became slippery and strewn with sharp rocks.

Then the Teacher appeared out of the gloom, wearing his usual long, black cape, which he opened and drew me into so that it enfolded me completely. This cape so often worn by the Zeta Teachers has always been symbolic of protection to me, and the warmth it provided was most welcome in the chilly dampness of the cave. We walked together beside a stream, and he placed a protective and steadying arm around me because the rocks underfoot were treacherously slippery with moss and moisture. The unsafe footing didn't seem to bother him at all, whereas I really needed to hold onto him tightly for support.

Eventually he led me to a flat area at the water's edge, and I lay down to rest. He then began draping many different colored cloaks over me. They were soft, fine and silken, and each was of a different rainbow color — all the colors of the spectrum. I pulled them up around my chin and felt very warm and safe. Little did I realize at the time that this was a clear precognitive message of the next major step the family had planned for me.

A priest named Paco whom Conchita and Manolo had known in Spain often used to turn up during meditation. On one occasion he placed a crucifix into my hands. He wasn't a past-life personality of my own, and he never attempted to overshadow me, but would sometimes give out messages. On three separate occasions he gave Irene the Spanish name "Juan" to pass on to me, which translates into English as "John." There was no doubt that the name was being given by a Spanish speaker, because of the correct pronunciation.

Not long after this I admitted new Tai Chi students, among whom was Ian, a man first mentioned in Chapter 1. During the class break we often spoke, and he told me that although he was working in the traditional medical field of nursing, he was also trained in therapeutic massage and was becoming increasingly drawn to natural and holistic healing, hence his desire to learn Tai Chi. Some years previously Ian had spent time in a Catholic seminary studying for the priesthood, but he had eventually left, realizing that it wasn't what he really wanted to do with his life after all. Right from the start he felt familiar to me, as if I knew him from somewhere.

Ian had been attuned to level-one Reiki, which I knew very little about back then. As a member of a circle conducted by a Spiritualist minister, I'd been trained in hands-on healing, and I tended to share their skepticism on a relatively new (to the West) healing technique that looked no different than what we were all doing, but which involved a quite expensive training and attunement process.

My skepticism soon evaporated, however, when Irene invited Ian to join our circle as a member, and I was able to experience Reiki first-hand. Even at level one, the first of three levels, the strength of the energy coming out of Ian's hands was amazing. Then and there I vowed that, given the opportunity, I would explore Reiki for myself.

As I got to know Ian better, the certainty grew that he was a reincarnation of the priest I knew as *Paco*, right down to the fact that he'd again trained for the priesthood in the present life. He now looked altogether different physically, not being Spanish this time around, but his energy field was very similar. Even his present name — Ian, is a form of *Juan*.

The meditation involving the rainbow-colored cloaks turned out to be a very accurate prediction of future events, because Ian later became a Reiki teacher, and attuned me to level one in early 1993. I then went on to do level two with him some time later, and I completed master/teacher training in 1996. It was only after learning Reiki that I found out that it is sometimes symbolized by a rainbow. Reiki works specifically on the energy/chakra system of the body, and the vibrational frequency of the seven main chakras corresponds to the seven colors of the spectrum — a rainbow. There was a strong Zeta connection here as well, with much more detailed teaching given by them on color and the chakra system some years later, which I now teach as part of the Reiki course.

Shortly after experiencing the cave meditation, my life path certainly did become very slippery and difficult over the following three years when almost single-handedly I was left to nurse a close family member through a serious illness. I thank Reiki entirely for helping us through and getting everything back on track. I was most definitely provided with assistance to enable me to walk the path safely — warmed, comforted and protected by the rainbow-colored cloak of Reiki that was laid over me, and which continues to play a major role in my life today.

I also owe the Zeta family a vote of thanks as well, for timely help provided during that difficult period of my life. One night I went to bed feeling very low and totally exhausted, to the point of seriously wondering how much longer I could keep going. I recall reaching out to "upstairs" with a thought of: "Please, *please* family — this is all *too hard* down here being human. I can't take any more — I just want to *go home*!"

Then I floated off into an altered state, clearly hearing the Teacher speaking to me. In the gentlest and most comforting voice I've ever heard he said: "Be at peace, my little one. Know that everything is going to plan — all will be well — have courage!"

Another amazing experience also occurred around that time involving someone else I'd known in the Spanish life. Catherine attended Tai Chi classes and was also in an open circle that Irene was conducting at the time. We became friends, but there was something about her that made me feel a little uncomfortable, not on the physical level but rather energetically. Ever since childhood I've been sensitive to the energy field around people, and this was where the problem lay — in her aura, but what it was I couldn't work out.

Catherine felt a very close link with *Manolo*. She had some clairvoyant ability and had seen him overshadowing me occasionally, and one night he appeared in her home while I sat meditating in circle. This occurred on the night before her mother's funeral, of which I was unaware at the time. He told her to include a touch of red on the otherwise dark-colored outfit she planned to wear to the funeral.

One afternoon I started feeling very tired, and I lay down on the bed to rest. Suddenly I found myself going into a deep trance-state, paralyzed from head to toe as happened in 1983. Wondering if the family was going to put in an appearance, I tried to relax more deeply, and immediately *Manolo* stepped into my body. It was *so* intense and the take-over so complete, that the "Judy" part of me disappeared totally. I *was Manolo*, seeing through his eyes, feeling through his senses and experiencing through his emotions.

Now this would have been fine, except for the fact that we were *really* distressed about something. In fact I've never experienced such intense anguish in my entire human life, and it was related to Catherine, or at least to the one she'd been in the past Spanish life, a woman known as *"Camilla,"* but it was also related to something that was happening with her right now, in the present. Bearing in mind that *Manolo* was a Zeta in human form, I always think of this incident whenever researchers insist that Zetas are robots and do not experience emotion. All I can say is — they *do*! I have truly never felt such intensity of emotion in all my life. He was beside himself with anguish.

Sensing through the consciousness of *Manolo/Oris*, I found myself fighting through a horrible, sticky, black fog. It was like the worst nightmare in which you are trying to run away from something awful, but you can't make any progress because your feet keep sinking into a bog, and your vision is severely limited by the darkness surrounding you. In this case however, I wasn't running away but rather trying to reach someone, and I knew very well that it was *Camilla*, Catherine's past-life personality. I was also aware of her being close by, but just beyond my reach. Straining every muscle in my body to get to her, I called her name over and over again, my voice breaking in anguish, despair and frustration, trying to get her attention, to make her listen to me, and it wasn't a physical matter of life and death, but rather a soul matter.

Waking from the trance, I couldn't move for some time. Tears were running down my cheeks and *Manolo/Oris's* presence was still strong. Finally rousing myself up and off the bed I tried to phone

Catherine to find out what was going on, but there was no answer. This was worrying because I *knew*, from the distress I'd experienced, that something was amiss. She eventually phoned, hours later.

Apparently at the very time I was "off," she'd gone to a secluded beach near where she lived, become drunk, and was on the verge of doing something extremely unwise. I found out later that she'd been playing around with some rather questionable "magical practices" in the company of a couple of like-minded friends, as she'd done in the past life when she'd refused to heed *Manolo's* warnings to leave such things alone. But for *Camilla*, as with Catherine, it all dealt with power/ego and therefore was both seductive and addictive.

While I was in trance, *Manolo* appeared to her on the beach with a look of pain and sadness on his face. He then proceeded to envelope her in a wave of such deep love that she immediately ceased what she was doing and sobered up almost instantaneously. She'd phoned to thank me, or at least to thank *Manolo* for his timely intervention. On the physical, human level I'd had no idea she was into such things or even that she had a problem with alcohol, appearing to be happily married to a good husband and seemingly quite well adjusted in her life. It was this hidden side that I was picking up on deeper levels from her aura. All these past-life/present-life/off-planet connections can be very confusing, but they serve to remind us how interconnected we all are and why we keep reconnecting as a soul group.

There are three more relevant events to be covered before I "close the loop" and bring my story back to where it began with those first worried phone calls from Ian and Helene, which was to set off a truly amazing saga. The first of these is the quite extraordinary circumstances surrounding the arrival on the scene of a third Teacher and family member by the name of *Serapis*. The second event, in 1995, which would prove to be another major turning point in my life, was a very profound and highly significant contact experience involving yet another upgrade with massive downloading of information and guidance from the Zeta consciousness.

I now know that Serapis is also the name of an "Ascended Master," but in 1993, I had never heard this name. As Serapis played a significant role many years later, I will briefly explain how I first got to know him.

The teachings had now been coming through on a regular basis since 1987, and I was aware that they were coming from two Teachers who were part of a group consciousness. These Teachers were Maris, and the one I knew as "*Manolo,*" who many years later would introduce himself to young Kira as *Oris*.

With the family presence in my life now firmly and comfortably established and their message starting to be spread through these writings, another name began haunting my mind on a regular basis. This name sounded like "rapis." I mentioned it in our circle to see if anyone could place it, but there was no recognition from anyone. For weeks it stayed there on the very edge of my mind, like a vaguely remembered dream, and I knew there was more to it — that "rapis" was only part of it, but what the rest of it was I didn't have a clue.

I was initiated to level-two Reiki in March, 1993, exactly ten years since the 1983 upgrade. In May a strong message started coming through that the time was ripe for new doorways of consciousness to open, so I consulted a Tarot reader for guidance.

In this reading I was told that contact would soon be established with a Teacher of a higher-vibrational frequency, and that in fact he'd already started moving into my energy field. She got the word "Leo" in connection with him, and felt that this was not his name but rather an indication that he would be making his appearance on the scene in the months of Leo — July or August, in other words. This woman was very much into astrology as well as Tarot, and brought the two together in her readings.

She especially commented on how "strange" he was — not human, but of another planet or even galaxy, which she repeated a couple of times, obviously quite intrigued: "A *very* strange vibrational frequency — definitely *not* of Planet Earth, but wise — wise and *ancient*!" She then went on to tell me this Teacher would be giving me something in the way of a gift or talisman.

The following Monday evening during meditation, I became aware of a large and powerful figure standing before me. Leaning forward, he placed around my neck a necklace of large seeds, pods and other forest items all strung on twine. Others in the circle also saw him clearly and commented particularly upon his wild head of hair. As he was facing me I couldn't see his back, but one sitting opposite described his hair as being like a lion's mane, very shaggy and extending partway down his spine. From the front he had what I would describe as a "South Sea Islander" appearance — big, dark, broad and strong, with a tribal look to him.

He was obviously the "Leo" of my Tarot reading. It was not that he appeared in July/August, but that he was a Lion-man. An incredible sense of love, strength and protection emanated from him, and I wished afterwards that I'd thought to ask his name, but his very unexpected arrival and appearance caught me completely by surprise.

A day or so later, walking in the garden, I spotted something shiny on the ground. Thinking it was broken glass, I bent to pick it up to throw in the rubbish bin, but on closer examination, I saw that it was a strangely shaped stone of a dark and shiny amber color, with smooth, glasslike facets. The thought struck me immediately that it was of the same amber color as the Lion-man's eyes. Perhaps this was his gift to me that the Tarot reading foretold — an amber talisman that I still possess. I kept asking for his name, and this "rapis" word always came into my mind, which just didn't make sense. I knew there was more to the name, but it would not come.

The following Friday evening I arrived at the Holistic Healing Center where I was conducting my weekly Tai Chi class, and I spoke awhile with one of the other staff members. She was into several alternative-healing modalities including meditation, and she asked me about the group that I attended. She particularly wanted to know if any of us channeled the so-called Ascended Masters.

I knew that the Ascended Masters Jesus and Mary were said to be among their illustrious ranks, as well as St. Germaine, Hilarion, and Kuthumi. Apart from this limited amount of knowledge, I was unfamiliar with all of them, and I was not really interested anyway, because of my predisposition.

In as diplomatic a way as possible I tried to end our conversation. I did, after all, have a class of Tai Chi students due to arrive, and certain preparations were involved, but this woman, obviously a true believer, was not to be put off so easily. Amazed by my lack of knowledge, she headed determinedly for the library room and selected a book on the Ascended Masters for me to look at.

Still wanting to get on with my class preparations, I quickly flipped the book open at random, and there, staring me straight in the eye, was the name *Serapis*, described as the ascended master of the Devic Kingdom. Here was the "rapis" name that had been on my mind for so long, and with a devic connection as well, which was how I still tended to think of the Zeta family. I must have gone quite pale with shock, because the Ascended Master woman pushed a chair at me so I could sit down, and believe me — I needed it!

The way *Serapis* was portrayed in this book didn't strike a chord with me at all. He was depicted as a way too perfect-looking "Aryan-type" human, but it did mention a connection with the Great Sphinx, the lion-man edifice in Egypt. I now know that the Zetas can portray themselves in whatever guise or belief system/mind-set is most useful to a given situation. They are masters of this, and can most certainly create screen images to hide behind if necessary. I've also read of the Leonines* — a race of humanoid cat or lion-like beings connected to the Sirius Star System to which I've always felt drawn, so maybe that is how I once knew him in a past life. He probably made use of the familiar vehicle of that past life to re-introduce himself to me.

After this experience at the Center I decided to do some research on *Serapis*, not from the Ascended Master angle but rather from ancient history. There is, as I found out, a connection between him and the Egyptian God Osiris, so he's been around for quite a long time. Oddly enough, many of those ancient gods of Egypt have the "is" suffix on the end of their names, like the Zeta Teachers I've come to know. Maybe there's a connection here somewhere!

Apologies to those who subscribe to the Ascended Masters concept, but this connotation caused me to back off poor old *Serapis* for many years, although I was always aware of his presence and protection around me — he must be very patient indeed! When eventually (probably out of sheer exasperation) he made himself known to me as one of the Zeta Teachers, I felt much more comfortable about him. It was a needed lesson in prejudice.

The second significant event occurred in 1995 when Irene's 1987 prediction of an overseas trip came to pass exactly as she'd described. It most certainly helped me to "find my roots," not only physically but spiritually as well, and it proved to be a major turning point in my life.

One evening in January my brother called about a family reunion to which we were invited. It was to be held in the UK the following July. He and his wife and youngest son were planning to

*Deane, Ashayana. *Voyagers II*, Columbus NC: Wild Flower Press, 2001, p. 60.

attend, and he wanted to know if I could join them. Overseas travel had never ranked highly on my "bucket list," but the compulsion to make this trip was *very* strong, so the next morning I told him to include me in their plans.

The following months were full of anticipation, preparation and a mad scramble to save up money, get a passport, and decide what to pack. I was *so* excited and looking forward to going, remembering Irene's prediction and presuming that it dealt with the family reunion, which was, after all, very much about finding my roots. People would be coming from far and wide to attend, only a couple of whom I'd ever met, and the guest list included a much-loved aunt with whom I'd been in touch by letter since childhood, but had never met in person.

We planned to spend two weeks in southeast England, visiting all the usual tourist attractions in London and making day-trips, and the third week we planned to tour Wales from south to north, then back to Stoke-on-Trent for the family gathering.

My brother's wife is half-English, half-Welsh, and she had been to the UK a couple of times to visit family, so we left our itinerary up to her. She asked me if there was anything special that I wanted to see, and without hesitation my choice was sacred sites — the Standing Stones such as Stonehenge and Avebury. This choice then set off an amazing coincidence.

A day or two later a letter arrived from a cousin who lives near Oxford. I'd not seen her since she'd visited Australia many years previously, well before either of us was married. We'd gotten on so well together all those years ago, like sisters, but we had eventually lost contact with each other as we went our separate ways. She too was attending the reunion, and she had managed to track me down through another family member who knew my married name.

She gave me her address, inviting us to come and visit before the reunion, and she too asked if there was anything special that I wanted to see, so in my reply I mentioned the Standing Stones. Imagine my surprise when she informed me that her husband, who was an archaeologist by profession, specialized in work on sacred sites and was deeply involved with protecting them from developers. He had written a book on a circle of Standing Stones not far from Oxford known as the Rollright Stones. She advised us to see the famous energy centers at Stonehenge and Avebury, but definitely to *not* miss the Rollrights. Being on private land and "in the family" so to speak, they're very special, and one of the most powerful and magical sites in Britain.

By what some would call "sheer chance," we visited our cousin in Oxford on the summer solstice, and with a picnic lunch packed, we headed out to the Rollrights. On the way she described her husband's work on this site, and the ancient artifacts that had been found there. Her sister, also an archaeologist, had worked on the Rollright project as well. My cousin lent me several books on this site, including *Circles of Silence*†, which was an account of some extremely interesting scientific tests carried out in the vicinity of the Rollrights. During our drive there she told us of a number of impressive crop circles that had recently appeared in the area. Unfortunately we never got to see any.

According to *Circles of Silence*, ultra-sound tests were carried out over several years, around and within the main Rollright Circle, which resulted in mysterious and rhythmical pulses being recorded. These pulses consistently rose in intensity at the times of the equinox, and dropped at the solstices. As I write this, a giant heartbeat comes to mind. Inside the circle was absolute and complete silence, like a vacuum, with a total absence of even the usual so-called "white noise" that always registers with any sort of sensitive recording equipment. This utter, complete and inexplicable silence was what gave the book its title.

Many strange stories surround the Rollrights. A ghostly dog named Black Shep reputedly guarded the site, and the area is well known as a dwelling place of the Fairy folk. The King Stone, a single menhir, stands alone and apart from the main circle, atop one of the most famous Fairy Knolls in all of Britain. It's said that on certain nights of the year, the Old Ones come forth from a hole in the hillside to dance around the King Stone. The Fairy Knoll also overlooks the village of Long Compton, which was once a major center for the Old Religion — the Craft of the Wise — with more practitioners per capita than any other village or town in the whole country.

There is a traditional association in folklore between the Fairy folk and ancient burial sites, and to me this is particularly significant in light of the link I've always sensed between the Zetas and the

†Robins, Don. *Circles of Silence*. London, England: Souvenir Press, 1985.

Devic Kingdom. For want of a better term I often referred to them in our group as the "Old Ones." I felt they were more interdimensional than extraterrestrial, but in fact they're both, and they are way beyond simply being a physical race of extraterrestrials from the Zeta Reticulan Star System. I now know that they're much more than this, being caretakers of energy and workers of the angels.

There have been several instances where Greys have been seen and even captured on film in the vicinity of cemeteries and ancient burial sites, and in fact they do play a significant role of assistance to humans in that inevitable rite of passage known on Earth as death. Perhaps the "Fairy" Guardians of such sacred sites are actually Zetas, and in fact this is an understanding I came to following the extraordinary contact experience that occurred sometime after my visit to the site, which I'll describe presently.

The Rollright Stones were on private land in 1995 and are now protected by the National Trust and looked after by a full-time caretaker. The site was almost deserted when we arrived, with only a few other tourists turning up later. My cousin introduced us to the elderly caretaker, who cordially invited us in to the center of the circle to experience the wonderful energy there.

Obviously passionate about his work, he was a mine of information once he realized that we were open to what he had to say. He described how on certain mornings at dawn the energy is quite clearly visible, like a white mist within the perimeter of the circle. He took me to a bare patch right at the very center, where he instructed me to close my eyes and just relax, thus allowing my body to sway gently back and forth with the energy force. He also had me stepping in and out of the circle to feel the difference in the energy. This, by the way, was all happening at midday on the day of the summer solstice, which had not been consciously planned and in fact didn't even occur to me until I read back over my travel diary some time later. I know the exact time only because we were keeping an eye on our watches, needing to return to Oxford for an appointment.

After spending time in the "The King's Men" circle, we crossed the border road between Oxfordshire and Warwickshire. Climbing a stile over the fence surrounding the Fairy Knoll overlooking Long Compton Village, we went to pay our respects to the "King Stone," which stands alone and apart from his "Men." The day was fine, warm, bright and windy, and it was quite magical sitting there on the

Knoll, eating our picnic lunch and watching the wind rippling through the long, soft grass. I sent a silent greeting out to the Old Ones, and I had to hold back tears when it was time to leave. I would've loved to spend a night there.

The following week we visited Stonehenge and Avebury, both very impressive and beautiful. Avebury was particularly magical, because unlike Stonehenge it is not fenced off, so you can walk among the Stones and touch them. We were there at twilight, about 8:30 p.m., but there was still enough light to take photos without a flash. Sheep grazed around the Stones, and a single church bell tolled in the nearby village, creating yet another magical moment to hold in my heart.

From the time I arrived home in Australia, awareness lingered that something extraordinary had happened. At first I put down to jet lag the strange inner sensation of shaking and a greatly increased sensitivity to energies around me, but when it kept up over a period of time, the realization dawned that something was going on at deeper spiritual levels. I found myself experiencing much deeper states of meditation and Tai Chi, which was wonderful, but the heightened state of sensitivity had a down side too, making certain aspects of my life — going among crowds in the supermarket for example — very difficult. Then one night, about three weeks after arriving back in Australia, I had a most incredible experience.

While in an altered state and in my astral body, I was taken by the "Old Ones" to a special place which turned out to be the Rollright Circle. I recognized it as soon as we arrived. My conscious recall the next morning was of being carried in an ancient horse-drawn cart with solid wooden wheels, and taken by a group of small, dark "children." At first I thought they were Gypsy children, but then I realized that no, they were adults, but with the fine delicacy of form and carefree, fun-loving way of children about them. It was as if the whole process was a light-hearted celebration of some sort. Strangely enough, the other tourist, an American woman who'd been at the circle on the day of my visit, was also present.

The next thing I recalled was being taken from the cart and laid down on the ground in the very center of the circle. Here I was held down firmly by many small but surprisingly strong hands, then, with great ceremony, a long needle was plunged into my third-eye chakra. This needle had a most gorgeous, large, light-blue faceted crystal on the other end of it.

I cried out and struggled, begging them to pull it out because of the intense pain. They withdrew the needle, and my mind went blank. The next morning I awoke with clear recall of all that had occurred, but I put it down to a particularly realistic dream — until I examined my face in the mirror and found a small red mark in the shape of a crescent right on the point of my brow chakra.

9

Directed to Write

Just as the 1983 "upgrade" had the effect of opening up paths of study for me in the form of Tai Chi, meditation and Reiki, this latest one had the same effect, only at even deeper levels. My first fully awake, conscious meeting and subsequent reunion with the Zeta family occurred *exactly six years to the day after my 1995 contact experience,* but a vast amount of clearing and preparation still had to be done to allow my Earth-based human consciousness to open up enough for this to take place. This was triggered by the third "amazing event."

At the time of my UK trip, Ian attended a gathering of Reiki Masters in New Zealand. There he met Maureen, a teacher who'd been carrying out in-depth and almost inaccessible research on some Reiki practices based on esoteric Buddhism and connected to the Mandala of the Medicine (Healing) Buddha. These advanced practices had never been released into the West, and Maureen's many years of research were made more difficult because much of the information had not been translated into English from the original Sutras (Buddhist scriptures). This was during the 1990s, when the first tentative contacts were being made between Western Reiki practitioners and their counterparts in Japan, where the system originated.

From her research, it seemed that only the outer teachings had been released to the West, whereas the information she was gathering had more to do with esoteric teachings. Some of this information dealt with the translation of a Reiki symbol known as the "communication symbol," which consists of a quite complex Japanese *kanji* of 22 strokes. The basic meaning of this symbol is: "The Buddha in me greets the Buddha in you." By using this symbol, a Reiki practitioner can send the energy to anyone or anything anywhere, even across time and space.

As a result of her research, our contact Maureen came to understand that the main part of this symbol is the first four strokes, which are an invocation of the Healing Buddha and his twelve assistants known as *Yaksha Generals.* The Healing Buddha is symbolized by the element of wood, pertaining to the five elements of Eastern philosophy — wood, earth, metal, fire and water, and the *Yaksha Generals* are the Japanese equivalent of Nature Spirits.

Maureen just happened to pass this information on to Ian, who in turn passed it on to me, knowing of my link with the devas. A strong message then came through from the family to make personal contact with her, which I did, and she in turn was very happy to hear from somebody else who was interested and open to what she had to say. At that time the Western Reiki community was feeling rather threatened by information that was starting to trickle through from some of the original Reiki practitioners in Japan and was certainly not ready to accept such controversial ideas from one of their own.

Several letters were exchanged between us, and Maureen went on to tell me of a series of initiations into the second level of the Healing Buddha mandala that she'd discovered through her research. The information indicated that Reiki, as it's taught in the West even up to Master Level, only allows the practitioner to access the first (outer) level of the Mandala, which comprises three levels in total. The traditional 21-day cleanse that must be performed after each attunement process deals with the 21 aspects of self-healing/wholing associated with this first, outer level of the Mandala.

The initiation process involved with the second level of the Mandala (note — this is *not* referring to the second degree of Reiki) that our contact had discovered through her research has a much more profound effect, because the healing and clearing is taken to even deeper layers of the psyche. This, in fact, is the deeply hidden aspect of our inner being that the Zetas mirror back to us during encounter experiences. *It is this part of self that must be accessed, dealt with and released if we are to truly achieve self-realization, which is the basis of all Buddhist practices.* Self-realization is what the Buddhist nun, Tensin Palma, was referring to as "the white transparent light at the center of the prism that one should ultimately be aiming to reach through meditation." It is this letting go of and releasing our personal issues and "stories" in order to achieve true self-realization that is referred to in the Katha Upanishad's Chapter 3, Verse 4:

> When all desires that surge in the heart are renounced, the mortal becomes immortal.

When all the knots that strangle the heart are loosened, the mortal becomes immortal.

Thus the “rainbow colors” that we must move past in our quest to access the white transparent light at the center are not just the visions and illusions of the astral plane, but also our personal “stories” that we present to the outer world, and more often than not fool ourselves with as well.

Maureen sent me detailed notes on the very precise ritual involved in accessing this deeper level, which we both subsequently carried out. This was all quite new and experimental to our Western minds, so she was very happy to have someone else to share and compare notes with. We now had an idea of what it must have been like for Mikao Usui, the founder of the Reiki system, when he first put it together from his already acquired knowledge of Buddhism, Shintoism, Shamanism, Samurai training and a deeply esoteric practice known as Shugendo. He apparently tried it out first on himself, family and friends, just to make sure that it worked before releasing it publicly.

What we discovered was that these are *very* powerful and profound practices that could not be done on anyone who hadn't already reached an advanced level of Reiki. The outer aspect needs to be cleared and balanced thoroughly before the inner levels can be dealt with, and as with all energy work, it must be approached slowly and respectfully, and not played around with or rushed into lightly. These newly acquired initiations, like all Buddhist initiation processes, were specifically designed to assist the aspirant onto the path of enlightenment and self-realization, and even with the limited amount of the practice that we are able to access (the parts that had been translated from the Sutras), the results were truly amazing, and exactly what was needed to connect back to the original “family roots” — in other words the true, or higher self.

The more our inner self is healed and balanced, the more our conscious awareness is awakened, which is what evolution in the Human Kingdom is all about, but this is never an easy process, and is the reason why contact with the Zetas is often highly traumatic, confronting, and in some cases very frightening. It can even be compared to the shamanic “Dark Night of the Soul.”

The first initiation into the second level of the Mandala of the Healing Buddha, followed by a 28-day cleanse, started the process within my psyche. I dreamed a lot, with some very profound shifts in consciousness that helped bring about an even deeper sense of connection back to the Zeta family. With this sense of connectedness came a much clearer understanding of exactly who and what they are and why they are down here. Although most Western researchers aren't aware of the fact, these beings are fully acknowledged by Eastern spiritual adepts.

Along with the various experiences and understandings that had come about over the years connecting my own past-life personalities with these beings, memories began surfacing which indicated an even closer interaction with the Zetas. On several occasions I woke in the morning with clear recall of carrying out work alongside of, and as one of, them. These experiences were subsequently independently confirmed by others who were involved at the time and have been recorded in the companion docudrama, *Human by Day, Zeta by Night*[*].

An example of such an incident occurred one night when my spirit form appeared in the bedroom of Catherine's youngest daughter Becky, standing at the foot of her bed with my back turned towards her. As I came around to face her, my appearance changed to that of an ET. When she showed fear, I said to her: "Please do not be afraid — it is only me!" I then took her ankles in my hands to give her healing, and a message was delivered in what we later discovered was Russian, which my Earth form does not know.

The next morning her mother rang to tell me what had happened. At first I assumed that the girl had simply experienced a vivid dream, but as we spoke the memory of a distinctive piece of furniture came into my mind. When I described it to her, she confirmed that her daughter did indeed have such an item in her room. I'd only visited their home on one or two occasions, and I had never seen the girl's bedroom.

This was not an isolated incident. Once my husband received the shock of his life when he entered a room where I was meditating and found one of the Teachers sitting where he expected to see me. I can still recall the look of surprise on his face and how quiet he was afterwards until he managed to summon up enough courage to tell me what he'd seen. Soon after, when I was sitting at the dining room

---

[*] Carroll, Judy. *Human by Day, Zeta by Night*. Columbus, NC: Wild Flower Press, 2011.

table doing some of my writing, it happened again. Luckily he was used to it by then and calmly informed me afterwards about the "shape-shift" that had taken place.

Through such experiences and independent confirmations, the understanding of the true depth of my Zeta connection was becoming increasingly stronger, but there was still a little corner of my very stubborn Earth human consciousness that was having trouble totally accepting it. The problem was this total acceptance was vital, because of a very daunting request that had been put to me by the family during the 1995 contact/upgrade. This demand was for me to write a book on ET/human contact, approached entirely from the Zeta perspective. This book was to offer the communication and information that the Zetas were so often accused of not providing, and also to hopefully counteract all the inaccurate and misinformed fear mongering that has been put out about them over the years.

During the contact they pointed out to me that, from experience acquired over a number of lives lived here on Earth, I would have the knowledge, insight and understanding to present the material from both perspectives, but in a way that Earth folk would be able to relate to more easily. They reminded me of the massive amount of writings they'd managed to channel through to me already, and they gave their assurance that others would be brought online at the appropriate time to help with this rather daunting project. Indeed, the promised help arrived, resulting in the companion volume, *Human by Day, Zeta by Night*[†]. As they said to me: "It will be a 'family project.'"

Now this was quite a brilliant idea theoretically, but putting it into practice was a different matter entirely. A million questions and doubts rose up in my mind. I understood entirely where they were coming from — I too felt deep sadness and frustration at the fear and blatant misinformation that was being spread, but I also felt very small and inadequate in the face of such a request. It was all very well for "upstairs" to come up with these great ideas, but down here on good old Planet Earth, things don't usually flow quite so easily. As it turned out however, all that was needed was a bit more faith and trust. The Zeta folk, like the Romany folk, look after their own. Family is important to them, and they'd never let me down before, so why would they abandon me now in the face of such a daunting task?

[†]Carroll, *ibid.*

As I wrote, help soon arrived in the form of a couple who contacted me through my local Romany association and came to me for Reiki. They were traditional Romany storytellers and published writers. Kate is the one on whom I partly modeled Mara, the old Gypsy lady in *Human by Day, Zeta by Night.* Mara is actually a combination of Kate, my own great-grandmother and another Romany Elder I was in touch with then who confirmed the link I'd long suspected that exists between the Romany Folk, the Zetas and the legend of the lost continent of Lemuria. This is part of the "Secret Lore" of the ancient past that Mara shares with Ali in *Human by Day, Zeta by Night.*

Whenever the couple passed through on their travels, they would come by for a Reiki treatment in exchange for in-depth instruction on writing and the art of storytelling. They put hours into proof reading my first manuscript, providing constructive criticism, ideas and endless support. As a fellow Romany, I felt a strong rapport with them, and the book really did become a "family project" as the Zetas had promised, but something else was needed. As much as I deeply appreciated this amazing help, I still felt very lonely down here, trying to carry out this massive project on my own.

More and more negative hype was being put out about the poor old Zetas, and it was really getting to me. God knows what I was going to come up against if I started writing books from their perspective. It wasn't the ETs I was worried about but rather humans down here, so how was I going to cope with this on my own? I really needed more tangible assistance. Surely I wasn't alone — surely there were others down here similar to me, but where were they? What still needed to be done? The answer? Yes, you guessed it *more* inner work! And the family obliged, as they always do.

The second of the five Mandala practices I undertook over the next few years was done in early 1998, followed by an itchy rash that broke out on my body at the completion of the 28-day cleanse. I was about to seek lice treatment when it occurred to me that no one else in our house was scratching. Then I remembered the *really* hard time I'd had with the cleanse, which had taken me 40 days to complete instead of 28. Something was obviously coming to the surface in a *big* way.

What followed was two years of major karmic clearing and rebalancing from the past Spanish life, which was orchestrated solely to bring the family back together again down here in physical form on Planet Earth after a period of 200 years of enforced separation. This process involved a return to performing and teaching flamenco, as well as working as a Reiki practitioner and teaching Tai Chi. It was at this point that I stopped attending Irene's group because of these other major work commitments.

During Christmas 1998 I went to visit a friend to exchange a psychic reading for a Reiki treatment. The reading's main message was that the following June I would be contacted by an ET teacher, and an opportunity for much closer contact would arise if I chose to accept it. The way it was described made it sound like actual physical contact, if I chose it to be. Free will applied of course, and it was most important that I grasp the offering with both hands if this was the path I really wished to take.

June 1999 did indeed see part of this prediction fulfilled when a very special little being came into my life in the form of Woody, a beautiful honey-and-cream-colored cat who decided to adopt us as her new family. The first night she spent indoors I went to bed feeling a bit uneasy because I had no idea how well house-trained she was, nor whether she would settle down quietly or get upset and perhaps have a little "accident" inside.

That night, with Woody curled up beside me in bed, I experienced a dream in which she appeared to me as a little gray worker. She then grew taller and transformed into the Zeta teacher Maris, who said to me,

> Please do not be concerned about any little accidents in the house. It is me, and surely you know I wouldn't do such a thing!

He actually made a joke of it, going on to reassure me that he *was* house-trained and would not mess on the floor or furnishings. He then woke me up straight away so I'd remember the dream. Mind you, over the next few years a slightly more pussycat-oriented side of Woody emerged, with the occasional fur-ball regurgitated in bed or wherever.

Woody had a most unusual habit that suggested her Zeta connection. Whenever she wanted to link into me on an energy level, she would come up really close to look deeply into my eyes, her pupils dilating until her eyes became huge and totally black, with none of the normal yellow cat's eye color visible. The energy and love that then flowed out of them was amazing, and quite tangible.

This was my first step towards closer contact with the ETs, because when I got to meet Oris in June 2001, he confirmed that part of their soul essence was being projected through Woody as well as through me. The Zetas can easily do shape-shifting, in which they change their appearance and form to some type of animal or bird. This trick is often used to project a screen image to block out more potentially traumatic memories of perhaps being taken up onto a disc. Cats, owls, wolves and deer are often used.

And so my story goes full circle back to Ian's desperate plea on an otherwise ordinary afternoon in June 2000, and from there to Helene's phone call the following day. What struck me most strongly during that first contact was the (then) inexplicable feeling of total recognition I felt on hearing her voice. I knew her so well from somewhere.

Little did I realize on a conscious level that I was reconnecting with my Zeta sister and twin soul from whom I had been separated since the crash of our disc all those many years ago. Our separate paths of travel were finally converging, and what a journey it was going to be!

10
TWIN SOUL

During that first telephone conversation, one piece of advice I gave Helene was to keep a diary, which was a valuable lesson learned from sitting in Irene's circle. What I've found over the years is that when a really extraordinary event such as ET or spirit contact takes place in your life, the inclination is to lock it away in a separate little compartment of your mind. It is so much *not* a part of everyday waking reality that you sometimes just cannot amalgamate it into your consciousness, and so it's forgotten, rather like a dream. I warned Helene of this, suggesting that she keep notes, and being the meticulous Virgo that she is, she followed my instructions explicitly. Consequently we have a wonderfully descriptive daily account of the amazing events that unfolded in the life of this family over the following four years, so from time to time I'll let Helene tell it in her own words:

Helene (H): When I first spoke to Jude on the phone, there was an instant feeling of trust and understanding. Our conversation flowed so easily. To be able to speak freely and openly and to be believed was so amazing and comforting to me. I'd been in such a confused, bewildered daze not knowing who to turn to, even at the point of thinking maybe my children and I were going mad, then to hear Jude's beautiful, calming and reassuring voice on the other end of the phone, like someone throwing out a lifeline to help me stay afloat.

Judy (J): Although Helene didn't realize it at the time it was a huge relief for me as well, to be able to speak freely and openly about my Zeta friends after so many years of "walking on thin ice." To many people, the only "good" ETs were the beautiful, blonde, blue-eyed, rather Aryan-looking Space Brother types. My Zeta friends didn't fall into this category at all. I'll never forget being told once by a supposed psychic to: "Just forget about those little Greys — they're nothing! It's the tall ones (meaning the blonde Space Brothers) you should be trying to connect with." The problem was, I felt no rapport whatsoever with the Space Brother-types.

With Helene there was none of this prejudice, and no preconceived ideas at all, which was a huge relief from my perspective. She was fascinated, because until that point none of her family had had the slightest interest in ET contact — hadn't even heard of it in fact. They were very grounded, down-to-earth folk deeply involved at that time in getting a family business up and running. But they were also open-minded, and by the end of our first phone conversation I felt that my words of reassurance had really helped her. During July we spoke regularly on the phone and things calmed down a little for the family. The nocturnal visits continued however, with their son Ben going off into his trance-state whenever the black-cloaked man was present.

H: In 2000 our family life changed totally, and our whole way of thinking got a complete overhaul when our son Ben started having what I called "night terrors." He was seven at the time, and he would wake up screaming and yelling out: "No!" I'd run to his room to find him sitting curled up at the top of his bed crying, his body shaking in fear and his heart pounding. Turning the light on and giving him a sip of water had no effect — even saying the Lord's Prayer made no difference — nothing worked. It was as if he didn't know I was in the room. This state could last up to 15 minutes, and sometimes happened several nights a week.

At times he would call out his own name very loudly, and speaking slowly would say: "I need this thing!" or "You don't understand — I'm very scared! *Thing following me." One time he told me his tongue felt like wood, and on another occasion that he felt "all stretchy." As time went by, I tried to learn more so I could help him, and during his trances he would say to me:* "I need you! Protect me! I'm sorry — I love you!" *One morning he told me that he'd had a dream where he was in Canada talking French to a man. There was no way Ben would have known that they speak French in Canada. We have no friends or relatives living there, and he was not learning such things in school. Often he would call out to me, and when I came into his room he would say: "Why do people —?" and then stop talking, forgetting what he wanted to ask and suddenly falling back to sleep.*

J: On several occasions Ben saw a man dressed in black pants, shirt, cape and hat, sometimes accompanied by a woman. Helene was caught in the difficult situation of knowing that there definitely was something strange going on in their family home, but not wanting to frighten Ben by openly acknowledging it to him. They'd all seen and heard so much around the house that could not be explained in physical terms.

She knew that trying to convince Ben that there was nothing there and that it was just his imagination was *not* the way to go either. Children are not stupid, and he would have known she wasn't telling the truth — there was just so much going on. Her coping strategy therefore was to acknowledge that yes, we are being visited, but they're our friends and are here to protect us, sort of like Guardian angels. This however was a difficult stance to maintain, at least until she was able to overcome her own uncertainty, and I was very aware of the fact that it was my job to help her do this.

One of the main points that worried her was the fact that the Visitor was dressed in black. I reassured her by explaining that the Zeta Teacher Maris, with whom I'm very familiar, always dresses that way. When he used to stand protectively behind me in the meditation circle he was often mistaken for the priest, Paco, and other people around me have also seen him in his long black cloak and hat, but he is totally benevolent, and a respected Teacher who does have a priestly quality about him.

I went on to tell her of the well-known experiencer, Whitley Strieber, who in *The Secret School*, is reminded of the Sisters of Mercy Order of Nuns when he describes the old female Zeta Teacher in flowing black robes who conducted the classes he attended as a child. I explained that the Zetas often cover themselves this way when approaching humans. After all, by Earth human standards they do look strange and rather frightening, and so take this precaution of covering themselves.

H: August 7, 2000, 9:20 p.m.

Ben was screaming. I went in, could tell he was in trance. He was very scared. I said the Lord's Prayer and then tried to ground him (technique used in Reiki where the ankles are held to ground the energy after a treatment), *but he wouldn't let me. I did a Reiki protection symbol over him. He went to the toilet, came out, still in trance. He looked at me as if I was someone else. My skin crawled. I told him to say "Go away!" He did, but nothing changed. He had a sip of water. He was jumping around the bed and screaming, shaking in fear. I told him they are here to love and protect him. What else could I say?*

Suddenly he grabbed my hands, pulled them forward and turned them over, then laid his hands on top of mine. I think he said something about "dance" and "babe" or "baby." He put his hands in my lap and wriggled his fingers. I (mentally) asked them to please go away and come back when he's older and more able to handle it, and asked God to love and protect him. Then it all stopped. I asked if he knew I was in the room. He said yes. Asked if he wanted a cuddle — he did. I told him I'm here to support and protect him. I asked if he remembered anything, and he said no, then he went straight back to sleep.

J: What young Ben didn't know was the fact that his mom had been suffering debilitating gynecological problems since his birth, with excruciating menstrual cramps every month. She and her husband were in the process of setting up a manufacturing business in camper-trailers, which meant spending long hours on their feet at camping shows promoting their product, and poor Helene was having major difficulties with this.

Young Ben of course had no idea of his mom's health issues, but when Helene described the way he'd moved his hands in such a strange way over her stomach area while in trance, it was obvious that he'd been doing a Qi Gong-type healing technique on her, under the guidance of whoever was present in the room. As the dreaded time of the month approached a week or so later, Helene waited with bated breath to see what would happen, and was ecstatic when no pain occurred, and she's had few problems since.

This amazing event seems to have been carefully orchestrated to provide Helene with further reassurance that what I'd told her about the black-clad Visitors was correct — that they were benevolent and here only to help us. At the same time, I too still needed a little reassurance on the conscious, Earth human level of my psyche.

During my 1995 contact, much deeper understanding was opened up for me on the role of the Zetas on Earth, and the reasons behind the various procedures they do on humans. This was all very well on an academic level, but now here I was being brought online to give help and reassurance to others going through potentially very challenging contact with these beings to whom I was intrinsically linked. The time was ripe for me to be given some first-hand experience of one of these procedures — as if the needle in the brow chakra hadn't been enough! The thing was, during the "needle" experience I'd felt scared and helpless, held down firmly as the painful procedure was seemingly forced upon me. Now it was time for me to take back my power.

One night I found myself sitting up on one of the tables in the clinic on the disc. Several of my Zeta friends were gathered around, and one was making a long incision on my leg. I felt absolutely no fear or pain; in fact I was in control and directing them, and I was just as interested in the procedure as those doing it. There was a clear awareness that my Earth body was nothing more than a "container" that I'd made available to be experimented upon, and I felt very little attachment to it. My Zeta consciousness was fully open and present.

At first when I woke the next morning there was only a very vague recollection of being "upstairs," but that day we were planning a trip to the beach, so before leaving home I went to apply suntan lotion to my legs and discovered the cut. Because I had felt no pain, I'd not noticed it previously, but as soon as I saw it, the memory of the procedure up on the disc came back clearly. The cut was about 6 cm. long, perfectly straight, and it looked really strange because there were tiny blisters along its entire length. It was situated on the outer side of my lower right leg, exactly where I remembered them working, and obviously quite deep, because a faint scar remains to this day. There was no pain at any time and it healed very quickly.

As with Helene's healing, positive things also started manifesting for Ben soon after the black-cloaked man came into his life, with so much improvement in several areas that his teachers noticed and commented upon the difference. Whenever his nocturnal activities became too persistent or Ben's fear became too intense, Helene would phone to let me know. Once I was consciously aware on the physical human level that things were getting too heavy, I was able to intervene on the Zeta level, easing the process somewhat and calming the situation.

It's very hard to describe fully the conflict of emotions this understanding brought up within my psyche. My human side experienced a deep level of disquiet in that it seemed to be a part of me that was causing such distress to a child, which at the time I couldn't express to Helene. My Zeta side felt deep sympathy too, but it had no choice — it *had* to be done. Nevertheless, this was a huge burden to carry, for I can't bear to see a child or animal in distress. At least "upstairs" was trying to do some positive things to make up for the traumas inflicted upon the family, and this understanding helped assuage some of my guilt, but it didn't stop me from being anxious over the situation.

H: August 19, 2000.

Ben came in at 6:00 a.m. this morning. He said he saw the shadow of a dog and then heard a beep, beep noise all around his room. He ran out and came to our room. He seemed scared but not terrified. Two days ago Ben read four books in one night — and did very well. He said he prayed to God to make him smarter, because he was having learning difficulties at school. This morning he noticed strange marks on his cupboard door. Our dog Shaka is acting strange and wants to be near us all the time.*

J: With these happenings going on in Helene's family, I wanted to provide them with more information on the subject of ET contact, but most books available back then, particularly those dealing with the Greys, were very fear oriented, which was *not* what they needed at that point in their lives. Not knowing what else to give them, I passed on the manuscript I'd been writing with the help of my Romany friends. At that time it wasn't even completed, so it was a good chance to get some feedback before the daunting task of approaching publishers.

The timing of everything that was going on was quite amazing. The Zetas put forward the initial idea for the book in 1995. The Romany story tellers then arrived just when help was needed in writing the book, and as a result, by the time Helene contacted me, I had a reasonably well-put-together manuscript to pass on to the family *exactly when it was needed.*

As I've learned from being down here in human form for a number of lives, we on Planet Earth are very much bound by time — timing is everything, and it is not linear as most people perceive it to be. This is one of a number of illusions that we think of as third-dimensional reality, and although it works this way for us on the Earth human conscious level, it's not the way things operate in the greater reality. It does however tend to control the unfolding of events on Earth.

*J: These were little reading books he was given for homework.

All those years ago when I appeared as an ET in the middle of the night at the foot of Becky's bed, I gave a message. I still have no conscious memory of this, but the next morning she could recall one word that I spoke. That word was "*vremya*." We searched and searched, trying to find out what it meant, and eventually by pure chance found out that it's the Russian word for time. On the conscious human level, I don't know the Russian language at all, but of course Maris/Ferenc does. As I have since discovered, a common message that is given to human experiencers by the Zetas is: "It is time for you to wake up!" I am now certain that this was the message my ET self was trying to get across to my young friend.

August, 2000.

I finally met Helene and Gary face to face when they came by to pick up my manuscript. Their son Ben and daughter Kira accompanied them, and they really impressed me as being well-brought-up kids. The family seemed very pleasant all around. During their visit Kira expressed the wish that she could see the "Visitors" as Ben did. She was 12 at the time, and little did we know that after this wish was verbally expressed and Kira and I had established physical contact, life was never going to be the same again, for any of us. Unbeknown to us, energies were being shifted on deeper levels, which immediately impacted on the whole family in a *big* way.

*H: As we drove home from Jude's place there was complete silence in the car, which was very strange for us, being a quite talkative family. No one spoke; we were all deeply immersed in our own thoughts. The sound of silence was actually the sound of reality hitting us big time. My thoughts during that drive were: "Oh my God this is real! We're being visited by some type of beings from somewhere out there in the universe!" Please excuse my language here, but "Oh s**t! Now what?" and "Why us?" When we got home our energies were all over the place. Even our dog Shaka sensed it and started acting strangely. Finally realizing all this was real was a total shock to our systems, to say the least.*

Not only was my life changing, but so was my whole way of thinking, the way I view the world, and the way I see myself. And we all came to the realization that we really do have strange neighbors living somewhere out there in the cosmos who are now visiting us, my children, my family — of all people! But why us?

Suddenly I felt as if I'd been asleep all my life. What a sheltered existence I'd been living for the past 40 years. My whole structure of life was crumbling and tumbling down around me, and my belief system was being tested to its limits. I was being tested to my limits, trying to understand and comprehend all of this, on top of having the responsibility of my children's physical and emotional wellbeing.

H: August 20, 2000.

We met Judy yesterday afternoon, and since then we have all been totally out of whack, even the dog. The whole family has been either having words with each other or else not talking at all.

August 21, 2000.

I'm feeling very unbalanced. I don't know where I am. I put some meditation music on, looked at Ben's photo on the wall, and burst into tears. A great urge came upon me to go down to the beach, where I sat on a rock wall and listened to the ocean. Closing my eyes I could see the color orange, and asked God for help and guidance, and to give me a sign to show me that I'm going in the right direction. A dark fellow about 16 was standing at the edge of the rocks near to where I sat. He turned and walked past without looking at me, then he suddenly stopped, turned back, and asked me for the time. He then moved on. A strong message came through:

Take your time — be patient!

Looking down I saw a stone with a smiley face on it. I picked it up to take home with me.

August 22, 2000.

Ian gave me a Reiki treatment. During it I felt two other pairs of hands on me besides his. He told me my aura was all silvery. I really needed the treatment to help gather my thoughts and clear my head. In one way it was wonderful to feel another set of hands working on me, and it felt very calming and comforting, but later on it seemed as if it brought all my feelings and emotions up to the surface, as Reiki tends to do. Everything was so overwhelming and confusing!

During the days that followed, life was foggy, stressful and exhausting. I remember walking outside one night and throwing my hands up in the air, crying and saying: "God, what have we done to deserve this? We are not bad people! Please help us!"

There were three things that kept me going through those early times — my lifelong motto, "Love conquers all," my new friend

Jude, and my love for my family. There was no choice anyway — I couldn't simply ignore these strange experiences and hope they'd go away, what with screaming, frightened children, flashing lights and strange noises in our home and crazy "dreams." And so I took just one step, one day at a time, with a lot of faith and sheer determination to get through this for all our sakes.

January 2001

Ben wakes five out of seven nights, wanting a drink and saying he hears footsteps or sees people. He normally wakes between 11:00 p.m. and 1:00 a.m. He came out with a statement: "I love the flowers. I can't talk to them, but they understand my feelings!" He's walked into our bedroom in the middle of the night three nights in a row. Normally he's too terrified to leave his room in the dark, and always bangs on the wall or yells out for us to come to him, but he just walked into our room and stood next to Gary's side of the bed, saying nothing. Gary woke in a fright and took him back to his own bed.

February 4, 2001

I went to bed at 11:00 p.m. and couldn't sleep. I asked the Visitors for guidance to help all of them — the ETs and Ben — and to please protect him from harm. I explained to them that I feel I'm starting to understand why they are here. I suddenly felt a hand with long fingers on my head, and my body felt crawly, as if I'd walked into a spider's web. I could hear noises in the house. I asked the ET Visitors if they could help me to more easily see auras and energy, and I told them I just want to help them all.

I asked them to give me a sign that they'd heard. A scratching sound started up behind the bed, like a mouse in the wall. In my mind I said to the mouse: "Please go away, Mousey, and eat somewhere else." The sound stopped immediately, which would be a bit strange if it really was a mouse — it's not like I spoke out aloud to frighten it. I was still awake at 1:00 a.m. when Ben called out that there was a big spider in his room. He called out a second time, complaining of a "crawly" feeling, as if bugs were walking on him, just as I'd felt earlier in the night. Then he called me in a third time, saying he'd seen a black shadow race across his room about a foot or so off the floor.

February 7, 2001, 11:30 p.m.

Ben woke, half sat up in bed, and said: "Mom, sometimes I have a dream, but it's not really a dream. I'm in a school doing

English and Math." He then said the letters Q, S, M, P, E, which he repeated again — Q, S, M, P, E. After that he said he was scared and didn't want to stay in his room, so I took him into ours.

Q	Quetzalcoatl
S	Serapis
M	Maris and Mara
P	Paco and Pan
E	Entil

J: Helene had no idea what these letters meant and phoned the next day for my opinion, but I didn't know either. A week or so later she called back, nearly bursting with excitement. As she'd read further into an early draft of my manuscript, the realization dawned that these were the first letters of the names of all the main ET characters in it.

Seven-year-old Ben had not read the manuscript, and couldn't have understood it if he'd tried. He was the perfect vehicle of communication to provide confirmation that there were other intelligences "out there" taking a hand in our affairs. It wasn't too long after this that Kira had her wish granted — the desire she'd expressed of wanting to see the Visitors for herself.

At first they simply appeared standing in the corner of her bedroom, one tall one and one smaller one, faces hidden but obviously watching her. Sometimes she would awaken during the night to find them seemingly giving her Reiki, with one at her ankles and the other at her throat. Kira was unaware that these two positions cover every energy meridian in the body, and so she was being given a very thorough treatment. But in her ignorance, she was terrified.

Each time the Visitors appeared in her room or touched her, she ran screaming to her parents' room, too scared to be left alone and begging to be allowed to sleep with them. My family link now became very useful, because as soon as Helene brought my conscious attention to Kira's fear, they pulled back a little. In fact they then tried to lighten the situation with humor. One morning I awoke with the bright idea, seemingly out of the blue, that maybe I should get myself an exercise ball. That very day Helene rang to tell me that the night before, Kira had woken to find the tall one, dressed in full Zeta Teacher regalia of black cape and hat, sitting on her pink exercise ball and bouncing up and down, as if trying it out.

This simple act was exactly what was required to help Helene move past her fear, and it served to bolster my confidence as well. For her it provided much-needed proof that there definitely was a connection between the Judy she had come to know as a trusted friend, and whoever these mysterious beings were that visited her family. For me it was further confirmation of my deep connection with them, which in turn gave me the confidence to be able to reassure Helene unconditionally that her children were safe, and that no harm would come to them.

I now knew without a doubt that I am still "me" in whichever reality I happen to be operating. My Zeta reality is not different than my Earth human reality when it comes to ethics, understanding and compassion. Sometimes a doctor has to cause pain or fear to a child in order to carry out a procedure, but this doesn't make the doctor evil or bad. Even though pain and fear may be involved, the procedure is done with the full intention of helping, protecting and healing the child. The doctor may well absolutely adore children, so frightening or causing them pain would be totally abhorrent to them, but the procedure must be done for the children's sake, to heal or protect them from illness. This is exactly how it is from the Zeta perspective.

H: April 18, 2001, 8:40 p.m.

Ben came running out to the lounge room complaining of being hurt. He seemed to be in a trance. I took him back to his bedroom. He kept looking around his room and towards the doorway, and he appeared fearful and worried. I assured him I was there and I asked if he realized this. His answer was, "Yes, but I don't know if it's you." He then got up and ran into the office wanting his dad. Crying, he put his arms around Gary, then he came back to the lounge, sat down and again complained of hurting all over his body. We took him back to bed. He'd start to talk then stop — and he kept mumbling. We told him to tell them to go away, and we said the Lord's Prayer. He said it with us, very clearly. Gary brought him a drink of water and he settled down and started to wake up.

He told me he had been at the beach, and they'd dumped a wave on him. I asked him how they'd done this, and he answered: "They have magical powers." I asked what they look like and he answered that they had the color orange on, and black hair. He couldn't see them very well but said they looked different from the others he'd seen. He kept complaining of a sore tummy, so I gave him some Reiki. He said, "I'm glad you're my mom!" then he fell asleep.

When I came back out to the lounge room, I could smell strong sandalwood incense; the scent of it was on my left hand. Maybe I imagined it because I do have some, but it's packed away in a cardboard box in our bedroom across the hallway. Ben's trance lasted about 20 minutes, until 9:00 p.m. At 9:30 I went into our bedroom, but I couldn't smell any incense. The day before I'd kept seeing a mist inside the house, and Gary thought he saw someone walking through the doorway between the lounge and office. Ben had also woken the night before, complaining of seeing someone and of a light going on and off.

May 2, 2001.

Kira felt someone move her foot as she lay in bed (about 9:30 p.m.). She was scared, so we swapped beds. Ben woke at 2:00 a.m. wanting a drink, and was surprised at how fast I came into him. I explained that I was sleeping in Kira's room, which is closer to his than ours is. At 4:45 a.m. he came running in wanting to know if I was all right. He'd seen flashing lights outside the window and heard footsteps down the side of the house.

J: Through all of this Helene somehow managed to keep quite a lot of the raw emotion to herself, which didn't occur to me until I asked her to write out a description of a typical night of "activity," including the feelings and emotions involved.

To say I was surprised at the fears and questions that she described being confronted with would be a gross understatement I was shocked to the core of my being. Not having been a mother, I'd never considered the situation from this angle — to have your children — your own flesh and blood — undergoing these extremely weird experiences and contacts that you cannot control or stop, cannot protect them from, and worst of all, cannot reassure them that it won't recur. Added to this were the questions that arose in her mind — why is this happening to us? Is it my fault? Who, or what are these beings, and what do they want? Will my children be hurt psychologically, if not physically? Are we all going crazy?

The only words of comfort I could offer were that I too had been through this as a child, including the fear that had Kira spending so many nights sleeping in with her parents, and Ben waking in terror at least one night a week. The only reassurance I could give was that I'd never been hurt in any way, and that the fear eventually dissipated. As I explained to her, once my consciousness opened properly to the Visitors, their love and caring was quite tangible, and her regular contact with Oris confirmed this, not once, but many times, as she got to know him better. The thing that struck her most about him was his sheer "human-ness." He displayed deep emotion — joy, sadness, kindness, and compassion, and sometimes impatience, although a lot of that originated with Kira.

In a quest to find another parent in a similar situation with whom she could communicate, Helene turned to the Internet. Only one response came in, from David in the UK, an experiencer himself, who also had a son undergoing Zeta contact. We kept up correspondence with David for a while, and a lot of mutual assistance was provided. This contact resulted in more incredible confirmation for me of my work "upstairs" when, during the course of our correspondence, David told us of a mysterious scar on his head which was the result of one of his many encounters on board a Zeta disc in which his "abductors" operated on his head.

A year or so earlier, I'd woken one morning with very clear recall of walking into a room on the disc where a man lay on a table. This room was the clinic, where the medical procedures are carried out. As I stepped through the door the man turned his head in my direction, and catching sight of me, the look of horror that registered on his face was beyond description. Even now, years later in my waking human state I can't forget it, and I can still clearly recall the profound sadness and frustration that I felt at the time.

As far as I know, this is the first time the other side of the so-called "alien abduction experience" has ever been expressed, from the Zetas' point of view, of how truly awful it is to be feared and hated to that extent. I really felt like crying, but there was a job to do — so I just got on with it, but it hurt me deeply. I tried my best to communicate with him, but I could not penetrate his fear.

The procedure that I and two others working with me carried out involved something being done inside his head. I can't recall exactly what we did, but there's a memory of wires being either attached or removed, and that it was for his own good — to protect him in some way. Details escape me, but I can recall opening his head and working inside. On waking the next morning, I could remember clearly what he looked like, and I knew that if I ever saw him down here, I'd remember him. After some weeks of communication with David, he sent us a photograph of himself, and I recognized him immediately. *He was the same person* I'd worked on "upstairs."

11

CONTACT

June 14, 2001.

Helene gave Kira a Reiki treatment. The two Zetas had been back in her room trying to work on her ankles and throat, but despite my reassurances she was still terrified of them. Ten minutes or so into the treatment she began telling her mom what she was experiencing — "I'm walking through a beautiful rainforest. Now I can see grandma in a living room somewhere." The children's grandmother, Laura, had died of cancer a couple of years earlier, and Kira was still missing her badly. Grandma spoke to her, telling her how much she loved her, telling her to keep strong and that she'd be fine.

Suddenly she was back in the rainforest, with a little girl coming towards her, giggling happily. She was about seven or eight, very pretty with blonde hair. They walked out of the rainforest to a beach, where they built sandcastles together. Helene asked Kira if she knew who the little girl was. At first she said no, so Helene told her to take a closer look. It was then she realized that the little girl was herself when she was younger, and looking so happy and carefree. The girl then grabbed Kira's hand and led her back into the rainforest. "I'm scared," she said, "but let's keep going." The next moment they were back on the beach, and Kira could see a man in the distance, dressed all in black. The little girl suddenly announced: "I have to go now — bye!"

Kira walked towards the man but felt scared, so Helene told her to ask him his name. He replied,

Don't be afraid. My name is Oris*, and I'm here to help you.

"Help with what?"

You'll have to find out for yourself,

"When?" asked Kira.

---

* Pronounced "aw-riss."

When you are ready!

"When will that be?" Kira persisted, now feeling quite comfortable and at ease with him because he seemed familiar to her somehow, and his energy felt very pleasant.

When you are ready!

Putting his hand on her shoulder, he told her that he would see her again soon. Kira put her arms around him and they gave each other a hug. His energy made her feel so good, and his smile was kind. She later described him to her mother as being very tall and wearing a black suit. He also had on a long black cape with a high collar, shiny black shoes, and a black, wide-brimmed Spanish-style hat with a red band and red feather stuck in it. The hat was pulled down very low to almost cover his face. His skin was a bluish-gray color and quite wrinkled, and there were four long fingers on each hand — blunt and rounded on the tips.

Kira then saw a house in the distance, and walking towards it she noticed how windy it had become. Gardening at the house was an old couple who seemed familiar. The garden was full of roses and daisies in many different colors. The woman waved a greeting and the old man said hello. Kira discovered later that this wind is caused by the proximity of a disc. The "house" was actually a screen image hiding the disc, which Kira wasn't quite ready to see at that point.

The next moment found Kira in a black room, feeling very scared. Helene reassured her by suggesting that this room could represent her fear, and that if she could trust and move past it, love would be there for her on the other side. Then she was back in the rainforest, but was again pulled back to the black room, sitting in a chair and feeling very frightened. Helene encouraged her again, telling her to be brave and to have trust that she could get through the fear barrier.

Kira then found herself playing happily in a beautiful green field with her friend and their two dogs, Shaka and Toby, but again she was pulled back to the room, and saw herself asleep, with a scared and stressed look on her face. At this point she woke from the treatment. At first she couldn't open her eyes, but she could see her mother's aura, which she described as all yellow, with an outline of reddish-orange color. After she woke properly she felt much happier and more relaxed.

June 17, 2001

Helene took Kira to Ian for a second Reiki treatment in which both of them worked on her. As she started going into an altered state, she realized she could "see" everything in the room even though her physical eyes were closed, and she proceeded to prove it by naming all the books on a nearby bookshelf.

After a few minutes Oris arrived. Ian could vaguely see somebody standing at her feet. Two of the smaller ones, which Oris referred to as Helpers, were present as well, and all three were assisting with the treatment. These little ones, about three feet or so in height, are also called workers, and are energetically linked to the older, taller Teachers. Towards the end of the session Ian suggested that he and Helene stand back out of the way to give the Zetas room to work, but as Helene felt, this really wasn't necessary, as they enjoy working beside us, and can quite easily even work through our physical bodies. She was now starting to feel very comfortable with the Visitors.

It was then Ian's turn for a treatment. He had a broken ankle, so Helene went straight to that, and Kira, sitting at Ian's head, could see Oris standing beside her mom, also working on the injured foot. One of the Helpers concentrated energy into the stomach area. At one point Oris stood behind Helene with his arms on either side of her and his hands under hers. She could feel something under her hands and thought it was Ian's foot, but on looking, realized her hands weren't touching him and that it was actually Oris's hands she could feel. They felt warm, just like normal human hands.

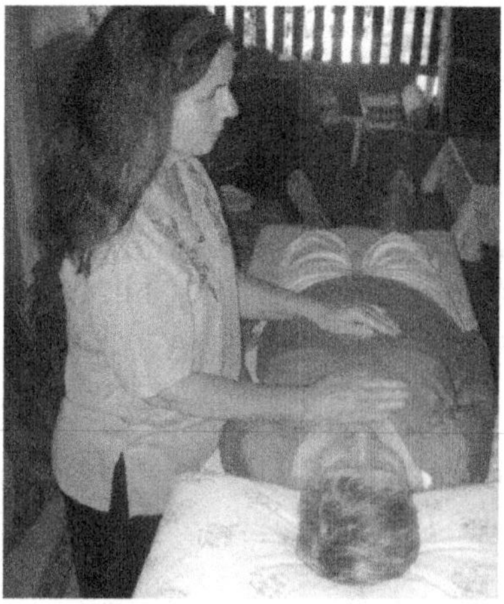

When she told me of this I thought back to the face and throat massage that I'd once been given in which very long fingers had reached far down into my throat, obviously working on my communication chakra. The explanation had been: "This is to help you to speak out." It was after this experience that all the teachings began coming through. Those hands too had felt warm, strong and very comforting.

Suddenly Oris relayed a message to Helene via Kira:

Cleanse the aura – now!

His voice sounded quite urgent, so Helene obeyed, but later questioned him about it. We had been taught to only cleanse the aura at the end of a treatment, which is the usual procedure with Reiki. He explained to her that the cleanse needs to be done much more often, and that when they (the ETs) do this type of healing, several of them work together, and one has the sole task of cleansing the aura repeatedly throughout the course of the treatment.

It was later explained to us that it's like when you're using a drill to bore a hole in wood. The drill works better if every so often you blow away the sawdust that has collected. When the treatment was over, Ian remarked on how profound it had been, despite the fact that they'd talked nearly all the way through it.

Over the following couple of years, both Oris and Maris gave us much information on Reiki, and evidence from an independent source has also shown the Zetas' strong link with Reiki healing — a book[†] by Adrian Dvir of Israel showed on its cover a Zeta-type being and is about Reiki-type healings being carried out by aliens.

After her two treatments, Kira felt more relaxed and comfortable with Oris, especially now that she knew his name, but the little ones still frightened her. Oris came when he could to give her healing, but sometimes the little workers came instead. What didn't help her fear was the fact that some of the little ones can be a bit rough and careless and are not always used to dealing with humans. They sometimes don't quite understand about human physicality and emotion. Some of them tend to just follow orders without much thought or sensitivity, and this has caused a few problems in Zeta/Earth human contact.

For example, when a worker came to give Kira healing on her throat, this worker suddenly appeared in Kira's room in the middle of the night and went straight for her throat with its long, thin, four-fingered hands. Of course poor Kira almost freaked out, screaming in terror and bringing both Helene and Oris running.

When he realized what had happened, Oris stepped in, first placing his hand gently on her shoulder then slowly moving across to

[†] Dvir, Adrian. *X3, Healing Entities and Aliens*. Israel: Gal Publishing, 2001.

her throat. Helene and I had a good chuckle about it afterwards, visualizing the poor little worker being on the receiving end of a stern reprimand by "The Boss" for not taking more care.

June 22, 2001

A visit to Helene's home was arranged so I could meet Oris. On the way there it suddenly occurred to me that it was exactly six years earlier that I'd visited the sacred site in the UK. I was also reminded of the 1998 prediction. Just prior to my visit, Helene mailed me copies of a couple of sketches Kira had done — one of a worker and one of Oris. At that point he still hadn't revealed his whole face to her, so this portrait shows him with his hat pulled down very low, almost to nose level.

The moment I saw it recognition dawned. The hat he wears has a flat top and wide, flat brim — very similar to the Cordobes-style hat worn in Spain, and despite his gray skin and ET features, I could clearly recognize *Manolo's* energy in him.

Helene had commented several times on the cold energy that always accompanied Oris's visits to their home, just as it did around me when *Manolo* was present in our meditation circle. A number of experiencers have spoken of this cold Zeta energy, and it took Helene and Kira quite a few months to get used to it.

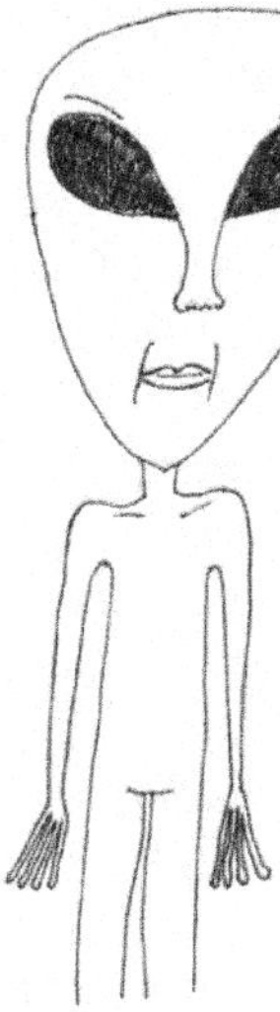

WORKER, BY KIRA

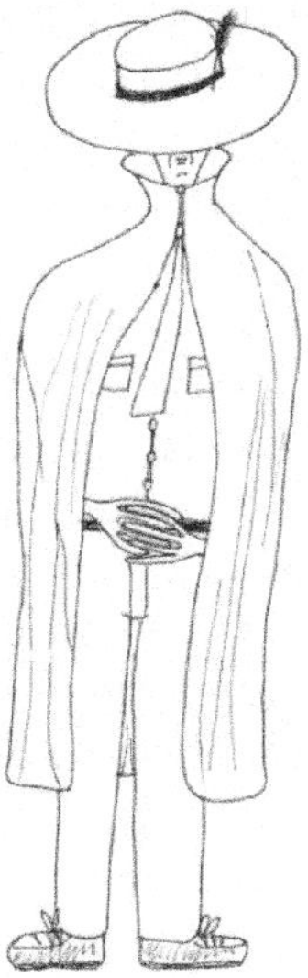

ORIS IN CORDOBES-STYLE HAT

H: When Oris visited us, the feelings were totally different from anything I'd ever experienced. Our bodies felt as if they were shaking from the inside out — as if your body were shivering on the inside only. I've never felt this sensation before. The inside of my body felt like it was vibrating faster, and at the same time my brain was slowing down. I found it hard to think and felt tired. It took us about a year to get used to his energies — the longer he stayed in the room the more we shook on the inside. Kira felt the same as I did. Sometimes he would be with us and talk for up to an hour or more. He was the one to decide when it was time to go, and I always felt strongly that he knew how much our bodies could handle, so never out-stayed his welcome. The room would also get colder and colder. Afterwards we would feel tired, relaxed and sometimes a little overwhelmed.

J: It was so good to make physical contact again, with all the activity happening around Helene's family. Oris was visiting their home and giving out teachings almost daily, and the day before my visit he had told them that he knew I was coming and that he'd be there for sure.

We decided that I would lie on Helene's treatment table and they would give me Reiki. When you open up in this way for contact with spirit, protection is really important, because you don't want any negative energies impinging. This was a valuable lesson learned in Irene's group. By doing Reiki we felt safe and protected from any negative interference, because one of the Reiki symbols is specifically for this. Besides, the Zetas love Reiki energy, and sure enough, about 10 minutes into the treatment Oris arrived, apologizing for his lateness.

Twelve-year-old Kira hadn't done anything in the way of psychic development, but she does have natural abilities in this area. These abilities are enhanced by the fact that she is a rather emotional individual with an excess of astral plane energy, which is typical of many natural-born psychics. The astral plane acts like a bridge between the physical and higher realms, and is always utilized for spirit communication. Oris once made the comment that her emotions were the reason why he was drawn to her. Her role was to be a messenger, to bring forward information on the physical side of Zeta life — what and how they eat, how and when they sleep, and how they relate to each other as a human-type culture. My role has been to access their spiritual teachings and messages.

Since the 1983 upgrade to my energy system, tapping into Zeta consciousness to access spiritual teachings has never been a problem for me. The difficulty lay in bridging the two realities, Earth human and Zeta, and bringing physical recall through from one to the other. This "selective consciousness" was chosen on purpose so that I wouldn't feel caught between two worlds, although this still happens to a certain extent, which can be quite disconcerting at times. Because of the type of work I'm doing, it's necessary to be fully grounded and totally focused into either one or the other. This is why a more astral-plane-oriented translator or bridge was needed, to assist in the conscious melding of the two realities. Earlier attempts had been made with two others, but in both cases ego and belief systems ended up getting in the way.

The astral plane is the plane of emotion, dreams and illusion, and unfortunately one can get too caught up in this area with visions, past lives and the various belief systems and mind-sets connected to past or present. Young Kira was a clean slate, so to speak, and ideal in that her family background is stable and not caught up too much in any particular belief system, including New Age ones. At the same time it was necessary to seize the opportunity to impart as much information as possible in the limited time frame available while she was still young enough to be completely clear. This is why the contact was so full on. In exchange for her assistance, she has been provided with as much teaching and guidance as possible while still respecting her free will, and a great amount of karma has also been balanced in the process.

Oris arrived soon after we settled ourselves into the Reiki energy, and I asked him if he was aware that it was exactly six years since I'd visited the sacred site where the needle with the blue crystal on the end had been inserted into my third-eye chakra. (See Chapter 8.) He answered in the affirmative and went on to tell me that this was why we'd come together today. He confirmed that it was a group of workers who'd carried it out.

We asked Oris, "How do you prefer to be called — aliens, Greys, Zetas, ETs or what?"

> Please, not aliens! Greys or ETs is fine, but what we would really like you to call us is family.

This then led to my next question, about the past life in Spain. I told him how I recognized his hat and that I could sense *Manolo's* energy in him, and was he there back then in human form. Again he answered in the affirmative, and went on to explain how we were a family.

He told us that he recalled being a dancer in a past human life in Spain, and added that he still likes to dance and was the one who helped me in my flamenco work. The old Zeta Teacher in Whitley Strieber's *The Secret School* also taught dance as an important part of the curriculum, and when students graduated, they were referred to as "dancers." By promoting flexibility of the body, dancing also helps to keep the mind flexible. This is a *most* important part of human evolution (mind expansion) that the Zetas are trying to impart, and it is why I teach Tai Chi.

The Zetas are badly misunderstood by many people down here, most especially by those humans who are blinded by ego. Oris has commented several times on how upset they get when people regard them as gods or demons. To quote his exact words:

> Humans either look upon us as Gods, or else they are terrified of us, but we are not to be feared or revered, for we are simply humanoid beings like your selves.

They are not infallible – they do occasionally make mistakes, just like humans. Sometimes when we've asked a question, Oris has had to go off to ask someone else, or check his records and get back to us later. Even though he's an Elder, he once had to ask a worker to help answer a question for us.

I asked him if he was helping me with my writing, and if there was anything in particular they wanted me to include. He explained that Maris is the one assisting me and that he'd get back to me on it. After consulting Maris, Oris later told me to include some illustrations, and to speak out about the negative forces causing problems for both Zetas and Earthlings. He also asked me to include information on the different levels of awareness that they refer to as the "Human Ladder," which I have done in Chapter 13.

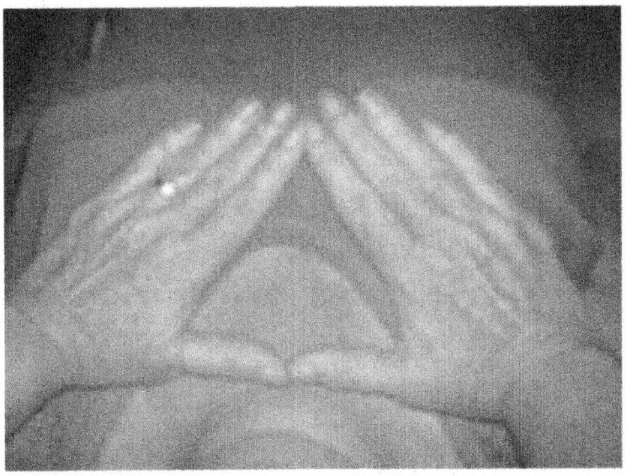

Oris also gave us some useful advice on Reiki, teaching us a special way of holding our hands to amplify the flow of energy. He referred to this hand position as the "peace sign," and went on to tell us that the well-known peace sign — the "Ban the Bomb" insignia that was introduced during the 1960s, is quite negative. Being formed from semaphore signals for N and D (Nuclear Disarmament) and appearing as an inverted cross, it actually draws negative energy. He explained that the Zeta peace sign is like a shield that deflects negativity, and since using it we find our Reiki to be stronger.

Independent confirmation was given on this hand position some time later, from two different sources. The first came from an elderly gentleman who attended my Tai Chi classes and went on to learn Reiki from me. He'd done a Tai Chi Course many years before with another school, and when I showed him the peace sign hand position during the Reiki seminar (not mentioning where I'd learned it of course), he recognized it straight away from his earlier Tai Chi training as a hand position referred to as "Tiger's Mouth."

The second confirmation came from a Roman Catholic nun who was also a Reiki student of mine. She had studied Qi Gong, and when shown the peace sign during the seminar, informed me that she knew it as "Diamond Hands."

On several occasions when Oris has stepped in to help Helene with Reiki treatments, he's made use of Qi Gong. Neither Helene nor Kira knew what he was doing as they have no knowledge of this. It was only later when they described his techniques to me that we began to realize the depth of his knowledge and understanding of energy.

There is similarity between the Zetas/Greys and the devas of the ancient Indian writings known as the Vedas. Deva is a Sanskrit word meaning "Shining One." Their discs are even spoken of in the Rig Veda, where they are referred to as "Vimanas." As far as I understand, all the natural healing methods of Eastern tradition which tap into life-force energy came originally from India, and I believe they were first shown to humankind by the devas, so it may have been the Zetas who brought them here to Planet Earth millennia ago. This is why we take note when they give us advice on Reiki.

During my visit that day Oris also showed us a rather complex aura-cleansing technique which is, as he explained, easier for the Zetas with their very long fingers. To compensate for our anatomical deficiency, he showed us how to link the energy flow between our fingertips. This lesson led to more amazing confirmation for Helene later that afternoon.

While I was there, Shaka the black Labrador came unbidden into the lounge room and went straight to a seemingly empty armchair in the far corner. When Helene scolded him, Oris apologized and owned up to having called the dog in. Of course Shaka had gone over to where he was sitting. Oris explained how much he enjoyed having the dog present, so Helene let him stay, sitting happily with his huge head resting on Oris's lap, which looked really weird as neither Helene nor I could see Oris physically.

Returning home from dropping me off at the train station later that afternoon, Helene asked Kira if she felt better after speaking to me. She said yes, in a way, but she was still worried that we'd think she was making it all up or else imagining it, as she was the only one who could see and hear Oris on a physical, conscious level. Helene reassured her that she did trust her and believed what she was saying, and went on to point out that there was *no* way she could have made up all the information that Oris had passed on to us during the course of the day. "I know that, Mom," Kira replied, "but I still wish you could at least hear his voice!"

Little did Kira know how soon her wish would be granted, nor did Helene even begin to guess that she was about to receive the shock of her life.

H: When we got home from taking Jude to the station, we sat down in the family room to talk over the day's events. I did this to help both of us acknowledge how important the day had been, for all our sakes. It really had been huge! I then suggested we refresh ourselves with the new teaching of the aura cleanse that Oris had given us. I felt it was very important, and being one who loves details, and being a bit of a perfectionist for making sure things are done correctly, especially with energy work, I thought I'd write down each step. After all, it is rather complex.

Well, what excitement! I'm busy practicing, and asking Kira if this is how he did it when all of a sudden I hear this loud, strong, authoritative but kindly voice say:

No, put your fingers together!

All the dogs in the street started barking except Shaka. I told Kira to run out front to see if someone was there, but nobody was in sight. As she walked back towards me she suddenly squealed with excitement, shock and realization: "Mom — that was Oris talking to you! You heard his voice just like I hear it!" Almost scraping myself up off the floor in shock I could only respond lamely with — "Really?" then, "Oh my God! Thank you so much Oris!" Kira threw her arms around me. She was so *excited and happy — and I felt totally stunned — relieved and pleased for her, but in a complete state of shock myself.*

As the reality of what had just happened began filtering through my brain — or should I say through my consciousness, it dawned on me — why in the world would somebody walk past our front door saying: "Put your fingers together!" And the voice was so *loud and powerful — enough to set all the local dogs off — except Shaka, who knows Oris and is therefore familiar with him enough not to respond in such a way at the sound of his voice. If it had been someone outside, Shaka would have barked too, so that doesn't make sense at all. Isn't it funny how, when we can't believe what we're hearing, we go looking "outside" for answers!*

J: When Helene told her husband Gary about this, he informed her that he had seen Oris on one occasion in Kira's room when he'd gone in to calm her fears in the middle of the night, and on another occasion had almost walked into him in the hallway. He'd felt too embarrassed to say anything at the time, which is a fairly common reaction with some people in connection with ET visitation and contact. A few days after Helene's experience, Oris confirmed that it had indeed been his voice she'd heard. He explained that he'd allowed her to hear him that one time, to put their minds at ease and to reassure them both of the reality of his presence.

So many who've been taken onto the discs and had half-understood experiences with the Zetas perceive them as cold, emotionless and even robotic, but this is simply not true of the Zetas we know. I believe a number of people have been subjected to faked "alien abduction experiences" in which mind-control techniques and even man-made robots created to look like Zetas have been utilized, but these experiences are totally Earth-based, and designed specifically to make the real ETs appear bad and to create a false sense of fear and threat. Unfortunately, as we have since found out ourselves, a number of researchers have bought into this, and because of their own ego or fear, simply refuse to look any further. Some are so entrenched in the negative and therefore more dramatic aspects that they don't seem to be interested in even looking at positive experiences, especially with the so-called Greys.

The Zetas don't have the same musculature in their faces as we Earth humans do, and in fact some of them don't even have biological bodies, and so they cannot express emotion physically through facial expression. But this does not mean they are devoid of feelings. Their hands and eyes are in fact very expressive. A deep sense of warmth, love and caring surrounds them, and they enjoy the presence of those who are not afraid of them.

Oris is no exception, and over the years he has never been cold or robotic in his dealings with us. In fact he's a very warm, loving and compassionate soul, with a wonderful sense of humor, as is Maris. Oris showed deep understanding and compassion in helping Kira to get past her fears and difficulties in dealing with them on an almost nightly basis, which continued, non-stop for several years.

At some time during the night following my visit to Helene's home, I awoke to find Woody Cat lying close beside me. I lay there thinking about all that had occurred, from that first worried phone call from Ian, then contact being made between Helene, Kira and me, and finally this incredible and almost tangible connection with these amazing beings whom I'd known for so long.

I thought of the ongoing contact with Maris over the years and the beautiful teachings he'd given me, but there had also been a sense of frustration and loneliness. Others around me, even some who were ostensibly into ET contact, were so caught up in their own belief systems of "Space Brothers," "Ascended Masters," etc., that my humble link with "those little Greys" was dismissed as something I would eventually get over and move away from as I became more "spiritually evolved."

There was deep sadness too because of the many supposedly authoritative books on the subject that promote nothing but fear. In the 1990s I could find only two authors who had approached the subject with an open mind. One of these was the late John Mack, a highly respected psychiatrist who took the subject of human/ET contact seriously and was one of the first investigators to recognize that it is all about expansion of human consciousness.[‡]

The other author, Courtney Brown, was even brave enough to suggest that it is simply the fact that the Greys look different that has caused so much prejudice against them, and that in many cases this automatic labeling of the more human-looking ETs as "good," and the Greys/Zetas as "evil" is simply another form of racism on the part of humans who cannot conceive of anything good or positive coming from such strange, non-human-looking beings. Brown has two books[§] dealing with an ongoing series of remote-viewing sessions carried out to investigate ET activity.

Remote viewing is an advanced form of psychic communication utilized by both American and Russian governments for spying purposes. It is not haphazard imagination but is carried out under strictly controlled conditions, with frequent checks and monitoring via a control system to guard against imagination or preconceived ideas creeping in to cloud the perceptions.

[‡]Mack, John E., MD. *Abduction: Human Encounters with Aliens*. Broadview Heights, OH: Wheeler Publishing Inc., 1994, and *Passport to the Cosmos: Human Transformation and Alien Encounters*. Orangeville, Ontario, Canada: Kunati Press, 1999.

[§]Brown, Courtney. Ph.D. *Cosmic Voyage*. New York: Onyx, 1997; and Brown, Courtney. Ph.D. *Cosmic Explorer*. New York: Dutton, 1996.

In *Cosmic Voyage*, Brown mentions an insignia seen on uniforms the Zetas were wearing. This insignia was described as a "heart" and a coiled snake. Bearing in mind that this was seen psychically rather than physically, I have to wonder if what was really seen was the peace sign that we were shown. This could easily be mistaken for a heart shape, and when worn as an insignia, does have a snake which Kira could recall. She had neither heard of Courtney Brown nor read his book, and I had completely forgotten the mention of this insignia, as it had been some years since I'd read the book. We've been told that this insignia is sort of like a family crest, and represents a shield of protection.

A more recently published book that we highly recommend for experiencers of ET contact is *Sacred Encounters — Spiritual Awakenings During Close Encounters,* by Dr. Janet Colli,[**] author of this book's Preface. Helene and I have been in touch with Dr. Colli for some time, and her "consciousness" approach to ET contact mirrors exactly what we ourselves have experienced.

[**]Colli, Janet, Ph.D. *Sacred Encounters — Spiritual Awakenings during Close Encounters.* www.xlibris.com/bookstore, 2004.

12

Mr. S

One Monday afternoon Kira arrived home from school all excited. "Mom," she announced, "the most amazing thing happened today. Mr. S (a teacher at her school) died on the weekend and I saw his ghost walking around this morning before class."

The news had been announced earlier to the other teachers, and one in particular was extremely upset. Kira watched in fascination as Mr. S's ghost went over to this woman and placed a comforting hand on her shoulder. She immediately started to calm down, but was obviously not consciously aware of his presence. Convinced by this that she was seeing a ghost, Kira bet her friend two dollars that Mr. S was dead. The friend told her not to be ridiculous — after all, he was still relatively young, and had been alive and well on the Friday. Then an announcement was made calling the whole school to a special assembly, where they were informed that the teacher, Mr. S, had passed away suddenly the day before.

Kira watched as her former teacher's ghost made his rounds of the school, as if saying goodbye, but then he looked directly at her, and she realized to her profound horror that he knew that she could see him. She ran off to class, hoping to escape his attention, but a couple of nights later he appeared in her bedroom. Her terrified screams brought both Helene and Oris running. Oris explained to her that Mr. S was "stuck," that he needed help to pass over properly, and that she could provide this help — in fact it was her job to do this.

"I don't want a teacher of mine visiting me at night!" Kira cried, thoroughly upset.

But I'm your teacher, and I visit you at night.

"But I never *liked* him!" she protested. "I *can't* help him!"

Helene then intervened, begging Oris to just get rid of him. Finally Oris gave in, calling on a worker to take Mr. S away, and poor Kira spent the next few nights sleeping in her parents' room, too scared to be alone.

H: I was just starting to settle down and get a bit more confidence, both within myself and also with Oris, especially after hearing his voice, then bang — another drama starts to unfold! I couldn't believe it. Here I am, trying to learn, trying to understand and trying to deal with Oris and his workers and now we have a ghost in the house! And not just any ghost — it's someone we know — one of Kira's teachers from school who's died. Oh joy of joys!

J: Late the following Saturday afternoon Oris arrived to warn Kira that Mr. S was going to come again that night and that they couldn't stop him. Of course she was terrified, but as Helene pointed out to her, they couldn't keep going on like this living in fear every night. She felt it would be best to confront him head-on.

They stayed up watching a movie that evening to relax themselves, and at 10:45 p.m. went to Kira's room to wait. Helene lay down on the bed and Kira settled herself on a camp bed on the floor. Suddenly she started crying and shaking with fear — Mr. S had arrived. Helene held Kira's hand and they asked him why he'd come. His reply was: "You need to help me." Kira called for Oris, but a small worker turned up instead, informing them that Oris was busy but would come as soon as he could.

H: By the time Mr. S arrived I'd really and truly had enough. Why would Oris allow any of this to happen? On one hand I felt very sorry for Mr. S, but honestly, I didn't feel he was our concern, let alone our responsibility. My only concern was for the wellbeing of my daughter. This was too much to handle and it didn't make sense to me at all. Surely it was up to the angels to look after him. It felt weird and creepy having him in my daughter's bedroom. Yuk!

J: A few years later we learned that in certain cases, some suicides for example, the energies engulfing the recently departed spirit are so heavy and negative that angels simply can't get near them. Under these circumstances it is the Greys, the workers of the angels, who are called in to carry out a "rescue."

In such cases, the Zeta temporarily takes on an angel-like form to help the spirit leave the physical body. I consciously recall carrying out this type of work as a Zeta. It can be extremely hard to convince some older folks that their time has come to move on — they're *so* fearful. How sad! Surely it should be the churches' job in the community to teach people the truth about dying — how it's simply an exciting rebirth into a higher state.

H: Kira was terrified and very confused, and the worker tried to explain to us that we had to help this person. My response was: "What! You've got to be kidding! How? Why us? When is Oris coming? I need to talk to him now!"

The worker kept insisting that Mr. S needed our help to move on, that his wife's grief was holding him back, and it was our job to tell her. I tried to explain that this was impossible — no one would believe us, and it could get Kira into a whole lot of trouble.

You have to – you are the only ones who can help!

There was a very uncomfortable silence in the room as we waited for Oris. My mind was spinning, and I was getting angrier by the moment. People would think we were crazy! They'd lock us up and throw away the key!

Oris arrived about ten minutes later and repeated what the worker had already told us: that it was Kira's job to help Mr. S. I couldn't believe what I was hearing, and I tried to explain to him that she was way too young to handle this kind of responsibility. There was no way I was going to back down. She was my child, my responsibility, and at that moment I didn't care who he was or what his orders were. I have truly never felt so empowered in all my life! As I stood up to this wise old being, I felt sheer grit and determination rising up from the very depths of my soul.

Looking back now, I can see and understand that Oris did this partly for my sake. I was seriously lacking in self-empowerment in those days, and he knew it. He also knew that it was only the protective-mother instinct within me that would be strong enough to override my lack of inner empowerment. To experience my own power and self-belief to this extent was certainly a breakthrough for me. Talk about Greys being "testers and tryers of souls" — what an understatement!

J: For a while Helene and Oris remained deadlocked, arguing back and forth, each equally insistent, but finally Oris gave in and came up with a compromise. He didn't know whether it would work or not, but he offered to call on the Zeta Teacher Garnibis, who is particularly gifted in the field of "rescue work." He went on to explain that Mr. S was stuck in the fourth dimension and they had to try to help him to move on to where he was supposed to be, otherwise he would be stuck for some time. I feel that Kira's link with Mr. S was the fact that she had known him personally on the physical level, but could also communicate with him on the astral level.

Part of the problem was his wife's extreme grief that was still holding him, not allowing his spirit to move on, hence Kira's appointed task to tell her to let go and release him. The Zetas have given us a lot of information along these lines, which I'll cover later in this book. There is just *so much* we don't understand down here about so-called death.

Oris also came up with the idea of somehow providing a book or information of some sort for the wife to read, which would assist her understanding and help her to let go. He went on to explain how people really have no concept of how much they can potentially block the progress of a loved one who has passed over to the other side through excessive grief, or by holding on to even a part of their remains. The next moment Mr. S disappeared, much to Kira and Helene's relief.

With the drama over, Oris sat down and made himself comfortable. He explained that this was one of his quieter nights, so if they wanted any questions answered he was happy to oblige. He went on to tell them of a young boy in Russia whom he'd been visiting. This boy was very ill with asthma and could see Oris, but he was still extremely fearful. Oris then proceeded to talk more about the Zetas, and where we all fit in. Within the Zeta culture there are different levels, depending upon the soul age and evolution of the individual.

He went on to explain that the younger workers, measuring about three to four feet in height, are the ones often seen by people during so-called "alien abduction experiences." Next up are the "Teachers in Training." These ones, about five feet in height, are sometimes seen to be acting in a supervisory capacity on board the discs. The Teachers are taller again, up to seven or eight feet in height. These are the highly evolved Elders who direct the work carried out by the others. All the ones of this latter group that we've met have names ending in "*is*," for example Oris, Maris, Serapis, etc.

Oris told them that at the worker level they go by number rather than by name, but in actual fact as far as I understand it, this was the only way he could describe their identification system to young Kira, who didn't have much concept of vibrational frequency levels, as even many older folk on Planet Earth don't. As Maris has explained since, within the Zeta culture, individuals are not labeled by verbal names as people here are. When they communicate with humans they may give themselves a name just for convenience and ease of communication, but within their culture everyone is identified solely by vibrational frequency. Things are not "named" as such but rather recognized by energy signature. Many down here seem to have trouble grasping this concept, because as a planetary culture we are very much into naming and labeling everything.

As a Teacher/Elder Oris travels widely and is sometimes delayed when called upon, depending on how busy he is at the time. He's never failed to respond, however, and if delayed he has always sent a worker to fill in for him until he can get here. On the day of my visit he was having a very busy time, but he felt so relaxed with us that he made himself comfortable in a chair in the lounge room, stretched his long legs out and took a quick catnap to re-charge himself. He commented on how pleasant it was to just relax for a while. On that occasion he came during the day because I couldn't get there at night, but they usually operate after dark because there's less interference on the electro-magnetic level, and less likelihood of anyone seeing them who is not intended to. Also, it's easier to work with people when their physical body is asleep.

Zetas, like a number of other ET types, can and do take human form, being born naturally like any other human and living out a life on Planet Earth. Many are not consciously aware of who and what they really are — otherwise life would be too difficult. After all, it's hard enough for people down here who have to uproot themselves to move to a foreign country to live and work. With memory of family, friends and native country still firmly entrenched in their minds, they often become homesick to the point of just not being able to make a go of it and having to return home. For someone from an off-planet culture like the Zetas, it could potentially be unbearable and just too different and "alien." Furthermore, the human brain simply can't cope with the massive amount of extra input. Even retaining some conscious understanding and memory is incredibly hard — any more would be impossible.

This being the case, during their conscious waking hours these ones are, to all intents and purposes, human, even in their own minds, with only a very vague memory of the other existence lying just below the surface of their waking reality, like a half-forgotten dream. As children they may even experience fear if any recall of being taken on board the disc at night bleeds through to their conscious mind. It is only when the mind begins to mature as they reach adulthood that this fear dissipates and deeper understanding unfolds.

These ones have a number of reasons for living this "double life" — to observe and gather information on the subconscious or super-conscious level of their mind — to learn, teach or heal — and to introduce ground-breaking research, ideas and concepts to assist in the opening up and unfolding of human consciousness to deeper and more expansive levels of spiritual evolvement. Some ETs are here to help Earth people understand the importance of balancing and harmonizing the life-force energy within the physical body. It is this understanding of the concept of universal energy that is the missing link between science and religion.

As Zetas age, their eye color fades, just as human hair grays with age. The younger ones have black eyes, which gradually fade to dark blue, then light blue, then white when they are close to death. They don't reckon their age by one lifetime alone, but rather take all their lives into consideration. When we asked Oris how old he is, his answer was: "Two million years." His eyes are faded to dark blue, and his skin is wrinkled and dark gray in color.

He also commented on how unusual it was that he could physically hear our voices. Generally they can only pick up human speech on a telepathic level. The most difficult thing they are up against is that Earth people are either scared of them or else look upon them as gods. All they want is acceptance and communication.

Helene invited Oris to ask questions, as he had so willingly given us information. He wanted to know *why* people are so scared and why humans need so much sleep. He then asked Kira about the posters she had on her bedroom walls. She explained to him that they were pictures of her favorite pop singers — the ones she really liked a lot. This then led to Helene trying to explain to him about well-known people on Earth such as film and rock stars. A puzzled and rather hurt expression came into his eyes, and he said to Kira:

> If these are all the ones you really love and admire, why haven't you got *my* picture there?

Poor Kira felt awful about this, but didn't know what to do. With school friends coming over for visits and sleepovers, she really couldn't have a picture of a Zeta ET on her wall. Then I thought of the little drawing done by my clairvoyant friend of *Manolo*, in which he looked like a Zeta in need of a shave (See Chapter 6). I made a photocopy of it, which Kira left on her dressing table. That night she awoke to find Oris leaning over looking at it closely, with a pleased expression in his eyes.

Oris said that he works with many Earthlings, and he finds Earth humans to be among the hardest life-forms to work with because of all the fear and ego that is rife on this planet. He explained that I do healing work both "upstairs" and down here, which is why I can recall (and have been seen by others) doing this type of work in Zeta form, and that part of my job here in physical human form is to bring the "family" back together again as a working unit, to connect us back to our soul group. I was told this long ago, but Oris was simply reminding me and providing confirmation through Kira, who knew nothing of this past message.

The reason why I've been drawn to working with elderly folks through teaching Tai Chi is that they will be reborn in the near future. Hopefully they'll come back here with open minds, ready to take in a much deeper understanding of

1. the all-important role of life-force energy in the process of staying balanced and harmonized as a human, and
2. the flexibility and expansion of mind that is necessary for spiritual growth and evolvement.

Reiki will have the same effect. This is part of what was discussed during my 1983 "consciousness upgrade."

H: Oris stayed with us until about 2:00 a.m., but eventually he had to go to pursue other work. The moment he left the room the energies dropped, leaving an instant sense of dread and nervousness that his strong presence had kept at bay. You could almost taste the fear and negativity. It was terrifying beyond belief — a feeling similar to walking down a dark alley expecting someone to jump out and attack you. But this was no dark alley — this was my daughter's bedroom.

Just when I thought everything had settled, with Oris finally giving in to my very firm request to take Mr. S away and then kindly and generously staying on with us to share his knowledge, now we were left alone to deal with these awful energies at 2:00 a.m. Suddenly the little worker appeared, telling us to leave the room immediately. Needless to say, he didn't have to ask twice — we were out of there like crazed, petrified mice — our bodies shaking and our hearts pounding.

We ran straight into my bedroom, waking Gary in the process. As I tried to calm Kira and reassure her that we were safe in this room with Dad, Ben suddenly woke from a bad dream and started yelling out to me. Leaving Kira in my bed to be comforted by her dad, I raced into Ben's room to attend to him, and I decided to stay there to make sure he would be safe as well. I've never *felt so nervous and unsettled in all my life, but sheer exhaustion finally took over and I fell sound asleep.*

J: First thing the next morning poor Helene was on the phone to me, frazzled, totally exhausted and in desperate need of support. At that point we weren't sure if Garnibis had managed to take care of Mr. S's spirit, or if he would come back again to bother them, and the unpleasant energy in the room was a worry. They were on my mind all day, and I kept sending Reiki through to them. At least now, with a conscious understanding through my human awareness of the difficulties involved, I hoped Oris would be able to intervene by enlisting Garnibis's assistance to help Mr. S.

I was still having trouble with my "identity problem," and suffering some self-doubt as a result. Looking back, I now realize that I was in denial as well. I've only now come to realize that it wasn't so much the Zeta side of my consciousness that I was having trouble accepting — it was more specifically the Teacher part, along with the weight of responsibility that came with it. Even to this day I tend to stand back from this, preferring to allow that part of my higher self to "do its own thing" without much conscious input from my limited human mind down here, which cannot always see the "bigger picture." The only time I tap into it is to allow teachings to come through.

Sure enough, the following night during a "dream" Oris took Kira for a walk along a beach, in fact the same beach where the first meeting had taken place during her Reiki treatment. Putting a comforting arm around her shoulders, he told her not to worry any more, and promised that Mr. S would not be permitted to bother her again. It would be taken care of and she wouldn't be asked to do this type of work again until she was older.

The reason for the feeling of negativity that had come into Kira's room after Oris left was that he vibrates at a very high frequency, so when he is present for any length of time, the energy frequency in the room is raised to a higher level. This is a quite tangible sensation that we all got to know very well and which is often an indication that one of the Zeta Teachers is around. However, when Oris left that night, the energy level dropped suddenly, leaving a sort of vacuum into which negative energies attracted by Mr. S's presence were drawn. They had been held at bay by Oris's presence.

I have conveyed the events that occurred as accurately as possible, but it's important to understand that the teachings given to Kira by Oris were imparted through the mind of a 12- to 14-year-old. In many instances he simplified his explanations, putting them into terms that she could more readily understand, and naturally all encounter experiences are interpreted and comprehended through the lens of the mind of the recipient.

H: Originally I decided to keep notes in the hope that this would help release some of the weight and tension off my shoulders. I was feeling very tired all the time and my head felt as if it were about to explode. I also thought that writing down our experiences and my thoughts might help me to understand the bigger picture in some way.

Other than Jude I had no one else to turn to, so my computer became my trusted friend as well. I also thought, "No one will believe me now, but maybe at some time in the future they will," and deep down I felt that all of this must have been happening for a reason. As I began writing the notes, I could feel the weight lifting off. It also helped me to release thoughts and emotions so I could move on.

J: Sometimes Oris allowed Helene to make notes on the spot and other times he didn't. She made careful note of the questions and answers from both sides, as well as the descriptions Kira gave, backed up by my own recall of interaction with the Zetas. What's not possible to convey in full is the emotion involved and the fear, especially in the early days.

Up until that time they'd not had any contact or interest in anything outside of normal day-to-day life on Planet Earth — family, school and work. ET contact was a subject they'd hardly even heard of, let alone taken an active interest in, and now they were suddenly confronted by these extraordinary happenings in what up until then they'd thought of as the safety and privacy of their home.

Those who've not experienced non-physical visitation of this sort on an ongoing basis have no way of truly understanding how disruptive it can be to family and home-life, most especially where children are involved. A mother's natural instinct is to protect her children, but in the case of ET visitation this is not so easy to do, and it took a huge amount of faith and trust from both of us to deal with it. What I had to fall back on was that I'd never been hurt in all my contacts with the Zetas, and I felt comfortable with them. The guidance and teachings they'd given me were positive and had radically changed my life for the good. Helene could see this, and she felt totally comfortable with me and trusted what I had to say, but this did not lighten the load of responsibility that we both felt.

As a mother she felt a deep responsibility for her children, but I too felt a great burden on my shoulders. Having faith and trust in the Zeta family was all very well for me on a personal level, but now others were involved as well, and they were somebody else's precious children.

My half-buried but still partly conscious memories of being up on the disc as a Zeta carrying out procedures on humans were now backed up by Kira's recall of seeing me up there as one of them.

Oris has something to say by way of explanation here. He usually communicates with me through the written word while I am in an altered state of consciousness, and this is what he "wrote":

> When Kira was brought up onto the Disc, Judy always appeared to her as a five-foot-tall female Worker. The reason for this was to provide reassurance. She was only 12 when this conscious contact began, and it was rather unusual in that it was a very full-on nightly occurrence. This was necessary to enable as much information as possible to be conveyed in a limited time frame. To help her through it, she needed to have somebody up there on the Disc with whom she could easily relate to on her terms – to be a friend and mentor to her rather than a Teacher. It also needed to be someone she could relate to comfortably down here in Human terms.
>
> Even though the "Judy" part was obviously a Zeta, she always acted in a very human way that a 12-year-old could feel comfortable with – making mistakes, doing silly things and getting into mischief. As bizarre as it sounds, at first she even kept her long plait so Kira would be able to distinguish her from the others. There were major fear issues that needed to be overcome quickly, and so this screen imagery was done to provide comfort, friendship, support and reassurance to assist her through what otherwise would have been an extremely daunting, if not impossible, task.

The appearance of Kira's deceased teacher Mr. S in her room was for three reasons. Firstly, he did indeed need help. As a 12-year-old child Kira saw him only as a bad-tempered and unpleasant teacher, but in reality he was a very unhappy and troubled soul. On the occasion of his untimely death, he was experiencing a huge amount of guilt over the fact that he had taken his personal problems out on his students. Forgiveness and understanding was what he sought in order to be released. This could only be provided by one of his students, and because of her heightened psychic sensing Kira was the only one he could get through to, hence the Worker's comment that she was "the only one who can help him."

In many cases of trapped souls such as this, forgiveness and compassion are the keys to their release, otherwise the process can be very difficult and prolonged. This underlines the fact that we are all intrinsically linked in Oneness, and so the thoughts and actions of one must always affect the whole. For optimal benefit this release needs to be carried out within a limited time frame, while the departed spirit still retains a close connection to the physical container, otherwise a massive karmic burden is carried over into the next life. This connection begins to weaken after three days, and dissipates further over a period of three weeks.

Now the question I hear you ask is: "Why didn't you explain this to Kira and Helene?" My answer to this question provides the second reason for the presence of the ghost of Mr. S in Kira's room. It was a test set up for her in order for me to gauge how much soul knowledge has been brought through to physical consciousness on such issues.

The third reason was as Helene has surmised: a learning experience to enable her to feel and savor her own self-empowerment for the first time in her life, and to prove to herself just what she is really capable of. It was truly inspiring to see her standing up to me in this way – expressing such strength of spirit and personal empowerment against a being whom she perceived as all-powerful and extremely daunting, in order to protect her child and safeguard everything she believed to be right.

These two factors were forcing me to accept the depth of my involvement. Added to this was the fact that I was able to exert some control over the children's experiences when things got too heavy for them to handle — all it took was a word in my ear from Helene. It wasn't that I feared they'd be hurt by the Zetas — it was simply the burden of knowing that I was at least partly responsible for what was going on. I never voiced these fears to Helene because she had enough to carry on her shoulders, and I didn't want her worrying any more.

H: From my perspective back then, I just thought that Jude had a great connection and "knew people in high places" so to speak. I used to imagine her storming down the corridors of the disc waving her finger at Oris or the workers, telling them to slow down a bit to give Helene and her family some rest. It was really only recently that it fully clicked with me that it was a part of Jude, or at least part of her Zeta consciousness doing all this to us. But then again, as she has confided to me, back then even she was not fully aware of the whole picture. She was aware of the Zeta part, but not that it was a Teacher working through her.

I still think of them as different entities, and it was a surprise to read (in this manuscript) what she was going through at the time. When I had Gary read these pages, he said, "Poor Jude — it would've been really hard for her!" I couldn't have said it any better myself. Oh boy! We've all come so far since then, with so *much more understanding and love with everyone involved, including Oris and his friends. I know very well that some of you reading this right now are thinking: "But how can this woman be so calm and forgiving, not only towards the Greys, but towards Judy as well?" All I can say is, as you read more you will understand.*

Looking back I now realize that there were many more lessons involved as well — more than can ever be expressed in words. During those years of full-on, almost daily conscious contact, we truly came to understand what the Greys being "Testers of Souls" really means. Between the three "boys," Oris, Maris and Serapis, we were made to dig down, bring to the surface, and closely examine parts of our being that we never even knew existed, let alone acknowledged.

Often we felt like old forgotten coats that had been pulled from the back of a wardrobe, turned inside out and upside down, minutely examined for moth holes and mold then given a good shaking to get rid of all the accumulated dust and cobwebs. God, it was hard at times, but it was worth every second! Would we go through it all again? Yes, yes, yes*! No question about it! As you read on you will hopefully come to the profoundly life-changing understanding that* *we have reached, thanks to our Zeta family — that we are all just pieces in a multi-dimensional jigsaw puzzle, which, when finally put together, forms a much bigger, clearer, and incredibly beautiful and magical picture.*

J: Over the years there's been much argument among researchers of ET contact, especially in connection with the Greys, as to whether that contact is positive or negative. Many are rather ambivalent about it, saying things like, "I just don't know about those Greys! Who *really* knows whether they're good or bad?" These are usually people who don't acknowledge the spiritual aspect and cannot sense the energy.

Part of the Zetas' work involves soul rescue, which is necessary in cases where a lot of negative energy surrounds a person's death. Examples are suicides and drug- or alcohol-related deaths. Normally it is the angels' job to help the spirit out of the deceased physical container (body), but angels vibrate at very high-energy frequencies, and so cannot enter the low and heavy energy field that surrounds a person who has died under these circumstances. This is where the Greys come into the picture as workers of the angels. It is their job to lift the spirit clear of the body and take it to where it can receive the necessary healing to enable it to move on.

My Zeta memory banks recall the sensation of sheer, mind-numbing aversion and cold dread on the rare occasions when I came into contact with such negative energy fields. Helene will back me up on this, having experienced first-hand the energy field surrounding Mr. S. The point is that there is *no doubt* when negative lower astral plane energy is present. When you're in the presence of real negativity and/or evil — you know it!

After all she'd been through with the children, Helene really wanted another mother to talk to — a mother whose children were also undergoing ET visitation. Having heard of close-encounter support groups that had started up around the world, we contacted the local UFO research association hoping for some much-needed help, but for them it all seemed a bit too much to handle. They were more than willing to spend time reporting on and investigating mysterious lights in the sky, distant sightings of discs, and "alien contacts" of the 1950s, but full-on, present-day visitation such as we were trying to deal with seemed to be a bit too much for them. Copious notes were taken — and that was it — no more contact, no help offered, and a lingering suspicion left that we were not believed. And so we battled on alone.

Since then, things have changed somewhat, with our local association asking us to speak at some UFO conferences. Furthermore, several members of the association have been extremely encouraging and supportive, providing very positive reviews on my books, and giving valuable assistance to me in promoting them, for which I am grateful.

Many times my phone would ring first thing in the morning, and it would be poor Helene, sometimes almost in tears and very much in need of support and reassurance over the previous night's events, including the night terrors that her son Ben was experiencing, sometimes twice a week. At times he'd run around the house as if trying to escape from something, and even attempted to get outside on a couple of occasions. Luckily Gary was on hand to help restrain him.

13
THE HUMAN LADDER

In June/July of 2001 we were given information on what the Zetas refer to as the Human Ladder, which had a strange sequel some weeks later. The Human Ladder was first discussed by one of the little workers, and it was explained later in more detail by Oris. This is a prime example of why the Zetas are sometimes accused of giving out wrong information. Both Oris and the worker told Kira that there are ten "galactic levels" in the universe, and that we live out ten lives on each level. Assuming that they meant galaxies, I questioned this. It obviously wasn't right because there are far more than ten galaxies in the universe, and the "ten lives on each level" didn't feel right either, because we all evolve at different rates.

They explained to her that it begins at level one, the lowest "rung" of the Ladder, which is where Planet Earth is situated at the moment, along with many other younger human civilizations. From there it goes up through levels two, three, four, etc., to level ten, which in our universe (which is not just physical but rather multi-dimensional) is the highest evolutionary rung, and inhabited by those beings that many Earth humans think of as "angels."

As I came to understand later, the information was given in this way to purposely cast doubt in my mind in order to make me think more deeply about the whole thing, because it is complex, and is, as far as I know, a totally new concept. But once we understood the full picture, it just made a lot of sense. These galactic levels are not places as such but rather *ascending and expanding levels of conscious awareness*. As Oris explained to me later, once a being evolves to human level, which is mainly a physical process, evolution then becomes a mind/spirit process. In other words, in the Human Kingdom evolution mainly involves expansion of mind and conscious awareness, thus humans of level one are able to tap into only about 10% of their potential conscious awareness, whereas level nine and ten humans (angelic beings) are able to utilize 90% to 100%, which is whole-mind conscious awareness, or in other words, pure mind.

The Zetas are at levels 5 to 8, able to utilize 50% to 80% of their potential conscious awareness. Even this is fairly impressive considering the fact, confirmed by psychologists, that if a human could even access *20%* of their potential consciousness they'd be considered a genius by Earth standards. As Kira's mind interpreted it, the "ten lives on each level" is only very approximate.*

H: It was beyond my wildest dreams to ever receive a teaching as profound as this. The Human Ladder really helped me to understand about Oneness, evolution and consciousness, but even more importantly, how we are all connected. It was definitely one of those "Ah ha!" moments. To come to the realization and understanding that Oris has been human before, as have the angels, Fairy folk and many other beings, brought very much comfort to me. We are all connected — they have all "been here, done that," as we are being and doing now. They truly do understand how hard it is to be human, having the use of only 10% of our potential conscious awareness — wow! But really, it all makes so much sense when you think about it. Everything in the universe is living — planets, people/beings, animals and plants, and we have all been created from God. We are all, every single one of us, on a journey of self-discovery. Everyone is learning and growing no matter who you are or where you live.

It is God's energy that keeps the wheel of life turning — this energy is Love, and it is Love that connects us all. Some are further along the path than we are, but at the same time there are ones coming up from behind as well. We are all moving along the path in our own perfect timing, and there are Teachers here to guide and help us wake up to our own hidden potential — just as Oris has done for me! In reality we are all just one big family, and all of us are God's children, so this explanation makes perfect sense and brings the whole picture together for those of us on the Human Ladder.

I'm very excited about this amazing information, and when the full realization of it dawned on me, I wanted to shout it from the rooftops and tell the whole world. It just explains so much on matters such as reincarnation, karma, consciousness and evolution, as well as answering such questions as: "Why am I here?" and "Are there really other people/beings living somewhere out there in the endless cosmos?" As for that second question — I certainly found the answer

* For more information about the Human Ladder, visit http://www.ufogreyinfo.com/zetagreyteachings.htm

to that one in a hurry, hey! There is an infinite order in this universe — living life and expressing love (God energy) is what we are all here to do, for our ultimate learning and growth.

Please excuse my outburst of enthusiasm, but I'm just so passionate about the Human Ladder teaching. It helped me so much on so many levels of my psyche and with my interactions with our otherworldly Visitors. I firmly believe that if other experiencers could come to understand this, it would help them move through their fear to find love and a brighter part of themselves on the other side, just as has happened to me.

J: We were very excited by this fascinating illustration of human evolution, so we approached several UFO/ET investigators with what we'd received. It made so much sense, and it seemed to answer so many questions. All of us, including Oris, were anxious to get this information out there to share with others, and we were curious to know if any other experiencers had been shown anything like this. But all we were met with was dead silence and seeming disinterest. Not one researcher ever approached us with questions, feedback, alternative information, nothing! We would be delighted to receive a bit of feedback on it — from *anybody — please!*[†]

The strange sequel to this event occurred several weeks later on the local TV news. Oris had done his best when describing the interdimensional spiral pattern of the galaxies and planets comprising the various levels to Kira, who drew an illustration of it as well as she could, but it was virtually impossible to draw or describe. They wanted me to put it in this book, but as we explained, reproducing it was going to be the problem. Kira tried to draw it as a series of "arms" spiraling out from the center, a bit like the sails of a windmill or fan.

A report came on after the TV news of the latest crop circle that had appeared in a field in Wiltshire, England. I was absolutely stunned to see a miniature but perfect reproduction of the pattern Kira had tried to draw. Luckily I managed to record it on video. A week or so later, Oris explained that this was what the crop circle was meant to illustrate, and agreed with us that it had indeed been hard even for them to re-create three-dimensionally in the field. They compromised by making it smaller, with only six spiraling "arms."

[†] Email the author at judy.carroll@bigpond.com

Several crop circles have been created to illustrate the Human Ladder.

In May of 2010 an Australian man, Brett Parrott, contacted me through my website. Brett feels an unexplained connection with ETs, and was excited about finding a positive and informative website on them since he has no conscious memories of ever meeting one. In the course of exchanging emails I happened to mention the Zetas' great sense of humor, and Brett agreed, going on to tell me of a joke played on him during a visit to the UK during the summer of 2001.

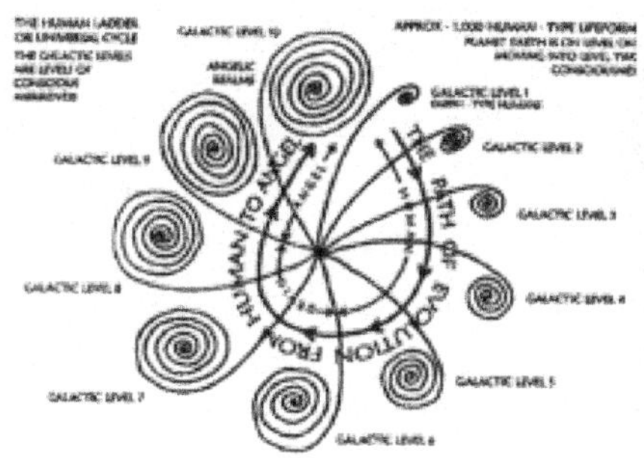

SPIRAL DIAGRAM OF THE HUMAN LADDER, BY KIRA

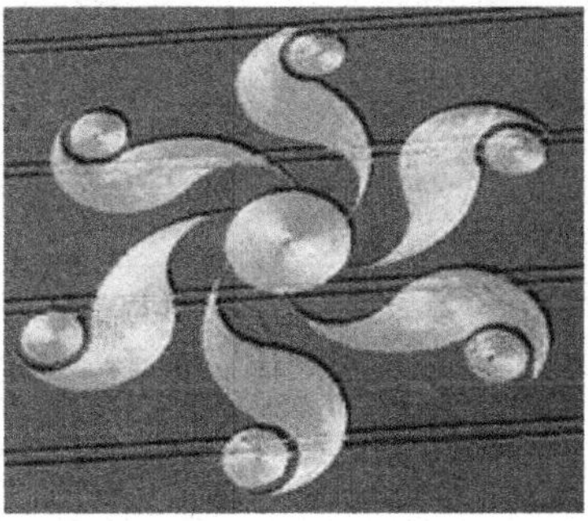

CROP CIRCLE FORMATION, WILTSHIRE, ENGLAND, 2001

He is a crop circle researcher, and right at the time we were putting out a request for help in the form of a crop circle to illustrate the Human Ladder, he was meditating at night inside a formation at the base of Milk Hill, in Wiltshire. During this meditation he put out a request for "the real circle makers" to create another one. Believing that it was Milk Hill Field where he sat meditating, in his mind he asked them to make it there. The next morning there was no newly created crop circle in the field, so he continued looking for other crop circles and thought nothing more of it.

Three days later he was checking out crop circle websites at an Internet café, and was surprised to find photos of a new formation in Milk Hill Field, that had been discovered *the morning after his request.* He couldn't understand why he hadn't found it when he'd specifically gone looking.

He went to investigate, and it turned out that the field in which he'd been meditating was not the one he thought. Milk Hill Field was actually above Milk Hill, and not visible from the road, whereas he'd been in another field at the base of the hill. As he explained in his email, "They gave me exactly what I asked for — not what I *thought* I'd asked for."

MILK HILL CROP FORMATION, NEAR ALTON BARNES, WILTSHIRE. AUGUST 13, 2001.

To add to the strangeness, this circle was one of, if not the biggest crop formation in recorded history, and as far as we know, the only one to make the TV news here in Australia, coincidentally (or maybe not) where the three people who simultaneously requested it, Brett, Helene and Judy, all live. Also, as Brett pointed out, how fitting that a crop circle representing the Human Ladder be created at the very top of the highest hill in the area. Above is an original photo of the Milk Hill crop circle, taken by Brett Parrott.[‡] Note the helicopter in the upper left, for scale.

One afternoon Kira and Helene were chatting, when Kira suddenly recalled being taken up on a disc. These memory lapses, or even complete blocks, are very common for experiencers of ET contact. They're put in place as a sort of safety measure to guard against the conscious mind being inundated with an overload of information that it may not be able to handle. This is why

‡ See http://www.theroswellcode.com/home.html for Brett's crop circle website. A global coordinated visualization project that is manifesting the 5th World, a long-prophesied better world of love, balance and spiritual strength, uses this powerful planetary healing pattern as its mandala. See http://5thWorldFund.org.

hypnotherapy is often employed to access information, but this still doesn't guarantee total accuracy, because the mind's built-in filter system tends to cause a certain amount of distortion. In Kira's case, however, with no fear involved by this stage, her memories were very close to conscious level, and a word or question often sparked off spontaneous recall.

One night Oris came to fetch her, and together they walked down the hallway. She was amazed to see him pass straight through the closed front door of the house, and went to try herself. She walked into it, unable to pass through. Oris came back to help her, touching it and somehow causing it to open. At this time, Kira didn't realize that it was her astral rather than her physical body that was being taken.

Following him out onto the front driveway, Kira accidentally walked into the sign advertising the family business, hurting her knee and toe, which were still sore and bruised the next day. Things that happen to our astral body in this way can impact upon the physical body, just as I woke with a physical scar on my forehead after the encounter at the sacred site. Oris turned around and told her to stop mucking about and being so clumsy. She snapped back at him: "I'm only *human* you know!"

"Oh yes," he answered, "I'm sorry. Sometimes I forget." He then slowed down and placed his hand on her shoulder to guide her, which she found so heavy her knees almost buckled under her. As they proceeded down the street Oris again led the way, and Kira noticed what she thought was a picture of an angel on the back of his cape. It was so beautiful, but only visible in the moonlight.

Continuing further, she suddenly noticed how windy it was, and then a "big blob of light" appeared. We later came to realize that this wind is an effect caused by the disc landing, which was what the "blob" turned out to be. It looked like a dome made out of light, with other different colored lights on it. There were two doors — a smaller one fitted neatly inside a larger one, both of which were of a rounded, oval shape. The two of them opened so Oris could pass through.

After they entered, they walked through what Kira described as a "gooey substance" about a foot in thickness. It resembled water but was more jelly-like, did not feel wet, and was of a most beautiful, shiny, pink/silver color that she'd never seen before. This description was proof to me that her experience was real, because this water/jelly has been described by others as well, but I'd never spoken of this to Kira and she'd not read anything about it. Like many young people, Kira was just not into reading books at all.

Proceeding into the disc, the floor they walked on was transparent and illuminated from beneath. They then passed down an aisle through the middle of many desks in what seemed to be a huge office area. There were even rubbish bins under the desks and it was quite noisy. Working at the desks were some small and some taller Zetas, writing on what looked like material. They were using a type of laser pen with a yellow-colored light on the tip that burned the script into the surface of the "paper," which resembled canvas. As they walked along, Oris kept his hand resting heavily on her shoulder.

Many of the workers were talking; some were eating or drinking from tube-like containers. Kira got to try this food sometimes, and found it to be in the form of a jelly-like paste, either blue or purple/pink in color, and their beverages were blue or yellow.

As they passed through, everyone stopped what they were doing to look, and Oris explained that not many humans come through this area. It's a part of the disc where they generally aren't taken. Kira noticed a large, round computer, and four of the "staff" were working on the touch screen.

She then noticed one of the taller Zetas sitting at a front desk working on a document using a laser pen. It started doing silly things to attract her attention — dropping its pen, getting up, tripping over things, etc. She was often taken through this office area when Oris brought her onto the disc — we joked that it must have been the tradesman's entrance — and that taller worker was always at the same desk, waving to attract her attention. Eventually Kira realized it was I in my Zeta form, which helped both Helene and Kira to feel better and to dissipate some of their fear.

Kira's understanding that I was on the disc also served to explain memories I had of travelling and working on discs. In February of 2000, for example, I clearly recalled being on board a smallish disc with two struts protruding upwards from the back. These struts had winglike appendages at the top. We flew over ocean and land, and at one point I flicked a switch on a control panel to adjust the interior temperature. I also later remembered lying down on a bunk to have a rest.

Another remembered event in June 2001 was of leaving an underground base in the Antarctic, and travelling up the east coast of Australia to an island in Moreton Bay off Brisbane. Strangely enough, the next day's news broadcast carried a story of mysterious sonic booms that were heard in that vicinity. As far as I know these have never been explained. This has an amusing side to it, because Helene's family was camping there at the time, and I'd joked beforehand that we'd pay them a visit or at least stage a "fly-over."

On yet another occasion, I used a prominent local building to get my bearings home in the early morning hours. We were approaching from high up, and I clearly remember looking down on it. A suspicion had lingered for a long time that I'd been leading virtually a double life, but I didn't realize to what extent until Kira recalled seeing me on the disc on a nightly basis. When we compared notes the following day, we found many consistent points.

As Kira stepped through the "gooey" substance and walked between the desks, she saw a bright light ahead. Thinking of the bright light so often seen at the end of a tunnel by those who've survived a near-death experience, she started to get scared, and told Oris she didn't want to die. Keeping his hand firmly on her shoulder, he assured her she wasn't going to.

They then passed through some even thicker "goo,"(about three feet in thickness), and ended up in Russia visiting the young boy with whom Oris was working. The boy was very frightened of Oris, and it was Kira's job to reassure him. Amazed to find she could communicate with him in Russian, she tried to explain about Oris and the others who accompanied him — that they were there to heal, not harm him. Having this communication and reassurance from a fellow human made the boy feel better. When the job was completed, Oris brought Kira back home to her bedroom and stayed with her until she settled back to sleep.

One afternoon Helene and Kira were chatting about something else when more memories began surfacing in connection with visits to the 15-year-old Russian boy. The first time they went, Oris gave him healing on his chest. Despite Kira's words of reassurance he was still very frightened, and they had to leave quickly when his mother entered the room.

On their second visit she was able to talk longer with him, and he asked a lot of questions about Oris and the little workers, which he could also see. During this conversation he and Kira started comparing notes, and each came to realize that the Zetas almost always worked on their throat and ankle areas. What Kira did not know is that these are the two places on the body where one can simultaneously access the most energy meridians. This comment she so casually passed on to her mother was good confirmation to me of the reality of her contacts. Another fact she was quite unaware of was that these were the two points Maris always worked on when he visited others to give healing.

The third time Oris and Kira went to Russia, the boy was very ill and in the hospital. The mother was present, so they left and returned the next day to find him in an operating theatre with a doctor working on his lungs. Oris and Kira were invisibly in astral form, of course. Kira noticed how small the boy's lungs were, so it was no wonder he had trouble breathing. Perhaps his lung deformity was a result of the Chernobyl disaster.

Her job was to hold his hand while Oris reached down into the chest cavity, placing his hands on the lungs and pushing hard. She commented afterwards on the bluish, bruised appearance of the boy's body, and when we mentioned this to our friend Ian, an ex-nurse, he provided further confirmation on the reality of her experiences. Ian explained that he'd seen many patients after major surgery, and their skin is usually bruised. Also the weakness of the boy's lungs would give his complexion blueness from lack of oxygen. Kira would not have known these points if she'd not seen him for herself.

July 1, 2001.

Helene arrived home after working all day promoting their business at the local show. She was feeling ill and exhausted and was suffering pleurisy pain in her chest, so she lay down for Kira to give her some much-needed Reiki healing. Worried about her mom, Kira called on Oris to come and help, but a worker came instead, because Oris was busy elsewhere. Helene sent Kira for pen and paper just in case their Visitor had anything interesting to say. He'd been to their place before, but he had not spoken. Lying there on her own, Helene could clearly feel the worker's hands on her chest.

H: My asking Kira to fetch a pen and paper probably sounds a bit strange considering I was so ill, but at the time we just never knew who would turn up when, and so much wonderful information had been coming through, so I really felt that I needed to grasp every opportunity in both hands no matter how sick I was. I had no idea how long they were going to keep on visiting us, so as the saying goes: when opportunity knocks, go for it!

While Kira was out of the room I could feel the worker's hands on my chest. This was the first time that I was really consciously and physically aware of "someone" placing his or her hands on me. The hands felt so big compared to ours, and I experienced this beautiful energy going through my whole body right down to my feet. The feeling was different than receiving Reiki from a human channel. It felt both tingly and "fuzzy" at the same time, and very calming and loving on a very deep level. Just wonderful! After the little worker left, the sensation stayed with me for about half an hour, leaving me in a state of pure bliss.

J: I could *really* relate to this sensation Helene has described, having had to abandon my writing on one occasion and lie down when one of the Zetas placed long, thin hands on my shoulders. The waves of energy that coursed through my body were just as Helene said — total bliss.

When Kira returned, she confirmed the worker's presence for Helene. They asked him for his name, and he explained that workers don't have names, only numbers, and gave them his: 5589. He told them that his work is healing, but he is also a Scribe, and then went on to remark that humans of Earth are the hardest life form to work on — animals are much easier. He spoke more about the Human Ladder, and he informed them that Oris is living out his last life on level eight and will then incarnate onto level nine.

On the subject of names vs. numbers for Zeta workers, I know that some experiencers have received names to identify the particular one who is their main contact during encounters. I'm also aware that some people down here may find the idea of numbers rather than names either off-putting, or else confirmation of the (inaccurate) perception that Zetas are nothing but robots.

Bear in mind that this information was given to Kira and Helene, neither of whom had much understanding at that time of vibrational frequencies nor what the Zetas call "energy signatures." This being the case, worker 5589 explained how Zetas identify themselves in terms that Kira and Helene could understand at their level of knowledge.

In June 2007 Maris gave a deeper and more accurate explanation on energy signatures, when he was asked in our encounter group, "How do the Zeta Teachers get their names?" Here is his answer, as I recorded it:

> We use names more as a convenience when relating to humans of Earth, where names and labels are so much an intrinsic part of your culture. Within our society identification is based more on vibrational frequency – each of us has our own individual "energy signature" that we carry throughout our lives. People of Earth have this too, but most of you cannot perceive it so therefore must resort to names for identification.

J: My feeling is that the worker was trying to get this concept across in terms that Helene and Kira could understand, which happened on a number of occasions. An answer would be given in simple terms that Kira could comprehend, but on closer examination, deeper meanings and information would be hidden within it, beyond her 12-year-old understanding. On some occasions a wrong answer would be given on purpose, to test our inner sensing ability and to make us look deeper. At the same time, Oris has made mistakes too, as we all do, for we are all human, regardless of what soul container we inhabit.

Another factor involved is that the Zetas do not generally think in terms of physicality but rather in terms of energy, or perhaps I should say the *underlying energy that is the true nature of matter.* They perceive everything, the whole universe in fact, in terms of multi-level bands of vibrational frequency. To them everything is multi-dimensional, and trying to get this concept across to a species such as Earth humans, who tend to focus only on the shallow, material, physical outer layer is not easy. Misunderstandings are bound to occur in the process. If researchers would only take this into consideration a lot more information would be forthcoming. Even their form of writing is multi-dimensional.

Kira asked 5589 why he hadn't spoken to her previously, and his answer was:

> I try all the time, but you won't listen – or you are too scared to listen!

He was so pleased that now they could finally communicate.

They asked him what he ate, and he confirmed what Kira had experienced — they eat blue or purple/pink jelly-like substances and their drinks are blue or yellow. During one of Oris's visits he took a vial of this liquid out of his pocket to drink. Oris inhabits a biological, or at least a part-biological body at the moment to carry out his work, hence the need to take in nourishment. Some Zeta souls inhabit "artificial" containers specially adapted for space travel. These bodies don't require food — neither do they need a breathable atmosphere. This type of container allows the "wearer" to travel anywhere in the physical universe in safety and comfort.

I recall reading of a 1988 TV special in which William Moore and Jaime Shandera, both famous for their investigations of MJ-12[§], interviewed two alleged American intelligence agents, disguised electronically and codenamed "Falcon" and "Condor," who claimed that the US Government was hosting alien visitors who liked strawberry ice cream.[**]

This interview was later denounced as being full of disinformation and untruths, and if I remember correctly, it was the comment about ice cream that was used as an example of the "absurdity" of the information given out. This revelation came to mind, however, when Kira described the sweet purple/pink paste. Perhaps in a bid to find something that the poor, toothless ET could eat and enjoy, strawberry ice cream was the closest approximation that could be found, to keep this being alive, at least temporarily. Oris explained that Zetas eat once a day, but in Earth human terms this would be about once a month. He added that they sleep for about 24 hours straight once a month, but also take short "cat naps" in between if required. I believe Zeta sleep is more in the form of a deep meditation state.

The younger workers don't quite understand emotion in the Earth human sense of the word, but they must learn about it to become Teachers. Many weeks later Oris explained that this is why I'm having lives here in human form. He said it's as if I'm here on a "study tour," learning to understand and experience human emotion as part of my training. Perhaps this is why I was guided into dancing

---

[§]MJ-12: a highly secret group of a dozen military officials and scientists said to have been appointed to investigate crashed discs and their occupants.

[**]See http://www.ufoevidence.org/documents/doc579.htm.

flamenco professionally. What better way to learn to express and experience human emotion?

During his visit, 5589 asked Helene and Kira about feelings and emotion. Helene tried to explain by asking him how they feel when Oris sets them a task to do and they carry it out really well.

He just gives us another one.

Helene persisted, "But what if you *don't* do it right?"

Oh, then he gets annoyed with us!

"Well then," said Helene, beginning to realize she was pushing the proverbial boulder up-hill, "if you get it *right*, you feel *happy* — if you get it *wrong*, then you feel *sad*! *That* is emotion!"

Oh!

He was looking totally perplexed when Helene gave it up as a bad job.

14

COLORS

July 10, 2001.

Kira awoke at 6:00 a.m. complaining of feeling tired, because she'd been on the disc all night. She could recall listening to Oris and the others speaking together in their own language, and at the time had understood some of what they were saying. This is similar to an experience I had, which is still quite clear in my mind:

I was on board the big disc, reading a page of instructions of some sort. Suddenly I started to lose my ability to comprehend what was plainly in front of me. It was unsettling, because the words were familiar but my brain seemed to be rapidly losing its ability to take in the meaning behind the words. It was as if the language was multi-dimensional, but my mind could only perceive the outer layer.

Then I realized what the problem was — I was returning to Earth human consciousness. As this happened, the previously clearly understood script became a page of strange-looking unfamiliar symbols. The only memory later was that they were Braille-like in that they were raised up from the surface of the page, and I was reading them by touch as well as by sight.

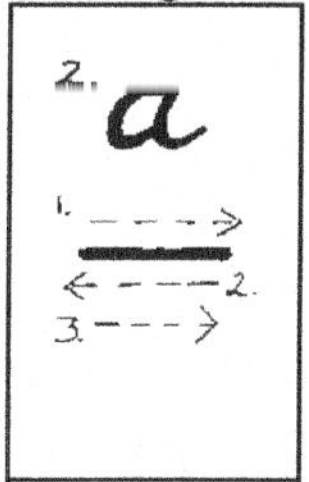

3D character learned by Jim Sparks

This script was at least three-dimensional, with strokes built up upon other strokes, so that one line or curve could actually be two, three or more "deep," and the meaning would change depending upon how many strokes were superimposed over the top. Jim Sparks experienced this with ET script.[*]

Kira could also recall using a computer on the disc, but she pressed a button too hard and received an electric shock. One of the workers told her to press it more lightly. When she awoke the next morning, her finger was still sore.

That day Oris turned up in her religious

[*]Sparks, Jim. *The Keepers: An Alien Message for the Human Race.* Columbus, NC: Wild Flower Press, 2006.

instruction class at school, visible only to Kira. The teacher asked the class, "What makes you different from everybody else?" With the ongoing contact Kira had been experiencing with the Zetas and her visits on board the disc every night, she caught Oris's expression and nearly burst out laughing. He'd very eloquently put both hands over his face and was slowly shaking his head from side to side — a sign of intense amusement in a Zeta.

When her turn came to answer, she couldn't very well tell the truth — that what made her different was that she went off every night with an ET Teacher on a "flying saucer" — so she panicked a bit and couldn't think of what to say. Oris suggested an answer.

> I am in charge of myself; I am on my own journey; and I am strong!

The teacher was totally amazed by the maturity of "her" answer. Oris also turned up in science class when they were learning about planets and the universe. This really upset him because some of the information being taught was not correct by his standards.

In another religious education class the students were given three questions to answer, and Oris spoke sternly to Kira.

> I trust you will not answer them, for they are very negative!

One question that really upset him was extremely judgmental, comparing "street" people with wealthy folk. The teacher became annoyed and scolded Kira for taking so much time, but she was hesitating because Oris was acting so stern and serious in not wanting her to answer. He then wanted to know why the teacher was getting so angry.

> When you are learning, you should never be spoken to like that!

"It's just the way humans are!" she explained.

That same afternoon Oris returned to clarify the Human Ladder further. He confirmed that the ten galactic levels are a path of evolution, from animal human to cosmic human (Earth human to angel). He explained that the Zetas refer to the angels as workers of God (or Oneness, which is a term they use for God — another term used is Source). They call themselves workers of the angels.

Once a soul has evolved through all ten levels, it returns back to Source then begins another round on a higher-vibrational frequency.

According to the Zetas, there are multi-universes of gradually ascending vibrational frequencies.

July 17, 2001.

Kira met Maris for the first time when he visited her school with Oris. A small worker accompanied them to take down notes using a laser pen. Again it was during religious instruction, which seemed to be one of Oris's favorite classes.

> Hi Kira! This is Maris, Judy's friend, and he's here to observe – and please don't mind about the worker – he'll be taking notes!

Maris gave her a friendly wave. The teacher was talking to the class about feelings, and how losing control of your emotions and yelling at someone gets you nowhere. The very next moment he was yelling at the students. Oris shook his head in total perplexity.

> He's just done what he's been telling you not to do!

Another of Oris's favorite classes was art. He seemed to really enjoy walking around looking at all the different colors and shapes, and he showed particular interest in some model animals that were on display. Having access to a far greater color spectrum than we do, the Zetas have a real "thing" about color. This is to do with the energy work they carry out with humans in connection with helping us to balance our chakra system, which in turn will facilitate human evolution on Earth.

Each of our main chakras resonates with one of the seven colors of the spectrum. Being more highly evolved than Earth humans, the Zeta teachers have "mastered all their colors" (balanced all their chakras). This is actually part of Zeta teacher training, and is the reason why, once they reach teacher level, they wear black. Black contains all seven colors of the spectrum, as opposed to white, which reflects all the colors, therefore black is "all colors" whereas white is "no color." The Zeta teacher can then reflect whatever color is appropriate to their student, to assist the healing and balancing process in the student's energy system. For example, I needed to balance my throat chakra, so my Teacher, Maris, reflects the color blue to me, as that is the color that resonates with the throat chakra and brings it back into balance.

The Zetas visiting Kira's art class would have been interested to see how well and how clearly the colors were being expressed through the consciousnesses of the children in the class. In this way they would have been able to get a feel of the energy signatures of the ones who had done the art work.

More support for the reality of Kira's experiences was provided that afternoon, when Helene asked her about Maris. A comment she made was that compared to Oris, Maris speaks more quietly and with an accent. I'd certainly never mentioned this to her, but Maris's voice is quite distinctive, and a couple of others who've heard him speak have also commented on this. He speaks slowly and carefully, like a foreigner whose native tongue is not English. He was the one who had spoken to Becky in Russian. Oris wears a red feather in his hat, while Maris wears a blue one, matching the color of the crystal on the end of the needle used on my third eye at the sacred site.

That night Kira dreamed that she was dressed in a Spanish flamenco outfit, dancing with a man she recognized as Oris. She felt that it was a past life in Spain. Details of this life were later given to Kira by Oris to help her understand certain lessons she is meant to learn this time around.

July 18, 2001.

Oris and Maris turned up again at the school, giving what appeared to be a guided tour to three or four other ETs.

July 19, 2001.

Helene and Kira went to visit their friend Dianne, to see her new baby. Dianne was suffering from bronchitis and the baby had a cold, so Helene and Kira gave them both some Reiki. While they were doing this, Dianne's mother arrived home. She'd had a stroke about four months previously, and so took them up on an offer of Reiki on her shoulder, which had been giving her pain. She could now walk, and her speech was returning to normal, but it was obvious that her right side had been affected, and she still couldn't move her right arm.

While Helene worked on her shoulder Oris suddenly turned up and started concentrating his attention on her arm, placing his hands so that his fingers were pointing towards each other, running energy along the meridian. Kira noticed that when he placed his hands on her, she sighed, and later on reported a tingling sensation in her arm.

As this was going on, Kira was giving the baby Reiki. She seemed uncomfortable in the chest and was having trouble breathing, so Oris came over to help, and he seemed to actually open the chest area, putting his hands right inside and squeezing hard. Blue-colored energy was visible coming out of his fingers.

Just then Betty, a friend of Dianne's, arrived. She knew about Reiki, and they chatted for a while as Helene, Kira and Oris (invisible of course to everyone but Kira) continued to work. Suddenly Dianne said to Betty, "I must give you back your camera so you can take a photo of the UFO!" Kira and Helene looked at each other, and Oris froze, looking very upset and concerned.

Later on in private Oris explained that a certain rebel group is here on Earth doing everything they can to disrupt the Zetas' work. One of the things they're doing is interfering with some people's third-eye chakras to open up psychic and clairvoyant abilities before the person is ready to handle these senses properly. This is causing a lot of confusion, and was what was enabling Betty to perceive the disc. The rebels work in other ways as well, by keeping some humans trapped in a state of perpetual amnesia on the physical plane, which causes them to forget that the body is just a "container" for the immortal spirit, which is what we all truly are.

Seeing Oris working inside the baby reminded Kira of a similar operation done on her "upstairs." It was not painful at all, but she could feel their fingers inside her. One of them reassured her, telling her not to worry and to just relax. Before she knew it, it was all over.

This in turn stirred up memories for me. In 1989 I too was taken up onto the disc, where a procedure was carried out in my chest. I asked Kira to check with Oris if my memory was correct, and he confirmed it for me. I clearly remember that once I was on board I didn't want to leave and that I got very upset and begged to stay with them.

When they finished and I got up, one of the workers asked me to help them lift a heavy bench. I never understood why this was asked of me, because although the Zetas appear physically weak and frail, they're really quite strong. I now believe that it dealt with the procedure. They were probably checking my heart rate under physical stress to make sure everything was functioning normally and that no damage had been done during the process.

By now, Helene was beginning to feel a lot more relaxed about this otherworldly contact. She'd developed a deep sense of trust with the Zetas, knowing her children would not be hurt and that they were cared for "upstairs" and protected. She'd come to a point of acceptance that there was a job to do, and that her own role was to guide, teach and be supportive. They'd moved through a huge fear barrier and found nothing but love on the other side. This difficult transition is the only way that experiencers of ET contact and their supporters can resolve their fears. Unfortunately there are many supporting humans who only cause more trauma and fear by assuming that the Zetas are negative. (See Chapter 7.)

Although I don't get to visit Helene's family very often in physical form because they live quite far from me, I still see them regularly. One night Kira saw me in Ben's room in my Zeta form, and on another occasion I awoke one morning remembering visiting Ben during the night, when he showed me his favorite pajamas with a distinctive color and pattern. The next time I phoned Helene, she confirmed my memory, and on my next physical visit, she showed me the pajamas, which I recognized immediately.

Oris's caring and protective nature has repeatedly shown itself. One night Helene was worried because Kira planned to sleep over with a school friend whose family was very dysfunctional — the parents separated and the children not well supervised. Oris arrived that night to take Kira up onto the disc, and when it was time for him to retrieve her, he wanted to take her home rather than return her to the other house. He insisted that the energies there were not good and he didn't want her staying there. Oris can be stubborn at times, and it took Kira a bit of convincing to get him to return her to her friend's place.

On another occasion, David, whose face I recognized from when I worked on him "upstairs," was taken up on the disc along with a friend. When it was time for them to be returned to their respective homes, David was dropped off at his friend's house instead of at his own, the reason being the friend wasn't feeling well, and David was sent back with him to make sure he was okay. David awoke the next morning totally disoriented, in a strange bed in a house that wasn't his. A lot of confusion followed, but strangely enough, once sorted out, the matter was never spoken of again. Obviously a mind block was put on everyone else involved, to prevent further enquiry and embarrassment.

People also sometimes find themselves outside the locked door of their home, unable to get back in. When the Zetas transport a person out through a locked door or window, they often place the person between them, so that the physical human body is enclosed in a sort of "corridor" of a higher-vibrational frequency that transcends time and space and enables the human body to be moved through solid matter. The problem is that, if they're not returned inside later, they can be locked out of their house.

In Kira's case it was only her astral form that was taken, so even if Oris had insisted on taking her back to her own home instead of returning her to where she was staying, he soon would have realized his error. He always assisted her back into her physical body, and he always waited to make sure she was settled before he left.

Despite the fact that the Zetas are "only human" and do make mistakes, these mistakes are sometimes done on purpose to make the human involved more aware — to "wake them up," in other words. In the case of Oris wanting to take Kira back to the wrong place, perhaps he was trying to get her to be more aware of the negative energies that are present in some places, and to be careful in such situations.

On one occasion Oris was too busy to come for her himself, and he sent in his place another who had only visited once before, wasn't familiar with the house, and so had to go looking for her. He couldn't remember which room was Kira's. Finally locating her, he accidentally woke her up. Kira then had to explain to him that she couldn't leave her body unless she was asleep, which meant he had to wait for her to drift off again. Instead of sitting down quietly to wait, he waited right beside her bed, watching her intently with his large black Zeta eyes, expecting her to drop off instantaneously as Zetas do. This, of course, made it just that much harder for Kira to get back to sleep again.

One day as Helene and Kira were busy doing housework, Oris appeared to explain about the color association of the chakras and the roles the various Zeta Teachers play in our lives.

Helene's lesson is self-empowerment, which relates to the solar plexus chakra and the color yellow. As the "red" Teacher, Oris works with those who need grounding and emotional balancing. Red is for physicality and emotion. Kira's lesson for this lifetime is to become more grounded and to learn to control the lower emotions — hence her association with Oris. We learned that green is for healing and balance; orange is for healing your inner child and trust; and yellow represents spiritual cleanliness.

Maris, being the "blue" Teacher, helps out with communication and artistic creativity — exactly the help I've needed in my writing and teaching work. Blue is for happiness, peace and calmness. It was after my experience involving the needle with Maris's blue crystal on the end of it (See Chapter 8.) that the idea of writing about the Zetas was conveyed to me. For those of us down here in human form, the Teacher to whom we're connected is our "telephone line" back to Zeta consciousness. The crystal on the end of the needle is encoded with the energy frequency of the data that is to be downloaded into our Earth human consciousness, rather like the data-encoded "energy stamps" that create the crop circles. It also carries our Teacher's energy signature. The Zeta Teachers have this crystal as an implant in the brow chakra. It's of a very high frequency, but occasionally it can be visible to clairvoyant sight.†

As Helene and Kira continued their housework on that "colorful" day, Oris followed them from room to room, happily chatting and answering questions, and as they moved from the bathroom to the bedroom, Serapis appeared.

H: By this time Kira and I were getting quite comfortable with our "upstairs family," as I now call them. Life was pretty busy in those days trying to run a business, a family and a household, and it got to the point that with Oris and his friends appearing so regularly and wanting to chat, I was having trouble getting everything done. Oris obviously realized this, and so he took the trouble to assure me:

Don't stop, Helene. I can talk to you while you work.

I had much to catch up on around the house, and I was pleasantly surprised by his insight and understanding, but it was a pity that he couldn't lend me a hand! I've always liked to keep a clean and tidy home, and now I realize it also keeps the energies better as well, which in turn makes it more pleasant for all.

---

† Paola Harris in *Connecting the Dots — Making Sense of the UFO Phenomenon*, (*ibid.*), discusses her interview with Col. Philip Corso, who was in charge of back-engineering material taken from one of the Discs that crashed near Roswell. Corso speaks of an ET contact experience he once had, during which he asked, "What can you offer me?" The ET replied: "A new world — if you can take it!"
Corso describes a red jewel or sensor imbedded in the glass of the ET's helmet, positioned right over the brow chakra. I was reminded of Kira's having seen a red jewel/crystal imbedded in Oris's forehead over the brow chakra and of the crystal-capped needle that was inserted into this same point on my forehead.

It was getting to where Oris felt like a trusted, old and long-lost friend, and I enjoyed his visits very much. Then when Serapis turned up, it was really more a surprise than a shock to me. How nice another Zeta Teacher was paying a visit! So unexpected! To my profound amazement, I could easily feel the difference in their energies, just like we have differences in our human personalities and energies. They were all starting to feel much more "human" to me. Oris felt strong, kind and wise, whereas Serapis felt sweet, gentle and all knowing. Both of them are very wise and knowledgeable in their own way, if that makes any sense.

Serapis explained to us that people are scared of his appearance because of a scar across his face and head. He went on to tell us that it was the result of a violent death in a past human life on Earth in which he'd been some sort of hermit monk living in a cave in a mountainous region of Asia.[‡] *One day a sick woman came to him for healing, and as he attended her, men wielding swords attacked them. Apparently many priests and monks were being put to death at the time. The woman was decapitated, and then they came after him. He tried to escape, and he ducked to avoid the blade of the sword, resulting in a horrific injury that of course killed him. The trauma of this awful death has obviously made a deep impression on his psyche, resulting in a scar still being visible on his Zeta body.*

J: Kira and I have both noticed on occasions that if we receive an injury "upstairs," our physical human body carries evidence of it for several days afterwards. So it stands to reason that such a serious and traumatic injury as the one which caused the death of Serapis's human body, could certainly manifest in his Zeta body, as the two are so closely linked. While he was talking to them, Kira needed to go to the toilet. Serapis was standing directly in front of the door to the bathroom, so she went to walk around him.

You can just walk through me if you like.

So she did. The sensation was like passing through the jelly-water substance we go through to enter the disc. I believe that some interdimensional portal is created wherever the Zetas are, particularly if they're in astral form. The disc itself is also like an

[‡]I later found out that Serapis showed me that scar to remind me of a past life I had with him.

interdimensional portal — certainly the big disc anyway, which the Zetas refer to as "the Workshop."

One day while walking through the local shopping center, Helene had a most incredible experience with Serapis when she spied an ordinary-looking, neatly dressed elderly man, probably in his late sixties to early seventies who was standing chatting with another man. As she walked past, the man caught her eye and smiled at her, leaving her wondering who he was. He appeared to know her, and he seemed somehow familiar, but she couldn't quite place him. Getting on with her shopping she forgot all about the incident until a day or so later, when Kira casually remarked: "By the way, Mom, I almost forgot — Serapis told me he saw you the other day at the shops. He smiled at you to say hello."

Helene and Kira finished their cleaning and moved into the garage/office area. They were now feeling perfectly comfortable having the Zeta Visitors around and looked upon them very much as members of the family. They knew that Oris and Serapis would follow along happily and keep talking if they wanted to.

One day one of the little workers was doing this, and being so friendly and polite, telling them what a nice house they had and how he enjoyed coming to visit. Helene smoked sometimes when they were around. As she said, "No one has complained yet — thank heavens!" Not long after that, Oris turned up one day feeling a bit out of sorts.

> Helene – will you please put that rotten thing out!

After Helene and Kira settled themselves in the office, Helene had more questions for Oris. They asked him what my worker number is, which he told them — 9756[§]. They then asked if the Zetas have a link with Buddhism.

> No, but we meditate with the Buddhas (enlightened beings) and convey messages through them, but that is all. Meditation is a form of healing for the soul. It is good even if you only meditate for five minutes each night in order to connect back to center. You do not have to sit in a cave for years! Relaxing is meditating – you only need to sit quietly and close your eyes.

[§]Worker numbers change as soul evolution takes place. The number is just a simple way of explaining "energy signature" to Earth Humans. Back then my Worker number was 9756. It's now 626. (An upgrade — I hope!)

Their next question was: Do Zetas ever get sick? At first he said no, that it's just an Earth human thing resulting from an imbalance in the energy system and emotions, but then he admitted that they can catch colds, but nothing more serious. He did, however, have a vague recollection of somebody developing some sort of serious condition that resulted in death, but it is apparently rare. If they do become ill, they take time out to meditate and rebalance their energy system through special breathing techniques, and of course there are always the magical healing chairs for a "quick fix." These chairs are very ordinary-looking chairs made out of a plastic-like material, but being energetically linked into and part of the disc's "consciousness," they have the ability to (a) mold themselves to comfortably accommodate whatever body sits in them, and (b) give that body an instant boost of healing energy.

Helene then asked him some personal questions about a worrying dream she'd had. He reassured her and explained its meaning more clearly, which caused a bit of a laugh, because Oris had appeared in this dream in a very nice-looking human form, and Helene cheekily asked him why he doesn't look like that all of the time. Quick as a flash, he answered back.

> Oh no, that wouldn't be any good at all! Everyone would fall in love with me, and I wouldn't get any work done!

It was around this time that the family rented the video "City of Angels," in which the angelic characters are dressed all in black, just like the Zeta Teachers. They asked Oris about this, and he explained that the person who wrote the story behind the film has an awareness of the Zetas (not necessarily on a conscious level), and he based the angel characters on them. There's one scene in the film in which all the black-clad angels congregate on a beach at dawn to face the dawn and listen to beautiful, celestial music. Helene asked Oris if the Zetas do this.

> No we don't, but it would be nice to be able to!

There was one very moving scene where an armed robber comes storming into a shop, waving a gun around and screaming at the man behind the counter to hand over the cash. He's shaking with nervousness, violence and desperation, and the victim is trembling with terror, expecting to be shot at any moment, but he is too paralyzed with fear to obey the gunman's order. An angel steps between them, placing a hand on each man's shoulder to calm the dangerous situation, which enables the victim to hand over the cash safely and the robber leaves the premises without any shots being fired.

Many months later Kira witnessed a similar incident at a police-supervised disco she was attending with some of her school friends, at which a potentially dangerous fight broke out between two groups of youths. One of these boys had smuggled a knife into the disco, and in a fit of rage he was threatening to use it. Just moments before, Kira had been sitting close to where this situation was unfolding when Oris suddenly appeared on the scene, suggesting to her to get up and have a dance. His voice was calm and quiet so as not to scare her, but he was extremely insistent.

Just seconds after Oris got her out of harm's way, the fight broke out, and Kira watched in fascination as Oris stepped up behind the knife-wielding youth and placed a gentle hand on his shoulder. The boy calmed down immediately, and the police who were running the disco took care of the troublemakers without anyone getting hurt. The Zetas often use this calming technique. Kira, Helene and I have all experienced it personally, and it's a lovely sensation, to have a long, thin, four-fingered hand placed on your shoulder.

Something similar happened to a female client during a Reiki treatment. I was sitting at her head, and as often occurs during Reiki, this woman started having an out-of-body experience. Not being accustomed to such a thing, she began to get frightened, but the next moment she became aware of really strange-feeling, long, thin hands gently taking hold of her ankles and guiding her back down. The hands then remained in position for the remainder of the treatment, holding her firmly by the ankles to keep her grounded and in her body.

After the question-and-answer session in the office, Helene and Kira went into the kitchen to make themselves a sandwich for lunch. As Kira was getting the food from the refrigerator, she kicked Ben's rubber ball that was on the floor. Helene noticed that it seemed to be kicked back at her. This happened several times. Finally, without even thinking, Helene said: "Will you two stop playing ball in the house!" Kira burst out laughing at the look of surprise on Oris's face that he'd been caught out, and Helene was quite shocked herself that she'd reprimanded an ET without thinking twice about it.

As they made their sandwiches, they explained to Oris about the different food groups and that these enable our body to stay healthy. They also explained to him that we need eight hours sleep each night in order to stay well and functioning at optimal efficiency. He commented on how easy they were to communicate with and how much he enjoyed this friendly interaction — even getting into trouble for playing ball in the house!

H: When I look back now at our conversation in the kitchen about food and sleep, I think Oris was being very polite, wanting to give us a sense of equality through an exchange of information, so we wouldn't feel that it was entirely one-sided. In a very subtle way I think he was also bringing our attention to how important it is to eat a well-balanced diet and to have the right amount of sleep. He often gently got us to focus on the important things in life by asking the appropriate questions.

15
Home Planet

August 3, 2001.

Another visit by Oris, and more questions answered for Helene. He was usually very cooperative when it came to answering questions, only occasionally refusing due to tiredness or lack of time. By this time he even had a favorite chair in the lounge where he always sat. Helene's first question dealt with whether or not he had assisted her with a Reiki treatment she'd done on her husband the day before. He answered affirmatively and told her that they often step in to help, and said she should call on them any time she needs assistance (hence my recent experience with the woman client). He added that they're always present during Reiki attunements. For example, very recently, some little workers were being a bit naughty and mischievous, mucking about with the music during an attunement I was doing. A clairvoyant friend who was present caught them "red-handed."

Another question: Can Zetas live out a whole life on Earth as a human, or do they sometimes just make quick visits, taking on human form temporarily?

The answer was yes to both. Some appear for just a short space of time in human form, looking exactly like any other ordinary person walking down the street (or standing about in shopping centers as Serapis enjoys doing when he has a few minutes to spare). Others come here to live out a whole-life experience for various reasons — to teach, learn, observe, etc., sometimes not even realizing on the human level that they are ETs.

I have since been told that a number of ET folk, some of them Zetas, are trapped down here in Earth human bodies. They are caught up in a permanent state of forgetfulness, living out one physical life after another, continually pulled back down onto the physical plane, unable to escape back to their true Home. This situation has been going on for eons, and the Zeta "rescue party" is trying to help break this cycle by waking us all up to the fact that we are more than just a physical body. All of us have God Essence within and are therefore potentially all-powerful immortal spiritual beings. This is our soul heritage that the visitors are attempting to restore to us, a heritage that has been deliberately blocked from our consciousness over many millennia.

They then asked Oris about his home planet, and he told them there are five countries, each about the size of the US. Three of these have been left untouched, and two are totally urbanized. One of the natural wilderness countries may eventually be developed for urban living, but two will always be left untouched for wildlife. He added that special fertilizer is used in the soil to assist plant growth.

The Zetas inform me that they have actually evolved from many different planets, not just the Zeta Reticuli system. They have now moved beyond the need to reside on a physical planet, as their home realm is of a higher and finer frequency that is beyond physical worlds. This realm doesn't have a name as such, but its energy signature denotes home, birthplace, and family.

The "home planet" Oris described to Helene and Kira was from a past existence, and the information was given not only to help them feel more comfortable and familiar with him, but also to give them something tangible that they could relate to.

Oris also explained more about the universe. The Zetas speak of the universe being a "Cycle," which is comprised of the various levels of the Human Ladder. Once a soul has completed one cycle, it reincarnates onto the next, and so on — in other words, infinite universal cycles, each resonating on a different frequency band. He said that the Zetas — the workers of the angels — are caretakers of life-force energy, or what is sometimes referred to as the Universal force-field, and in this role have been called "Watchers," "Guardians," "Keepers," and "Gardeners of the Earth."

The illustration on the following page is limited to our perspective in the Universe and our relationship with the Zetas. Clearly there are many other varied types of beings that are not on this chart.

He then went on to speak of what he calls "the family of 13," which is a Zeta Group whose job down here is to help people overcome their fear. They are here to help bring balance and healing to the planet.

A very important point Oris brought up was the fact that there is a group of negative beings down here who can appear as Zetas, but their eye shape is different. They give humans frightening and unpleasant experiences with so-called "Greys," and thus cause a deep sense of fear and mistrust, which feeds these negative ones. They're also responsible for causing a false sense of ego in some contactees. I believe they've been brought through from the lower astral plane specifically to cause feelings of hatred and prejudice against us real Zetas in order to block the positive work of transformation that we're here to carry out. We were told about this in August 2001, and since 2005 some of the more well-known researchers have started speaking out about this. The Zetas have hinted at some kind of a Nazi-type link here that is being promoted through the Aryan ideal concept of "beautiful, blonde, blue-eyed Space Brothers."

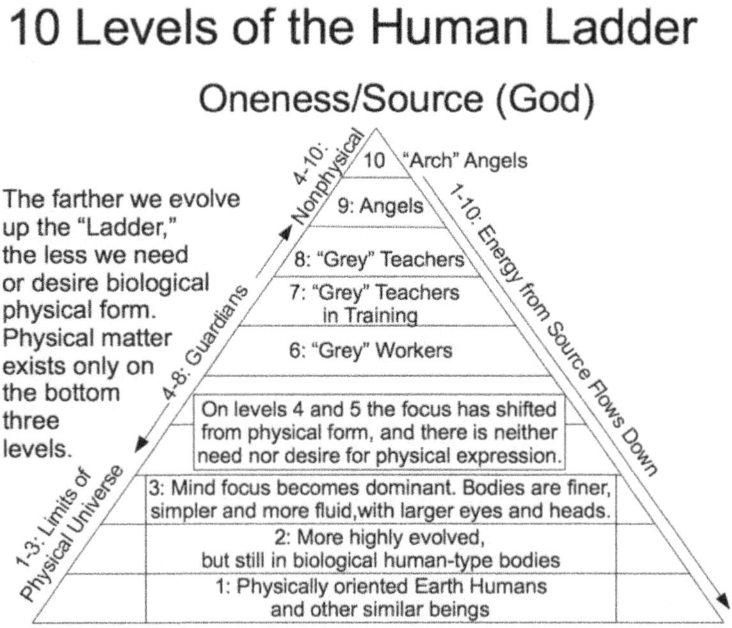

A SIMPLIFIED ILLUSTRATION OF THE HUMAN LADDER

In some cases however, the frightening experiences people go through with ETs may be likened to the Catholic doctrine of "Purgatory," according to which the soul must pass through the so-called "Fire of Purgatory," a highly unpleasant, almost Hell-like state, in order to be sufficiently purged or cleansed to allow it to enter "Heaven."

I asked Oris whether the concept of Purgatory may have arisen out of the shamanic "Dark Night of the Soul" experience that sometimes involves seemingly frightening or bizarre ET-type encounters, and he answered affirmatively and went on to explain —

> It is only when fear and egotism are overcome that real spiritual progress can be made, and the only way to overcome fear and egotism (which is simply a facet of fear) is to face it head-on. People need to be pushed out of and beyond their "comfort-zones" if they are to achieve real growth and evolution on the soul level.

During this question-and-answer session, Helene had sandalwood incense burning, which Oris particularly loves. He amused himself by causing the ash to curl around in a spiral pattern, which has been carefully preserved in honor of his visit. He also played with the smoke, forming it into the shape of a tree, a wave, and a long, thin line. Helene commented on how beautiful and relaxing it was to watch, and he explained how this could be used as a way to meditate. Since then, Oris has created some amazing shapes with incense ash, and they don't collapse afterwards but rather keep their shape permanently. His first "spiral" is still intact years later, and Helene has to buy new incense holders on a regular basis, as she doesn't want to destroy his handiwork.

August 11, 2001.

One of the negative ones was annoying Kira at school, but when she yelled at it, it disappeared. Oris later told her another good way to deal with them is to simply ignore them — they *hate* being ignored. As Oris once demonstrated to me, a good kick up the back end works well too.

August 12, 2001.

Two of the "negative Greys" came into Kira's bedroom, threatening her with a ball of purple energy that they claimed could "take her soul." She ran terrified to her parents and ended up changing beds with her mom. Alone in Kira's room, Helene simply told them to "rack off," then promptly fell asleep, not bothered in the least.

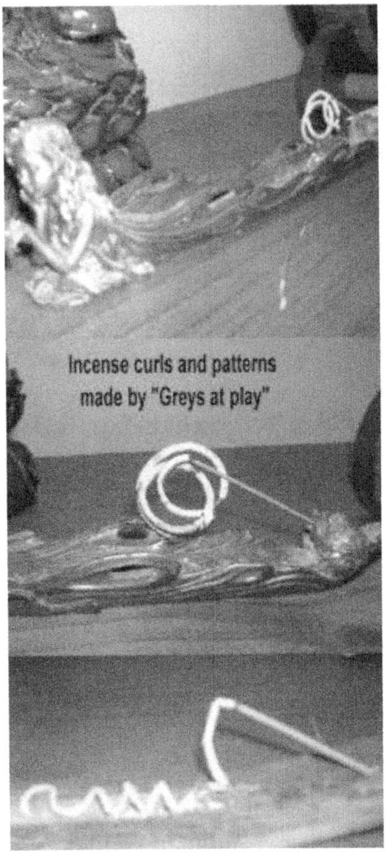

August 15, 2001.

Helene and Kira came to visit me. My intention, prompted by Oris, was to attune Kira to level-two Reiki in order to assist her with the negative energies that were still bothering her. Just prior to the attunement a very tangible change came into the room's energy — it got *very* cold, and just as this happened, Kira announced that Oris had arrived.

During the attunement process a number of Zeta Teachers were present, standing in a circle around us and doing symbols over us. Oris stood opposite me and we worked together, mirroring each other. A small worker was also present, continually cleansing Kira's aura as they do during a Reiki treatment. Kira later commented that the "yellow" Teacher (Helene's Teacher) had rings on his fingers, some plain gold and others set with stones. I wonder if anyone else has seen a Zeta wearing jewelry! His name is Anarkis.* Gold is symbolic of the Sun, which is interesting because he represents the solar plexus chakra.

That same evening one of the "negative Greys" turned up in Kira's room, scaring her badly. Helene tried burning sandalwood incense, and they both tried using Reiki symbols on him, but he told them these would not work. Helene felt no fear whatsoever. Looking back I strongly suspect that this may even have been Oris in disguise, testing Kira to help her push past her fear. His immunity to both the incense and the Reiki symbols tells me this, as well as Helene's lack of fear. She is very sensitive to energy, and having been in the presence of real negative entities on a couple of occasions myself, I

*pronounced *An-AR-kis*

know that she would have been aware and felt the unpleasant energy if it had been real.

Helene, not aware that it was Oris, asked him why he didn't come over to our side, because it was much nicer. His answer was that he had a job to do. Kira was still terrified, so Helene tried to get her laughing (another good antidote to negative energy) by telling her to visualize him with a funny hairdo, pretty dress and high-heeled shoes, but it didn't really help. She was still frightened.

Helene then started acting silly, pretending to scream in fear. "There you are!" she said to him. "You *scare* me — so now you can go!" All he did was comment on what a strange human she was. This at least got Kira giggling. Helene then got her to pinpoint exactly where he was in the room so she could give him a hug, but he didn't react at all. She tried to get Kira to do the same, but as she approached him he produced the purple ball of energy again, causing her to jump back in terror.

They tried taking the incense over to where he was standing, even stabbing at him with it. He just kept moving away, trying to trick them by telling them that incense is bad for your eyes. They got closer to him and he started coughing as part of his pretense at being "negative" and therefore adversely affected by the incense, then finally disappeared. Poor Kira spent the rest of the night on the floor in her parents' room.

H: When Kira told me that the negative ones had threatened to "take her soul," I couldn't believe it. My first reaction was: "No, they can't do that, surely. They can't just go around killing people off!" Now that I was sort of getting used to weird happenings in my home, I was becoming aware of my gut feelings growing stronger — or I was learning to listen more to my inner voice. Looking back, I now realize it was my own self-empowerment that was beginning to wake up and strengthen. How interesting!

As for taking Kira's soul, it just didn't make any sense at all. I remember thinking: "Surely God wouldn't allow such a thing to happen!" This whole thing was going weird on me again, and a million questions and thoughts popped up in my mind: What if I'm wrong? Could this really happen? Has it ever happened to anyone else? What if something does *happen to Kira? I would never forgive myself — she's my child! I love her and want to keep her safe and protected, but how, and from what exactly? I don't know how much more of this pressure I can handle. I'm her mom — I feel what she feels and I worry about her so much! How in hell are we all going to come through this sanely without any psychological scarring?*

And so it went on, and on! Just as I was becoming more confident in dealing with "upstairs," here was another blow coming at me from right field! But all I could do was just keep moving, one step at a time! As my mom always says, "It would all work out in the wash." But this wash felt like a bloody big load! I kept telling myself, "Just breathe Helene — breathe!" All I can say is thank God I had Jude to talk to and bounce ideas off and to share my thoughts and feelings. I hoped and prayed she would have some more answers for me like she always had in the past.

J: Helene was really worried and in need of reassurance when she rang me the next day to share their experience with the "negative Grey." A strong feeling immediately came into my mind that Kira needed to allow the purple ball to be thrown at her and that she needed to catch it. This would be a real test for her, because she'd been told that if the ball hit her, it would "take her soul." This was why she was so scared.

I knew very well that this was ridiculous, but at the same time I'm aware that negative energy is very real and can certainly impact upon us in one way or another, so I hoped to heaven that my advice was sound. There was no way of knowing for sure, never having come up against such a thing myself. In my experience, Reiki symbols have always provided protection.

I had no idea then that Oris was actually communicating this advice through me, so really it was a test of faith and trust for all of us, which is why he didn't communicate with Kira directly — we were all being tested on various levels. Luckily Helene had enough faith and trust in me to pass this advice on to Kira.

August 22, 2001.

Kira arrived home from school to tell her mother that workers had been turning up all day to warn her that the negative one was coming. One of the workers had come into the religious education class to explain to her that many of the religious figures in Earth's history were really ETs. He informed her that many of their teachings were misunderstood, including the concept of the Holy Spirit. The trinity of Father, Son and Holy Spirit actually represents our multidimensional self. The "Father" is the God part of our being, the "Son" is our physical form, and our "Holy Spirit" is our higher self.

He went on to tell her that the correct position for the hands to be held during prayer is with the fingertips touching but the palms apart. In this way the hands are in a pyramid shape, with the apex pointing upwards. Several years later I learned of the "*Gassho*" position for the hands in Japanese Reiki and Buddhist traditions, which matched exactly with what the worker told Kira

That evening Kira went to bed feeling very scared, and wanting to sleep in her parents' room. They refused, feeling that they needed to take a stronger stand with her. She tried desperately to change their minds, but they dug in.

H: Poor Kira was so scared and uncertain about everything at that stage. She'd been sleeping on the floor in our bedroom for nine nights in a row, but we just couldn't keep going on like this. Gary and I thought "No, we have to be stronger with her — we can't let this go on any longer." It was about 10:30 p.m. and we were almost asleep when the most terrifying scream came from Ben's room. My heart started pounding and instant fear took over. "Oh, God, no! What now!" I did not expect to hear from Ben tonight! Gary and I ran into his room and saw immediately that he was in one of his trances. At this point I'll let Jude finish the story. I still find it hard to talk about and revisit my feelings from that night. It was so intense! I felt so much pressure to protect them both and to do the right thing. All I can say is, I somehow just got on with my job as their mom as best I could, but God, I hated seeing my children feeling terrorized in this way.

J: The next moment, still in trance, Ben jumped out of bed, ran into Kira's room and threw his arms around her, giving her a big hug. Kira could see the "negative Greys," as she called them, coming into her room after him, and her room seemed to be full of them. Ben then ran back down the hallway to his parents' room and climbed into their bed. Helene asked him if he'd had a bad dream and he answered: "Yes — Kira was dead — they killed her with a pillow!" I must add here that none of the family ever discussed the subject of ET visitation with or in front of Ben. In fact they went to great lengths to keep it from him so as not to feed his "night terrors" further, so he knew nothing of Kira's experiences with the "baddies."

A few minutes later she came running in, jumping up and down with excitement, saying she'd caught the ball. Her poor father was totally confused and had no idea of what she was talking about, so Helene told him she'd explain later. Kira gave Ben a hug to reassure him that she was okay, and now that he'd calmed down, she and Helene took him back to his own room, where he quickly settled down to sleep.

They then went to Kira's room to talk about what had happened. She explained that a whole group of "negative Greys" had followed Ben into her room when he'd run to her during his trance, but the leader of the group had remained in his room. Kira could see him from her bed and told him to come to her. He refused, telling her to come to him, so gathering her courage, she went. He then threw the ball at her, and she caught it, which felt like the "gooey" substance we go through to board the disc. Then Oris arrived to congratulate her and to tell her she'd "passed the test." He instructed her to take it over to Ben's night light and to place it on the light, where it promptly disintegrated.

Kira shed some tears of relief and asked her mom to cleanse the room with Reiki, because the energy still felt a bit mixed up. Helene gave her a hug and she settled back into bed, still not quite able to believe she'd passed the test. Just as the Reiki symbols were put in place, Oris arrived, and Helene said to him: "Aren't you proud of Kira?"

He smiled and answered: "What do you think?"

She then asked him if he had orchestrated the test, but he answered no — it had come from God. He went on to explain that Kira had called Ben into her on a subconscious level, and Ben had been aware on the soul level that she needed help and was concerned for her safety, hence his dream of her death. (I really think his role was more to distract the parents so Kira would have to face her challenge alone.)

H: You know what is really strange? After all that happened that night, I still had no animosity towards Oris. I was just relieved and so glad that it was all over. Jude did say to me that it must have been a test for Kira, but who would've thought that it was a test for us all? In fact not only were we given a test, but we were also given a very big lesson in trust and faith with each other — Jude, Oris, Gary, Kira, Ben and me.

J: A really funny "Grey moment" (as opposed to a senior moment) occurred when Helene was typing up her last two notes to email to me. As she explained, when she got to the description of hearing young Ben scream and how she and Gary ran into his room, a whole lot of obviously very deeply buried emotion came flooding to the surface, and her eyes filled with tears. She clicked on *send* to forward the email through to me, then decided to check her own in-box while she had the computer on, just to distract her mind away from the whole painful episode.

Unknown to her, right at that very moment I was also at my computer checking my emails, and among them was a joke sent through by one of my Tai Chi students. It dealt with not being concerned if you gain weight as you age — that in reality it's the weight of the vast amount of wisdom and knowledge you've accumulated over the years, so it's all in the head rather than on the hips and bottom. Oris immediately came into my mind — a tall, thin but very large-headed Zeta Elder who most certainly carries a weight of knowledge and wisdom around with him — so I forwarded the joke through to Helene along with a little note saying: "Who does this remind you of?" and signed it "Oris." As she read it, her feelings of painful emotion dissipated instantly, and she became acutely aware of Oris's very strong presence behind her saying,

> There now, Helene – that should cheer you up and make you feel better!

16
9/11 Impact

While all of this was going on with Kira and her family, poor Oris had his own problems to contend with involving a negative attack on the big disc, which caused computers to go down and important files to be lost. This computer glitch involved a surveillance system the Zetas use to monitor happenings down here, and it resulted in a major catastrophe that took place three weeks later to the very day — one that has gone down in our planetary history as the infamous "9-11" attack on New York's Twin Towers.

I wrote earlier of Manolo/Oris's distress that I experienced first-hand as he was trying to get through to Catherine. This was nothing compared to what he and the other Zetas went through in their desperate attempt to get the Earth surveillance system up and running again before any major disasters occurred down here. Unfortunately they did not succeed. We've always wondered if any other experiencers were aware of the chaotic situation aboard one of the big discs on Tuesday night, August 21, 2001 (our time) just prior to the 9-11 attack.

August 22, 2001.

My first hint of problems "upstairs" was waking the following morning with a sore spot on my face that looked rather like a pimple, but was more painful. This was unusual for me as I'm not prone to skin problems, being one of those "tough nuts" who can handle fertilizers and such with my bare hands with no ill effects. I recalled Kira once mentioning that she'd received an injury one night while doing her "upstairs" work, and that it had manifested on her human body as a pimple-like mark that took several days to heal. The same morning that I woke with my "pimple," Helene phoned with details of the attack on the disc.

I had retained a vague memory of something dramatic happening "upstairs" and I asked Helene to ask Oris for more details. I wondered if one of the "baddies" had had a go at me — after all, Kira often mentioned how she always saw me at a front desk in the office area. Oris's explanation was that I'd dropped my laser pen on the floor, and accidentally burnt myself when I bent down to pick it up, but surely I couldn't be that silly — *surely*! After all, I'd *much* prefer to put my injury down to a brave act of heroism, defending our disc and valuable computer equipment from invading negative forces. But Oris can be a bit of a tease at times, so I guess I'll never know the truth. All I do know is that it took weeks to heal, and I still have a small scar.

September 12, 2001.

We woke to the tragic news of a massive terrorist attack in America. Helene had been picking up something on deeper levels of her psyche, with pain in the heart chakra, which started at 8:30 p.m. on September 11 (our time), and lasted for nearly 48 hours. She'd noticed such physical symptoms on several occasions, in the way of pains experienced in various parts of her body in response to outside influences, and has now learned to take note when this happens.

Kira made the comment that she would probably have to go onto the disc that night, as there'd be major work to carry out — and she was not wrong! Psychics have been predicting disasters like this for decades, but usually nothing happens, so I wondered why did it occur this time? Then it hit me like the proverbial bolt out of the blue — the sabotage of the computer system on board the big disc!

The Zetas use the computer system to monitor happenings on Earth and elsewhere, and in this way they often intervene as far as they can to avert major disasters. This is why "strange coincidences" often seem to occur, such as bombs failing to detonate or else exploding earlier or later than they're supposed to, thereby saving many lives. On other occasions someone is guided to the right place at the right time to thwart a potentially lethal act of sabotage or terrorism. But exactly three weeks earlier, to the day, the Zetas' own computer system had been sabotaged, along with their ability to monitor happenings down here.

Looking back we recalled how stressed Oris had been at times during those three weeks, and sometimes he was not available to come or else was called away suddenly. It was obviously "all hands on deck" to get the system functioning again, because they would have been fully aware of the huge potential for disaster.

That evening I too was aware of "upstairs" work to be done. I was alone, so I turned the TV off, with its continual, emotionally charged broadcasts of the event, and I settled myself with calming meditation music. I really didn't want to listen to any more news reports when we'd be going there in person (or in spirit) to help out.

The following morning I woke up feeling *very* sick. Unlike Kira, I don't generally have much conscious recall of my "upstairs" work, but the physical after-effects can be very obvious, and sometimes quite disruptive to my day-to-day human life. I woke with a splitting headache and nausea so bad that I had to spend half the day in bed, hardly able to stand. Luckily I had no classes to attend to. Helene rang first thing in the morning to report on both Kira's and my experiences, which Kira could clearly recall, but I couldn't even come to the phone, so I passed a message on via my husband for them to please send me Reiki.

Not consciously aware of what our work had entailed, it wasn't until later that I was told why I was so sick. Apparently on that first night, faced with an unspeakable scene of devastation and concerned about young Kira, who was with me and coming up against this sort of work for the first time, I broke the first rule of being a Zeta worker — I allowed human emotion to impinge upon my senses, which is a problem for those of us who operate on both levels.

Kira told her mom of our journey to America on the disc, and of Oris taking her to "Ground Zero." He showed her how to lift herself above all the ash and debris, which we knew about before it was described later on the news reports on TV, "so her feet wouldn't get dirty." She didn't know how, so he told her to just concentrate and she would be able to do it. Sure enough, it worked, and she was totally amazed. She commented on how it reminded her of Jesus walking on water.

Then she caught sight of a severed arm, and she told Oris she didn't think she could handle seeing dead bodies, especially mutilated ones. He wisely gave her the job of helping to calm and strengthen the rescue workers instead, showing her how to place her hands on their shoulders or backs. What a "coincidence" that she'd been attuned to level-two Reiki only weeks before! I came over to work beside her to make sure she was okay and to keep a watchful eye on her, as Oris was busy elsewhere. We had to be extremely careful to shield ourselves from all the raw human emotion, but on that first night (first day over in America) it was almost impossible.

For the next few weeks Kira and I spent every sleeping moment in the U.S. doing healing work, and each morning she gave her mom a report on what she was able to consciously recall.

H: What a very sad time indeed. On one hand I felt proud of my daughter going over to America to help out in her sleep state, but on the other hand I was very worried as to how she would handle seeing such devastation. At least it was comforting to know that either Jude or Oris would be by her side keeping a close eye on her. One part of me understood that it was "all hands on deck"— help was needed from far and wide. But the other part, the human mom part, couldn't help worrying about how she was going to cope and deal with all of this on a personal level.

As we all know, this event was so *horrific and there was so much chaos. I didn't know whether to tell Gary about Kira's involvement or not. The feeling was that I needed to get my own head around the whole situation before freaking him out as well. When she told me she'd been given the job of calming the rescue workers I was very relieved. When Oris showed her how to put her hands on their shoulders and back, this reminded us of the time when Kira's teacher Mr. S died. She watched him calming his very distraught teacher friends at school in the same way.*

During those first few days she used to wake each morning feeling agitated and tired, and to top it all off she had exams on at school as well. I felt very strongly to keep her human side of life as normal as possible, giving her Reiki frequently, along with a lot of love and support.

Thankfully it didn't seem to affect her as deeply or severely as one would have thought. It was as if when she was working in her "other dimension," there was some sort of filter system in place so that it didn't impact fully on her consciousness down here. Sure, she could remember some things, but it seemed separate and not all encompassing in her daily human life. I actually felt that in time this would be a very good lesson for her, to help her acknowledge and appreciate how good life is here, and to give her the practical experience and feeling of helping others under very difficult circumstances. What an amazing lesson for a young teenager to have!

J: It was during this time that I really came to understand, via Kira but also through some conscious recall of my own, the extent of the work we are involved in. It was a long time before we could bring ourselves to speak out about this to others, and it was never brought up at any encounter groups we attended because there were just too many sensitive issues involved. Even now at this point of writing we still haven't spoken out about 9/11 very much at all.

I recall both Helene and I sitting in on one such group listening to somebody venting their spleen about those *dreadful, negative Greys* who do such *unspeakable* things to their "human victims," and how badly they treat *those poor little hybrid children* up on the disc. Helene got up quietly and walked outside, feeling sick in the stomach and unable to stand listening to any more such nonsense. Taking a deep breath to help me keep my cool, I asked this woman if she'd ever actually been up on the big disc and seen this "mistreatment" for herself. Of course she hadn't — but she assured me she'd *read all about it* in a book. When questioned on the identity of the author, it turned out to be someone who is well known in the field of ET/UFO investigation for being extremely one-eyed and prejudiced against the Zetas. This author was saying exactly what she wanted to hear, so no further investigation was carried out. Unfortunately this is what we've come up against so often.

Another problem we've faced when trying to openly discuss some of the more mundane aspects of our "upstairs" encounters and activities is that many investigators seem to find it all just too much to take in. They get very excited hearing about "lights in the sky," and are most interested to listen to peoples' seemingly negative or frightening encounters with so-called Greys, but when these Greys are presented in a more positive and friendly light they just don't seem to want to know.

Another revelation that came about through our American experience was the differences, but also the similarities, between being in Zeta and human form. Apparently my way of getting Kira (and myself) through the more gruesome and unpleasant aspects of our work was by telling her jokes, and having her tell me ones, just as many people do in situations of extreme trauma, where humor is sometimes the only way of coping. I do admit to having a bit of a twisted sense of humor when in human form, and apparently it carries across quite strongly into my Zeta form as well. In fact as a Zeta, and this is where the main difference lies, I'm much more comfortable and self-assured, which sometimes gets me into trouble.

The Zetas were there to help the living, both victims and rescuers, and the angels were there to assist the dying. The ones that Earth humans think of as "angels" are simply more highly evolved beings (both ET and inter-dimensional) who occupy the very highest rungs of conscious awareness on the Human Ladder. The Zetas, or Guardians, to give them their proper name, are from Levels Five to Eight and can access 50% to 80% of their potential conscious awareness, whereas the angels are at Levels Nine and Ten, with the highest ones having moved past the need for physical form, being pure mind/consciousness, can access full-conscious awareness. These ones are "God energy" expressing in its purest form.

In the early stages there were still people trapped alive in the building, but to reach them the rescuers had to get through a five-story-high mountain of rubble, which was quite impossible in the time they had. The Zetas stayed with these people (not that the people were necessarily consciously aware of their presence), giving them healing and comfort until they were either rescued or died.

There were instances in which angels had to intervene to stop the Zetas' healing efforts because it was the person's time to die, but the Zeta healers didn't want to give up. I have to wonder in the case of some of the people who survived, if they later woke in hospital with vague memories of being seemingly fought over by two very distinctive-looking beings. One would have been all dressed in black, which the poor human would assume was the Grim Reaper, and the other would have been perceived as a white-clad angelic being come to "save" them. Little would they understand that in fact it was the other way around — that it was the angel trying to "take their soul," and the black-clad Zeta trying to keep them alive and kicking.

Kira recalled seeing a man moving about in a small room deep inside the building. He was physically unhurt but starting to have trouble breathing because of the smoke and dust. He was unsuccessfully searching for a mobile phone to call for help.

Both Zetas and angels were making use of the same aura cleansing technique that Oris has shown us — the Zetas before commencing treatment on the injured, and the angels before lifting the spirit out of the body. How they do this is by reaching out towards the dying person and telling them to take hold of their hands because, it is time for them to wake up — then they simply lift the person's spirit form up and out of the body.

Because of the fact that angelic beings don't have physical form as such, we perceive them through the filter system of our own personal conscious awareness. They are able to tap into this and *create a form for themselves that agrees with what we think an angel should look like.*

To Kira's perception they appeared as perfected humans, with fair hair but quite dark skin, as if all the racial colors of Earth had been blended together into one. To use her words, they looked like really good-looking, very suntanned "surfies." She saw the females wearing long, flowing white robes, and with long hair decorated by a small wreath of flowers. The males were in white suits and capes, like the black suits and capes worn by the Zeta Elders. Their hair was shorter than that of the females, and the wreath they wore was made of leaves. Their eyes were large and slanted, rather similar to Zeta eyes. My perception of them is more as perfected Zetas.

H: So much confirmation of the information we'd received previously seemed to be pouring through during these times. Talk about lessons in Oneness! Here was more proof of the Human Ladder, and how everyone is connected — everyone from different dimensions working together as a family for the good of all. Zetas working alongside angels and angels alongside Zetas, all united to provide aid and comfort in this time of desperate need. If only humanity could wake up to the true reality of our universe and the beings who reside in it.

To think we had been taught this same aura cleanse that was being used by not only the Zetas but the angels as well! It just makes so much sense when you really think about it. We are all connected — we all want to help others to heal — so it makes perfect sense that the aura cleanse is universal as well. After all, the energy is the same no matter what dimension you live on. The only difference in the energy is that it vibrates faster or slower depending upon where you reside.

J: As Helene has pointed out, "upstairs" we all know each other and work together, and this led to a funny situation. Those of us who are presently residing on Planet Earth in physical form must each be aligned to a particular planet within this solar system. When we're all working together as we were at "Ground Zero," the angels usually refer to us by our planetary name. Mine apparently is Saturn and Kira's Uranus. On one occasion an angel called out to Kira — "Hey, Uranus!" — placing the accent on the first "u" rather than on the "a." It sounded so funny, and she turned around and said very firmly: "Will you *please* just call me Kira!'

Back home the following Friday, Oris turned up at Kira's school, greeting her with

> How is my angel in disguise? Come on, let's go – we need some help.

She had to explain to him that she couldn't just walk out of school like that.

> Oh no, of course not – I'm sorry. I forgot! I'll see you tonight then.

Poor Oris — he was getting very tired by that stage.

Sitting here doing a rewrite on these notes taken down as the dramatic events of 9-11 unfolded, I've suddenly realized that today is September 11, 2007, the sixth anniversary of these happenings. How weird is that!

September 15, 2001.

Helene woke feeling very tired and light-headed. I wondered if she might have been helping us out, either over there with us or at least by contributing energy. Kira and I worked very closely, as she had to eventually face going among dead bodies. Some of those still alive were so badly trapped they couldn't move, and tried to keep each other going by talking about their lives and their families. It was really horrible, with body parts strewn everywhere. I woke one morning with a clear recall of losing my concentration for a moment and almost stepping on a torso — no head, no arms, and no legs — just a decomposing trunk. Although in Zeta form at the time I can still recall the incident and how I felt about it. Such things are not easily forgotten.

On a lighter note, I apparently kept my human hair on so that Kira could distinguish me from the others who were there, which must have looked *really* weird. Like many people, she had trouble telling us apart, and at one point in all the confusion approached a Teacher she thought was Oris. He told her,

> No I'm not – Oris is over there –

and pointed her in the right direction.

There were desks in the offices on which sat cups half-full of coffee and half-eaten sandwiches. It made us realize just how quickly it had all happened. Kira was having fun with her only recently acquired ability to pass through solid walls in her spirit form. She had *so much* to learn so *very* quickly. She was amazed to find that again it felt just like the "gooey stuff" (to use her words) she passes through to go onto the disc.

She kept practicing, walking backwards and forwards through the walls, until I told her to stop doing it so much or she'd have a pain in the stomach the next day. On the human level I have no idea why, but as a Zeta I must know about such things. Funnily enough, not long after this, independent confirmation was given on the matter.

September 16, 2001.

Helene and Kira came to my place for a visit. We had a number of things to talk about, including the work in America, and also some information on crop circles that Helene had got off the Internet during the week, one of which was our Human Ladder one. They also wanted to show me what Oris had taught them about the new hand position for giving Reiki treatments, and we wanted to do more practice with the Zetas' aura cleansing technique.

A couple of days before, he'd promised to come along that Sunday to give us a teaching on near-death experiences, but when he arrived, Kira said he looked really tired. He'd been working non-stop in America right from the first day, with no break at all. We were sitting under the house in the area I use for Reiki, and there's a very comfortable bed in one corner. Poor Oris was so tired he ended up lying down on it and falling sound asleep, with his feet draped over the end on a conveniently placed chair. He's nearly eight feet tall, so the bed was a bit short for him.

When it was time for Helene and Kira to go home, I very carefully leaned across him to retrieve their bags, getting Kira to guide me so as not to kneel on him accidentally. Needless to say we both got the giggles at the sheer bizarreness of the situation, and also because we were trying so hard not to as we didn't want to wake him. Really, I don't think we could've anyway because as I understand it, when Zetas sleep they turn right off and leave the body completely. After Helene and Kira left, I cleaned up as quietly as possible, shut the door and left him alone to catch up on some much-needed sleep.

After asking his permission, over the next few days we tried sending him Reiki. This proved to be a *most* interesting experience all around. He was as eager to find out what it would feel like to receive healing from physical, terrestrial channels as we were to try sending healing to an ET, and he really pulled it in, just as strongly as any of our Earth-based clients. In fact it was quite amazing just how hot our hands got.

The next thing that happened was a request from Maris — he wanted to try it as well, and pretended to be jealous, teasing us with: "That's *not fair*! You send *him* Reiki and forget all about me!" Needless to say, we quickly made up for our oversight, sending him a good dose of Reiki energy on the following night, for which he thanked us profusely, telling us how much he enjoyed it.

We've been witness to several instances of the Zetas good-naturedly teasing each other in this way. Once when Kira drew a particularly good portrait of Oris, he teased Serapis about how he was now going to be the famous one, and how his portrait was going to be seen by *thousands and thousands* of people *all over the world.* (Poor Serapis gets teased "upstairs" about the Ascended Master label connected with his name). We had a go at Oris about it at the time, but little did we know back then that this portrait would eventually end up on Richard Boylan's website, as well as on mine, and probably *has* been seen by thousands of people the world over. He'd complained to Kira when she was doing it that she was putting too many wrinkles on his face, and what if he ever became famous, with everyone looking at his portrait. Helene teased him by saying: "Now, now Oris — I'd have thought someone as old and as highly evolved as you are supposed to be would be well past such vanities!"

September 19, 2001.

We were all feeling tired that week, with Kira and I off working every night, and probably drawing on Helene's energy as well. We decided that she was our "anchor." Oris had been so busy that he often didn't have time to fetch Kira himself, so sent a little worker instead to bring her on board. Helene felt reasonably okay with this, as she'd learned to trust the Zetas, but as a mother she still worried a little, knowing her 13-year-old daughter was being taken off on a disc every night.

It was the thought of Kira being collected by a worker instead of Oris that caused her some concern, because they can be a bit thoughtless and careless at times, but I was aware of keeping a watchful eye on her as well, so really, she was quite safe.

Not too long after that we did have a bit of a drama in which I apparently intervened. Kira was always in human form when she worked "upstairs," which was useful in that she didn't cause as much fear as the Zetas tend to, but in another way it was a disadvantage, as it meant she was more vulnerable to injury.

As the human rescue workers were finding out, "Ground Zero" was a dangerous place to be, with broken glass and twisted steel everywhere, and one night Kira tripped over something and fell backwards, hitting her head. As she did this, a sharp metal spike penetrated the back of her leg. The last thing she remembered was my rushing over to her.

She then became aware of moving at incredible speed, cradled in long, thin, gray arms, as her rescuer carried her back to her room. I understand that they needed to get her back into her physical body as quickly as possible, grounding her astral form by connecting it back into the physical.

As soon as she was back in her body, she woke up, crying out in pain with the injury to her leg. Her "rescuer" begged her to please quiet down or she'd wake the whole street. Helene heard her of course and came running to see what was wrong. Back in her physical body, the injury was manifesting as a bad cramp, so Helene gave her Reiki, which soon settled her down. Her leg was quite sore for several days after.

September 22-28, 2001.

Kira's family went off on one of their regular camping trips, but Oris still turned up each night to take her (in astral form) onto the disc. The first night he arrived there was a large kangaroo close by, which he patted. Animals and nature fascinate the Zetas, and Oris always enjoyed looking at the drawings of animals in Kira's art class at school. Helene was impressed with how polite he was when he came to collect Kira from their campsite. When camping, they all slept together in one section of the van, so he never came right in but rather called her from the doorway.

On one of their camping trips, Kira had a very amusing conversation with Oris when he spotted a large tourist bus parked near the grounds. "What is that?" he asked.

"It's a bus," she told him.

Oh! ...What is a bus?

"It's for carrying lots of people around," Kira explained.

How many?

I'm not sure," she answered, "probably about 60 or so."

Sixty! But how do they fit all the computer equipment on board?

"Humans don't have computer equipment on board their buses," she told him. "Buses are designed for carrying lots of people."

Oh come on! You say buses are designed for carrying lots of people – then that is not a bus!"

The tourist vehicle was dismissed with a wave of his four-fingered hand.

That is a bus!

he said, pointing to the huge suburb-sized disc.

H: Thank goodness we'd planned a camping trip for the September school holidays. After all the "upstairs" dramas we were really in need of a bit of rest and relaxation. A couple of other families that were good friends of ours were camped close by, and we were all set for some fun, laughter and time out from the rest of the world. Well at least I thought so, except for one hiccup of trying to explain to our friends why Kira had come running back to camp one afternoon crying her eyes out, extremely distressed.

Now remember, none of our other family members or friends knew of the "strange and unusual" circumstances that surrounded our immediate family — I just couldn't bring myself to tell anyone. Talk about feeling like an "alien"! Isn't it a shame the way human nature can be so ignorant but at the same time so judgmental of what they don't understand, and how this close-minded lack of understanding can be harmful to everyone involved in such a situation. Are humans ever going to evolve past this? I sometimes do wonder! This seems to be such a restrictive aspect of our spiritual growth. But then again, as they say, where there is love there is hope.

Now just picture this: Kira comes running into our campsite, crying hysterically. Conversation stops dead as everyone turns to look at her, wondering what in the name of heaven has happened. I grab her and quickly get her inside the camper van to try to calm her down and find out what the heck is going on. She then proceeds to tell me, between heart-rending sobs, that a Zeta worker had come to let her know that one of the two men she'd been helping in America had just died.

During the last few nights (days over there) she'd been with them, giving them Reiki and listening to them talking about their families and their lives. She was really hoping that at least one of them would survive, but to no avail. The other man died a couple of days later. They were just too far away from the rescue workers and could not be reached in time. At least they hadn't died alone, even the last one to pass over. One of the Zetas would have stayed close by to comfort him right to the very end. I had a long talk with her, explaining that we have no control over such things. It's all about a person's free will — it is their own soul contract/journey. Once I'd managed to calm her down, it was time to face the "wolves" outside.

Our friends were naturally very concerned and worried, wanting to know what was wrong. I was so thankful for the fact that she was 13, which enabled me to respond with: 'Oh, nothing much — she's just being a dramatic teenager at the moment. You know what they can be like!'

Everyone nodded in agreement and understanding: "Ah yes — teenagers!" Phew, I got out of that one by the skin of my teeth!

I later apologized to Kira for this, but she totally understood and even thanked me for thinking of it — but really, what else could I have said? I lay in bed that night thinking to myself: If only they knew the real situation. I desperately wanted to share our amazing experiences and our newly acquired knowledge on matters of life and death, of God, of Angels and of the ETs with everyone, but who would ever believe me? It was SO lonely and frustrating at times. I've always been a very upfront and honest person, but now felt like I was living a double life. Whoever would have thought! Not in a million years did I ever dream I would be part of such an amazing thing.

Kira later commented upon how on a couple of occasions she'd seen Zetas pleading for the lives of humans, trying to point out to the angels that if only a few could be seemingly miraculously saved it would give the rescuers a little joy and hope. The problem was, they were just too far away from help, and nothing could be done. She also saw angels almost having to force Zetas away from badly injured people, because it was that person's time to go, and they had to be allowed to die. It was not easy for anyone involved — tears were shed, and not only by humans.

The memory of what went on in America stayed with Kira, and her way of dealing with it and clearing her mind was to write a poem.

The Day the Towers Fell

by Kira, 13

I didn't know him very well
Until the day the towers fell.
I went along to lend a hand
And became friends with an American.

I board the Ship
As I do every night,
To help the people in their plight.

I saw the pain
The country was given;
They didn't want to move on
Or continue living.

People in tears
Streets covered in dust,
Firemen working hard
Just because they must.

But one man was strong
And survived the fall;
He always stayed brave,
Was the strongest of all.

He spoke of his family
Friends, work mates too.
He wondered how I got there;
Did not have a clue.

I'm his guardian angel,
Friend and helping hand;
I will always be there
On any demand.

He lived on coffee beans

And little dreams.
I started to cry
As I watched him die.

Smoking ashes and burning flames. Mark was to be a father too,
His life was over. His child born February 2002
I know his soul will keep on living,
Because he was always so happy and giving.

October 2, 2001.

J: After all the dramas of 9-11 it seems that the Zeta consciousness, or at least our little corner of it, needed some light relief which I apparently provided, much to my embarrassment although there is no conscious memory of it whatsoever. Selective amnesia is very useful at times! If it really *did* occur, then the only excuse I have, and I do believe it's a good one, is that we were all very tired and are, after all, only human so to speak.

Just in case it really did happen, I won't go into any details on the matter except to say that a human "guest" was taken up into the disc in physical rather than astral form, and then returned to the wrong place — in fact the wrong city. In other words, a Zeta "stuff-up" of major proportions, which even made it onto the evening TV news program. I squirm inwardly just writing about it!

The next morning Helene rang early to tell me that Kira, on seeing the news report on TV, burst out laughing with a comment to the effect of — "*Now* I know what Judy was getting into trouble about up on the disc last night!" She'd then gone on to describe in graphic and giggling detail exactly what had happened, that it was *all my fault*, and *boy!* had the Elders chewed me up over it.

"Oh, God no!" I groaned, not having any recall of it whatsoever. "*What* have I done *now*?" It was exactly like waking up in the morning after a particularly convivial and alcoholically charged party, with no memory at all of your antics, but with your friends breaking into uncontrollable fits of giggling and hinting at naked dances performed on table-tops with nothing but a party hat perched at a rakish angle on your head. Not that I'm speaking from past experience of course!

Kira clearly recalled the pair of us talking and mucking about on the big disc, as we do, while I was in the process of sorting out some files. Somebody walking past said something to the effect of: "Hey

Number 9756 (my worker number), hadn't you better concentrate on what you're doing — you'll get those files all mixed up!"

"Oh no," I replied breezily, "I'm so used to doing this I could do it with my eyes closed! It'll be right!" Famous last words — I got the files mixed up.

People are very rarely taken by the Zetas in physical form — this is more a MILABS (*mil*itary *ab*duction*s* disguised to appear as the work of the Zetas) phenomenon, but it does happen occasionally. The usual procedure is to take the astral form only. Somehow the files on someone who *is* collected physically and someone who *isn't* got mixed up.

Kira also remembered walking in on a conversation the following night between an Elder and myself. She informed me that the Elder was *really* annoyed, and telling me off over something (which turned out to be the file stuff-up), and I was protesting loudly and vehemently that I hadn't *meant* to do it, and that it had *not* been done on *purpose*! It seems that I am somewhat feistier in Zeta form than in human form.

Although I must admit to being more amused than appalled at my mistake, and was obviously not the least bit fazed by the annoyance of my "boss," I did feel very sorry for the poor human involved and hope sincerely that on some level of consciousness the opportunity was provided for me to offer an apology. Zetas are *not* robots, they *do* have feelings, and *do* make stupid mistakes at times for which they feel really, *really* sorry about afterwards.

17
Zeta Reality

On the subject of Zeta Reality, more information was being given on our friends "upstairs." Some of it seems strange and rather fantastic, but remember it was being filtered through the perceptions of a 12- to 14-year-old, and some was very likely in the form of screen images, which are projected by the Zetas and sometimes they're created by our own subconscious mind. Bearing this in mind, I'll tell it simply as Kira relayed it.

The Zetas have dragons to protect them, in the same way that we have guard dogs. These dragons provide protection from negative energy, which they eat. They're generally small but can transform to a much larger size. According to Kira, Oris warned her not to be afraid of them or else she would get bitten. She told us that she patted one and it felt soft and velvety, rather like a snake. Many folk wouldn't agree, but snakes do feel nice to touch. There were many of these dragons on board the disc, and one guarded Oris's office.

My interpretation of this is that these "dragons" are members of either a Reptilian ET group or else are Repterrans, an ancient Earth-based species. Like the Zetas, the poor old Reptoid folk have been given some very bad press down here by certain researchers in this field, but truly they don't deserve it except for one small rebel group. The Repterrans evolved out of the dinosaurs, as opposed to modern humans who developed out of primate stock. I believe some of them act as protectors to the Zetas, performing a guardian-type role. They are younger souls (but older than modern man), and the Zetas are very fond of them, valuing the work they carry out.

The rebel group, however, certainly does feed off negativity, and this is why they do their very best to create turmoil and fear on this planet. Maybe there's a connection here with Oris's comment on the dragons providing protection by "eating negative energy," and his warning to Kira to "not be afraid or you'll get bitten." In other words, it's fear that causes so many of our problems.

My feeling is that they work side by side with the Zetas, but this one break-away group, sort of like the fallen angels of the Bible, are uncooperative and in fact quite dangerous. They could be likened to a pet dog that has rebelled against human ownership and gone feral, becoming mean and vicious in the process. Rather than simply feeding off negative energy as do the guard dragons on the disc, these rebels actively create negativity and fear to provide themselves with sustenance.

On one occasion Oris took Kira to visit his home planet to meet some of his friends. This is the planet mentioned before. It was in one of the undeveloped areas that this family lived, and the family was comprised of two parents and three children.

They lived in a small home with a floor made of what looked like bamboo. There was Eastern-type meditation music playing, and the CDs were square in shape rather than the round ones we use down here. I wonder if they're related to our floppy discs, which are inside a square plastic casing (so I've been told by somebody who is into such things). They sleep on "mattresses" on the floor, rather similar to Japanese futons, and the chairs are made of a plastic-like material that adjusts itself to the size and shape of the person seated in them. These chairs are also used on the discs, and sitting in them also provides a healing and energizing effect on the body. Kira saw monkey-like animals in the area, and other animal types she'd never encountered before.

Everyone is taken care of — no one is rich or poor but rather equal. When they're young they choose the type of work they wish to carry out, and it becomes their vocation in life to which they are totally committed. They work most of the time, but their work is also their pleasure, and is never considered menial or drudgery as on Earth. They do however take time off for recreation. The urbanized countries have large, tall buildings like apartment blocks.

The few houses that are built in the wilderness areas are constructed out of natural materials — mud bricks, thatch and bamboo. Here the people understand that they are the trespassers, and adjust their lifestyle accordingly so as not to pollute or interfere with the natural environment in any way.

The Zetas can travel by simply using mind power to think themselves somewhere. For them, stepping out of the container (physical body) and travelling to wherever in spirit form is child's play. If they want to transport things physically they use the discs.

The discs are actually interdimensional portals and "time machines," and there are three basic sizes, all of them sentient, "consciousness enhanced" vehicles — almost living organisms. The really huge ones are like small towns in that they contain everything needed in the way of living quarters, medical and scientific facilities, recreation areas, etc. They're totally self-contained, and quite a number of people live in them permanently.

Then there are smaller discs that carry a crew of up to about six, and really small "mini-discs" that carry two people, the operator sitting in front and the passenger behind. Even these little ones have an on-board computer, but they're directly operated by the hands and mind of one person rather than a crew. I have a strong and quite clear memory of driving one of these under the supervision of Maris.

I was in the front operator's seat and he was behind me, leaning over my shoulder as "back seat driver." We were moving *very* fast, which was extremely unnerving. The eyesight in my Earth body isn't perfect, so I need glasses for driving, and this perception carried over into the Zeta experience. It's so confusing working between two bodies! This apparently is why I choose not to generally recall much of my "upstairs" activities — it's bad enough as it is. If I could remember everything I'd be in an awful tangle. Because of this Earth human-oriented need for glasses, my Zeta perception was that I couldn't see where I was going properly, and consequently wanted to pull over, but Maris wouldn't let me. He was trying to push me past this human-oriented limitation.

The disc seemed to be travelling along some sort of track that cannot be described in physical terms, and to keep it on this track took a *huge* amount of mind focus and concentration, which I'm usually fairly good at from my years of Tai Chi. It was however extremely difficult to keep it steady, and every time my mind lapsed slightly, the disc started to wobble and deviate in its path, as if about to go out of control. On top of this, the speed was incredible, adding to my sense of panic.

I felt annoyed with Maris for seemingly pushing me beyond what I felt capable of and comfortable with, and insisted that I could *not* do it and *really* needed to pull over. He on the other hand was adamant, and made me keep going, trying to push me past my fear barrier. I was angry with him for being so heartless, and was almost on the point of disobeying him, pulling over and flatly refusing to go any further. It was a real "Mexican stand-off." My last memory before waking up in a cold sweat was of protesting angrily that — "I *can't see properly, damn it!"* And an icy-cool, calm, quiet and emotionless voice answering from behind me — "Bulls**t! Just keep going!"

Once tempers had cooled, it was explained to me that I'd died in a Zeta life in a crashed disc, and this trauma has carried over into the present life, resulting in a fear of high speed and dislike of driving. Helene apparently died along with me in the disc, and has similar problems, getting panic attacks behind the wheel of a car. Maris was trying to get me past this problem, and has succeeded to a certain extent. But again I say, so much for Zetas being emotionless robots — what I experienced that night was cold-sweating terror and very real emotion, as anyone feels when faced with such an experience of being pushed beyond their personal comfort zone.

The sequel to this occurred a few weeks later when Kira happened to mention that Oris had given her a go at operating one of the little discs. Not letting on about my own experience I asked her to describe what it was like. Her description tallied exactly with my memory — the terrific speed, the need for mental focus to control the disc, and the strange "track" it ran along. She got an awful fright when the disc suddenly dropped, like a 'plane hitting an air-pocket, leaving her stomach behind somewhere in the cosmos. She apparently screamed and jumped, letting go of the controls in her panic. Oris had to lean forward and grab them quickly to get everything under control again.

After much soul searching, Helene had finally decided to do her Reiki Master level. Oris in fact prompted her, which helped her come to a decision. She never felt she was worthy enough, but Oris and the others knew what *huge* potential lay within, just needing to be brought to the surface.

Oris advised that Ian and I perform the ceremony together, which would bring more Teachers in. Ian wanted to be initiated to the next level of the Healing Buddha Mandala, which I'd been taking him through step by step, so we decided to do both initiations. The timing was perfect, because Helene had just celebrated her birthday in late September, and school holidays meant Kira could be present to watch proceedings and tell us exactly which members of the Zeta family were present, and what they were doing.

Ian and I arrived at 9:30 a.m., and set ourselves up in the lounge room where we were to carry out proceedings. Oris was the next to arrive, making himself at home on the three-seat settee and giving Kira the giggles because he was accompanied by seven little workers who promptly settled themselves on the settee beside him, all squashed up together, waiting for the "Show" to begin.

As soon as we started the ceremony all the other Teachers arrived, forming a semi-circle around Helene along with the workers. Just before we began, the one who is Helene's Teacher, Anarkis, stood behind her with his hands on her shoulders. During the initiation she could feel a throbbing sensation in her brow chakra, and Kira told her afterwards that Oris had placed his hand there.

While we worked, all the Teachers stood around in a circle doing symbols over her. According to the Zetas, the number 13 is very significant, representing transformation and also divinity, so during Helene's Master initiation we had 13 candles burning, and at the end of the ceremony Ian got her to choose one of them. Oris told her that the one she selected represented courage. During the ceremony Maris gave Helene a guided meditation, causing her to first visualize herself in a beautiful rainforest, then as an eagle in flight — all her very favorite imaginings! I then performed Ian's Mandala initiation, during which Oris, Maris and another teacher did symbols on him. The other Zeta teachers who were present stood holding their hands in *Gassho* position while the workers placed their hands on him.

October 7, 2001.

Helene did a Reiki treatment on Ben, and telling me about it later she mentioned that he kept stretching. Maris sent the message through telepathically to me that this is a way to get the Qi (energy) flowing more freely through the meridians (energy system of the body). While he was receiving this treatment he told his mom that he could see somebody's reflection in an overhead light. With no prompting on her part Helene asked him to describe the person, and his answer was that they wore a black cape and hat. Because of his "night terrors" they'd been very careful not to speak of Oris or the "Visitors" in front of Ben, so it wasn't that he was just making things up from what he'd heard or imagining what he was seeing. She then asked Ben if there was a color on the hat, and he answered,

"Yes, red."

Oris was sitting in a chair close by, but Ben could only see his reflection on the gold base of the overhead light. The next morning Ben woke at 5:00 a.m. complaining of seeing a shadow in his doorway. Helene came in to calm him, and could see Oris's shadow on the wall next to the bed.

18

A TEENAGE HISSY FIT

When Helene's call came through on the evening of October 11, I had little idea that we were on the verge of a whole new era of understanding with our ET/human contact experiences. Many of the interactions we'd had with the Zetas up until then had been described by others as well, but what was to follow lifted our relationship with them to a totally different level that may be unique in the field of human/ET contact. I wouldn't dream of making such a claim outright, but all I can say is that over the past few years we've done a lot of reading on the subject, and so far we have not heard of any other experiencer having such a profound level of contact and "family relationship" as we went on to establish with the Zetas. I do believe we came to see a whole new side of them that has rarely been perceived down here.

Towards the end of our perfectly normal telephone conversation, Kira came bursting in on Helene, crying her eyes out. She was a typical young teen with all the ups and downs of "teenage angst," and that day had been a "grumpy" one. Finally, to the rest of the family's relief, she'd retired to her room to listen to music, which usually helped to improve her mood. But all of a sudden there'd been a flash of light and a big bang. The light in her room had flickered off then on again, then her CD player went dead and she couldn't get it going again. From the other end of the phone I heard her come running to her mom, crying and scared, and we promptly terminated our conversation so Helene could go to investigate.

The next morning Helene called to tell me that when they went back into the bedroom, Kira started crying hysterically, and she spent the rest of the night in her parents' room. Helene worried that perhaps there'd been an accident of some sort — that the disc had crashed or that Oris was hurt, but I doubted it. By that stage I had enough faith in my connection to know that I'd be aware of such an occurrence if it had happened. But by the weekend Kira still hadn't heard a word from Oris, or, for that matter, from any of the others.

On the following Monday Kira finally admitted to her mother that on the previous Wednesday night, the night before the incident in her room, she and Oris had had an argument. He'd wanted to take her somewhere to show her something and she'd told him she was too tired and not interested, and had refused to cooperate. He'd responded with: "Okay, if that's the way you feel, then you can just go home!" and immediately he sent her off with a little worker. It was, I thought, definitely a case of everybody's nerves still being on edge after September 11th.

The week that followed was most unpleasant for everyone involved. Kira was extremely upset, especially with Oris, and in typical teenage fashion was taking it out on everyone around her. I too was annoyed with Oris, and I felt that he should have known better, but at the same time it really highlighted his "human-ness," and stirred up clear recall of the past Spanish life when he was down here as an Earth human.

His behavior also made me stop and think more deeply about emotion from the Zeta perspective, and truly it's not all that different, but this angle is rarely taken into consideration by researchers. Certainly there's a deeper level of non-attachment, and the ability to experience unconditional love is much more developed, but at the same time, other emotions can definitely be felt as well. Vices such as greed, lust, jealousy and hatred are not experienced, but frustration, sadness and annoyance can definitely be aroused.

At the same time, this incident of an argument between Oris and Kira was so strange, and something I'd never come across in any account of human/ET contact. Sure, there are plenty of cases of anger and resentment expressed towards the Zetas by terrified humans who have yelled and sworn at their perceived "abductors" who were seemingly taking them by force onto the disc. But this case of ours was completely different and quite bizarre. I'd never heard of anyone ever being kicked off a disc for bad behavior.

That night I went to sleep with the strongly held intention of trying to get things sorted out between them. I was annoyed with Oris and wanted to let him know. Soon I found myself on board the disc and walking down the corridor towards his office, my hand raised to pound on the door and my mind full of exactly what I planned to say to him. Just then a female Teacher appeared in front of me, gently but firmly blocking my way. "It's all right," she said, "just calm down. You don't have to talk to him. That is my job and

I'll take care of it right now. Everything will be all right, so don't worry."

October 21, 2001.

Helene went to Ian's place to teach some of the Reiki people how to do the Zeta aura cleanse, and when she got home Kira was in a better frame of mind, having seen Oris fleetingly. It seems he'd appeared briefly just to "test the water," because he'd walked past very quickly, probably feeling guilty, holding his hat in his hands so Kira hopefully wouldn't recognize him. To her perception, all the Zeta Teachers looked alike, and she could only identify Oris by the color of the feather in his hat.

When Helene suggested this explanation to Kira in a bid to offer her reassurance that Oris would eventually return, a teenage "hissy fit" erupted. Kira got angry and told us to back off, blaming us for telling Oris that she was having trouble handling the contact. Helene reciprocated by telling her to stop blaming others and to start taking responsibility for herself. She pointed out that we have no control over what Oris does or doesn't do. Then Helene walked away and burst into tears. What she'd been through emotionally over the past year or more was finally catching up with her.

Poor Helene had experienced *so* much over *so* many months that no one without first-hand experience of such a situation could even begin to understand. It all began with the initial fear and confusion that quite naturally accompanied the weird happenings that had suddenly intruded into their perfectly normal and peaceful family life. A gradual acceptance and acclimatization process then followed, but this required some very significant changes in her whole psychological outlook and perception of "reality," and these changes had to occur in a very short space of time.

On top of all this were the natural concerns of a dedicated and loving mother knowing something like this was going on with her children over which she had no control. Over the months she'd done everything in her power to make it easier for Kira, firstly by accepting her initial experiences as real rather than simply dismissing them as "just imagination," as so many parents do with children undergoing contact experiences.

There were many disturbed nights of swapping sleeping arrangements so that Kira (or Ben, who through all this was having night terrors/trances on a regular basis) could share a bed with Mom, while poor Dad got banished to a single bed in another room, a situation that went on for several years, naturally straining the marriage. Luckily Gary is a reasonable and understanding sort of man who'd seen the Visitors for himself, and so he knew that something more than just imagination was involved.

Secondly, Helene totally supported Kira, encouraged her to talk openly about her contact experiences, and continued to accept what she said. Thirdly, she put in many hours studying the subject, researching it and doing her best to understand it herself rather than simply retreating into fear and denial, as many do when faced with such happenings. Apart from me, she had no outside help at all, with only one response to the plea she'd put out on the Internet for advice or at least support from another parent in a similar position.

Helene is an extremely strong and resilient person, even though she wouldn't admit this, even to herself. When we've shared our experiences with people over the years, some really haven't quite known how to take us because we seemingly treat the whole thing so casually and even flippantly at times. Little do they know or realize the depth of feeling, and, in Helene's case, the very deep emotion that is hidden beneath the surface. She's a strong and positive person, and not one to dwell upon the drama, but unfortunately it seems to be the fear and drama that many investigators of ET contact like to focus upon and tap into. As we've both experienced on a personal basis — it's moving past the fear and drama that is the transformative experience. If you cannot or will not do this and remain stuck and focused in it, you will not move forward.

What with all the major trauma they'd been through, including the emotional turmoil Kira had displayed since her argument with Oris — she was absolutely sure he'd abandoned her forever — all Helene needed at this point was a teenage outburst by her daughter blaming her for it and announcing that it was all our fault.

After having a good cry, Helene prayed — to God, to the angels, to the Zetas, to *anyone* — asking for help, guidance and support. Oris obviously heard her plea and came straight away, going in to Kira to sort things out. He apologized to her, she told him how much she'd missed him, and they both shed a few tears. So much for robotic, emotionless Greys! Kira came out of her room a half-hour later with a drawing she'd done of him (see below). He'd sat on the bed and posed for her. She wouldn't tell her mother what they'd spoken about, but she offered the portrait to her mom to keep or else to pass on to me, seemingly as a peace offering. Kira and Helene were quickly coming to a realization about Oris that I'd learned in my teens — a few well-timed tears will always melt these Teachers' hearts. Over years of ongoing contact I've managed to build up quite a comprehensive personality profile on them — perhaps the first ever made on Zeta personalities, and both Kira and Helene have independently confirmed all that I found.

The Zetas' outlook and character is obviously influenced by their past human lives, just as our outlook and character is influenced by our past Zeta lives. As Zetas, they *are* still human, and not all that different from us down here. And as humans, we are still Zeta inside. The same soul consciousness flows through them as flows through Earth humans. The only difference is that the Zetas are able to access a greater amount of this consciousness.

ORIS, CHARCOAL BY KIRA, 13

MARIS, SKETCH BY JUDY CARROLL

Oris is a strong, "physical" type, who speaks loudly. Having once heard him for herself, Helene describes his voice as deep, strong and kind. He can be a bit bossy and stern, and even gets annoyed at times so he can be quite "human" in that way, but soon all is forgiven and forgotten. He is very protective, kind and loving, with a deep sense of responsibility for those in his care and he is also very ethical and respectful.

Maris is reserved, quietly spoken and rather serious — a bit more like Earth folk commonly think of Zetas. He speaks like a foreigner who has carefully studied the English language, and sometimes he displays a very dry sense of humor. For those who've followed the Harry Potter series by J. K. Rowling, Maris bears a strong likeness to Severus Snape, minus the sarcasm. He's actually extremely gentle and kind, but does not suffer fools gladly.

Serapis, the third Teacher we work with, is an absolute sweetie — kind and gentle, with a *wonderful* sense of humor and fun. Nobody could possibly be scared of Serapis, as the energy that emanates from and surrounds him is almost angelic.

A while back when I was typing this manuscript into Word, the computer froze up. Not being very computer savvy, and not yet realizing that it was a "Zeta problem" rather than a computer problem, I phoned Helene for help.

She said that computers simply *couldn't* freeze as I was describing. It was opening the file with no problem at all, scrolling through the 70-odd pages of manuscript, but every time I reached a certain point in one particular paragraph, the cursor would freeze, and I would be informed that the program was not responding.

I scratched my head, wracked my brains, swore at it, used Reiki symbols on it and made reference to the computer's questionable parental background and circumstances surrounding its conception and birth, as one does at such times. Then a message came through from "upstairs":

Please don't write that – people may misunderstand.

So I stopped and looked carefully at the wording and I could see the point they were trying to make. My description of them could be misconstrued and encourage fear. Once the sentence was deleted and reworded, everything went smoothly, and an expression of gratitude was clearly and tangibly conveyed to me. No wonder they don't like being called aliens. They can be so sensitive!

The day after Oris's return, Kira was in a much better mood, but everyone else was still feeling rather out of sorts. As Helene said, the best of families have their ups and downs, and Zeta families are no different. However, this falling out between Kira and Oris had provided proof of what I'd suspected for a while — that this link we had with him involved past-life issues as well, and was far more complex than it had first appeared. Without knowledge of past-life connections between Earth humans and ETs, investigators and researchers studying human/ET contact cannot perceive more than the very smallest tip of the iceberg.

October 24, 2001.

Kira seemed happier and more settled, making no further mention of contact with Oris. Helene was keeping an almost daily journal of happenings, and arriving at some deep understandings.

H: I have now come to realize that there are multi-layers within everything that happens.

J: We were also regularly seeing the number three coming up, and we have since been told that this number represents Balance and Creation. Applying this understanding to the multi-dimensional concept, we now always look for three reasons when something seemingly significant occurs in our lives. It's quite amazing how much we've learned about ourselves and about life by doing this, and are eternally grateful to our Zeta family for teaching us to think in this way. It brings so much more depth, understanding and clarity into even seemingly negative situations, and it assists us to look always at the bigger picture.

Some time back when Helene and I were doing a book signing at a local shopping center, someone asked her: "What is the main thing you have learned from the ETs?" Her answer was that we've learned to look at everything much more in terms of Oneness. Thinking about this afterwards, I decided to ask the Teachers for input on this, and their answer was:

> Yes, that is correct, but don't forget to think in threes – what are the three main things you have learned?

The three main things I have learned

1. To understand the universe in terms of Oneness.
2. To understand the universe in terms of energy.
3. To understand ourselves in terms of Oneness and energy, thus enabling us to choose love over fear.

19

CHOICE

October 25, 2001.

Kira dropped a bombshell on her poor mom when she announced that Oris had told her she had to choose between a Zeta life and an Earth human life, and that she could not have both. In a flood of tears she told Helene, "I don't know why, but I chose human life — up there everything is *perfect*! I am perfect — thin and really clever. Everybody is so loving and caring — not like *humans*! [distressed and angry voice] I *chose* to stay here as a human because I didn't want to leave you!"

Helene was totally dumbfounded and thought that Oris must have threatened to take Kira's soul. She pointed out to her daughter that the Zetas couldn't just kill her off like that. It didn't make sense. With that, Kira stormed off in a huff, while poor Mom scraped herself up off the floor. She called me for help and actually managed to chuckle when I responded exactly as she had, with dumbfounded disbelief. Then followed a flood of intense gratitude for the close link I'd had with the Zetas since early childhood, and also for the recognition I'd been given of Oris's past human life. Armed with this knowledge and understanding, I felt confident reassuring Helene totally. I knew Oris would not say or do such a thing.

Since then we've both done a lot more research into other peoples' so-called "abduction experiences with Greys," and it seems that this concept of the soul being taken is a basic instinctual fear that many humans experience. *The problem is that people don't generally understand the difference between the astral form (spirit) and cosmic form (soul).* Most Earth folk who are taken onto the discs go there in astral form only, and it's the conscious sensation of their astral body being assisted out of the physical body that they wrongly perceive as their "soul" being taken.

I was certain that some sort of misunderstanding had occurred between Kira and Oris, and later that day I tried to speak with Kira over the phone, but could only get yes and no answers out of her. It was obviously a case of Oris trying to convey a deep and multi-dimensional spiritual concept through the mind and vocabulary of a 13-year-old child. This conversation between them had apparently taken place on the Sunday evening when Helene had prayed for help, and Oris had gone to Kira's room to talk to her. The feeling I had was that he had indeed given her some sort of ultimatum dealing with her attitude and behavior, which she'd taken the wrong way.

With a complex group mind that operates a little differently than ours down here, Zetas can be hard to understand at times. Great chunks of information come flooding in on a very subtle telepathic level that even mature adult minds have some trouble sorting out, let alone a child. It's no wonder experiencers of Zeta contact do misinterpret things on occasion.

In our phone conversation I tried to find out from Kira exactly what Oris had said, and she continued to insist that he'd given her the choice of staying with her family as a human or going with them as a Zeta. Since this still made no sense, I determined to tune into Oris myself to hear his side of the story.

He was as dumbfounded as Helene and me when confronted with Kira's claim.

> I didn't tell her she had to choose between a Zeta life and a human life!

It was a forceful telepathic reply, accompanied by a shaking of the head and a covering of the face with four long thin fingers in a Zeta gesture denoting a high level of frustration.

> What I said to her was that going by what happened the other night up on the disc, I can see that a point has been reached where she must choose between continuing with her training for a future of helping, healing and teaching others, or else [she] must focus more upon her own physical human life on Earth and concentrate her energies into healing and balancing more aspects of herself.
>
> I know she is capable of so much, but I can also see that she cannot continue to do both, so this is the free-will choice that she was asked to make. On the physical human level she may be a child, but on the soul level she does have the age and maturity to make such a decision for herself in regard to this particular life journey. Please help her to understand this, and reassure her mother that we are not going to take her soul!

H: This episode certainly caused a lot of tension in our home and family life. Kira was totally distraught, emotional and angry. Gary was uptight and angry as well, while I felt numb, exhausted and confused. I didn't know what to think or how to act or react, but deep down inside I could feel someone saying to me:

> Come on Helene – where's your trust and faith? It will all work out, and you'll understand in time.

I was tired, bewildered and confused, but what else could I do except take one step at a time, and with each step there was this little mantra going on in my head

> Have trust, have faith – Have trust, have faith.

J: Talk about family dramas! Oris's frustration was really tangible, and it wasn't about Kira's choice. That was okay — it was her free-will choice, and he respected that. His frustration concerned the fact that she'd misunderstood his words, and in so doing, she was causing herself and her family deep distress and worry.

He had felt bad about getting annoyed with her that night up on the disc when she'd refused to cooperate and he'd sent her home with the worker, and had indeed put in a brief appearance afterwards to "test the water" with the intension of apologizing to her, as Helene had guessed. This however did not alter the fact that he was becoming more and more aware of the difficulties Kira was experiencing in trying to cope with being consciously aware of the "upstairs" work as well as her day-to-day human life.

This "dual consciousness" had been necessary over a short period of time for a number of reasons, but it could not continue indefinitely. Even the way she reacted to her mother's attempted reassurance convinced him further that the situation was becoming too much for her. It was time for her to choose where her energies would be focused, and it was a free-will decision that only she could make.

He was right there listening when this exchange took place between Kira and her mom, and he followed Helene into the lounge and saw her break down in tears. He was tuning right in to her distress, and he heard her desperate prayer — to God, to the angels, to the Zetas, to anyone — asking for help, guidance and support. He responded immediately, going straight in to Kira to apologize, and this was when he presented her with the choice — between a Zeta/higher-self-oriented life of devotion to helping, healing and teaching others, or a human/lower-self-oriented life of devotion to healing self. He told her she could not have both, and she chose the latter. It was not a physical, but rather a soul choice he was offering her. This is where the misunderstanding occurred.

Looking back on my own life, I knew that Oris spoke the truth, because I too was asked to make this choice at around Kira's age when "*Manolo*" (Oris) came into my life. Unlike Kira, I chose the Zeta/higher-self-oriented path — the one she misinterpreted as "giving up human life entirely and going up onto the disc to live as a Zeta," but it's not like that at all. I have continued to live a productive Earth human life as well as a Zeta life, even after my second major choice was made at 30, allowing a further Zeta upgrade. Despite some of the claims that have been made about them, the Greys do *not* "take peoples' souls," and as I was able to reassure Helene, I am living proof of one who has freely chosen the "Zeta life" over "human life." Oris urged me to write down what had really been said between himself and Kira and to pass it on for Helene to read, so she would know the truth of the situation and stop worrying.

Oris now had a problem. It was obvious that trying to deal consciously with a dual existence was just too much for Kira, which was perfectly understandable. I know that I couldn't do it. However, to suddenly lose the fully conscious connection she had with him was equally distressing for her. His final decision was to allow her to continue for a while longer, and then to withdraw the full-on contact gradually over an extended period of time thus allowing their connection to shift to deeper, less conscious levels of her being. This withdrawal took place very slowly over a period of several years, but meanwhile, there was still work to be done and information to be imparted.

October 30, 2001.

Kira arrived home from school bursting with excitement — Oris was back! Despite our reassurances, she'd been absolutely sure he'd gone forever. Having seen and felt things from his perspective, I understood his depth of feeling and determination regarding matters concerning this soul.

His return had been triggered by a free period at school in which some of the girls in Kira's class produced a Ouija board to play with. It was such dabbling in a past life that led to earlier problems for her, so Oris was not going to stand back this time and allow it to happen again. Also, as Helene said, "We pay for good education in a private Catholic high school, and *this* is what they get up to!"

At first Kira did refuse to join in, because Oris had warned her against such things, and she knew very well from the "purple ball" experience what it can be like to get involved with negative energies — and then Oris suddenly appeared out of nowhere, apologizing to her for "being late."

Her reaction was total puzzlement and amazement: "What do you mean 'late'? I didn't think you were ever coming back! What are you talking about?"

> What? Didn't the worker tell you I was coming?

"No!" she answered.

> Oh dear! It is hard to get good workers these days! Now go over and join in – we have work to do.

So saying, he indicated that she should join the group playing with the Ouija board. Kira protested that he'd told her never to do such a thing, but he insisted, repeating that there was work to be done, and he needed her help to teach them a lesson they would *not* forget.

Kira obediently took her place in the circle of girls around the board, explaining to them that she'd changed her mind about joining them. They invited her to place her finger on the pointer, but following Oris's telepathic instructions; she didn't actually touch it, but rather held her finger above it so the others could clearly see that there was no physical contact. It was Oris's finger that moved it to spell out a dire message:

> I give you warning of all spirits both good and evil, for they can harm you!

Needless to say, the Ouija board was quickly abandoned. Oris's advice on the danger of calling in spirits brought to mind a Reiki technique that is often taught at level two in which symbols are used to call in the thought form of a person who has requested a distance healing. We asked him about this and his reply was short and sharp.

> Don't do it! You do not, under any circumstances, have the right to draw another person's thought form to you – it is too dangerous!

He then went on to give us instructions on how to visit others to give Reiki healing. As he explained, we are attuned to the Reiki symbols, and so we are safe and protected, but the other person may not be.

His further advice on playing with a Ouija board was:

> Don't! If you wish to contact spirit, the best and safest way is to go to your favorite place, preferably not inside your house but rather outdoors. Place some of your favorite objects around you – pretty flowers, shells, crystals, some incense, and anything you feel gives you protection, such as a bible, a cross, a pentagram, etc. Then just sit quietly and call them in.

The next day the girls brought the board out again, but Kira refused to join in. Helene was proud of her for being strong and not allowing the others to draw her in to their silliness. That evening the whole family attended an awards night for the college and was thrilled to see Kira receive an award for application and effort. Helene wondered to herself if it was only from the school that Kira was receiving the award or from the Zeta family as well. She'd been very worried over the past few months about her daughter coping with both worlds, so the award was received with gratification, relief and amazement.

In an attempt to clear matters further on the misunderstanding that had occurred, Oris asked me to sit down quietly one day with pen and paper so that he could convey information through to Kira on the past life in Spain. He wanted to do this via me, because after the last disastrous attempt at communication, he didn't want to risk it happening again. In fact his nervousness was quite tangible, not only because he desperately wanted Kira and Helene to understand the whole matter more clearly (hopefully so that Kira wouldn't repeat mistakes of the past, which was really worrying him), but also because of the sensitivities involved.

Once the writing was completed to his satisfaction, I passed it on to Helene to give to Kira. When she took it to her room to read it in privacy, Oris arrived, taking a seat on the bed beside her to make sure the information was clearly understood and that she was okay with it, because it did touch on some fairly heavy matters. She shed a few tears, and apparently Oris did too, but at least now we all had a much clearer picture of past and present.

About this time I had a couple of interesting experiences. One night I woke from a "dream" in which I'd been carrying on a conversation with someone I knew very well. As I awoke, I became aware of a loud clicking sound in my left ear, which stopped suddenly. My first thought was that an insect had somehow got into my ear or the pillow on which I was lying, but nothing was there. Thinking about the strangeness of it, it then occurred to me that the clicking sound had been a continuation of the voice of the one with whom I'd been having a seemingly quite normal and ordinary conversation.

A day or so later on the phone to Helene, I tried to describe the sound I'd heard. Kira was in the room with her mom, so Helene told her of my experience. Like me, she guessed it was "Zeta speak," but couldn't quite describe it either. Kira always referred to the Zeta language as "gibberish." She then left Helene on the phone in the office and walked through to the lounge room where the TV was on.

The next moment she came running back into the office, where Helene was still on the phone talking to me. "Mom, Mom!" she called in excitement. "I know what the Greys' language sounds like! Just as I walked into the lounge they showed a *dolphin* on TV, and it was making a *clicking* sound! *That's* how the Greys speak!"

While she was saying this to Helene, I was on the other end of the phone saying, "I know what the clicks sounded like — a *dolphin*!" Helene was receiving the exact same message in stereo from both Kira and me at exactly the same time.

A few mornings later I again woke with a clear memory of leaving my physical body during the night and walking through the house to the closed back door, which appeared totally transparent rather than solid. Looking through it, I could see Maris standing, waiting for me at the bottom of the back stairs. He'd obviously come to fetch me, and the disc must have been close by, as a strong wind was blowing. At this point the human part of my mind must still have been functioning consciously, because I can clearly recall those first few moments of looking down at him standing there in semi-transparent form, dressed all in black with his cape billowing out in the wind, and the fleeting sensation of fear that passed through me.

He didn't know I was there, as his back was turned towards me, and it took some courage on my part to step through the closed door and walk down the steps to join him. As I reached the bottom he turned towards me, and my human consciousness faded as Zeta consciousness took over, causing me to feel perfectly comfortable and familiar in his presence. He opened his arms and I stepped into his embrace, melding my essence into that of my Teacher, thus becoming one with him.

It was quite some time after this that Kira happened to mention in passing that Maris, unlike the others, always appears in semi-transparent spirit form on the disc.

November 16, 2001.

H: Judy phoned to let me know that a friend had just called to inform her that there could be another terrorist attack, and this time it could happen in Australia. Jude and I weren't convinced, and discussed how fear on this planet was certainly getting out of hand and spreading like wildfire. It's such a pity that good news never seems to travel at the same pace and with the same amount of energy behind it. That afternoon Oris arrived, so I decided to have a chat with him about terrorism and the amount of fear that it was generating. I asked him if our hometown were attacked, would Jude and my family be safe.

> As with all souls, if you are meant to die at that particular time you will, as you have chosen to do so at that point in your journey. But on the other hand, if you have not chosen to die that way then "something" will stop you. For instance, you may get a flat tire on your car and have to delay your plans, or you may decide to take a different route on that day.

He said it's very important to always listen to your gut feeling. This is the connection to your higher self that guides you in the right direction for your soul journey.

I also mentioned to him how helpful it's been to have Judy in our lives — we are forever grateful. I've even given her a new nickname — my "Walking Encyclopedia." The amount of knowledge and wisdom she has acquired truly amazes and surprises me every day. Oris responded with:

> Judy is a "Bible of her kind."

Gee, Oris, for someone who is more used to talking telepathically, you have a wonderful way with words, and express things so well!

J: I really am totally embarrassed and did *not* want to include that, but Helene threatened to go on strike if I left it out. However, I do love the quaint way Oris has with words, and that phrase he used, coming out via Kira, was such good proof that she really was just repeating his words. There is *no way* Kira would ever have come up with such a phrase out of her own vocabulary. In fact I don't know of any 13-year-old who would.

At that time we were planning a visit to the local UFO association meeting, which is held on a monthly basis. Oris encouraged us to attend, telling us we needed to speak out more. Researchers in ET/human contact often complain that the Zetas should be more open in their dealings with humans, and that their contact should be face to face on the physical level. But what these researchers can't seem to understand is that they operate on different brain-wave frequencies than Earth humans. Their contact generally has to be made on a personal, one-to-one basis, and when the human contactee is in an altered state, such as sleep.

The "body asleep, mind awake" state (as described by one experiencer) is the best for contact. This is the sleep-paralysis state that is so scary at first, until you become accustomed to it. Our fully awake conscious state is of a lower frequency and the ETs' is of a higher frequency. The astral plane is the common ground so to speak — the only frequency band that is reasonably compatible to both. This is why, if any real progress is to be made in understanding the Zetas on a deeper level, the evidence of *genuine* experiencers needs to be listened to carefully and studied.

However, the problem of human illusion, emotion and "static" that is present at the astral-plane level must also be taken into account, both on the part of the experiencer and the investigator. Astral-plane perception is inevitably distorted by the person's own mind-stuff, even if it is being accessed via hypnosis, and this is vitally important for investigators to understand. This is why you need to get past the fear of the paralysis state; *otherwise your own mind can create a seemingly negative experience.*

The Zetas have encouraged us to speak out right from the start, but what we've found again and again is that the information is taken down, stored away, and disappears from sight forever, never to be seen again. *It seems to me that the communication problem is more with the humans involved rather than with the ETs*! Why UFO groups and individual researchers cannot be more like the Zetas and operate in unity and oneness I really don't know. So much more would be achieved if they'd only cooperate with each other more instead of jealously hoarding the information they receive and keeping it all to themselves "just in case someone else gets hold of it."

November 26, 2001.

We were having our Reiki Christmas party at my place, and Helene and Kira came early so we could have a quiet chat before everyone else arrived. Oris of course turned up, not wanting to miss out on the fun. We asked him if there was anything else we needed to teach in Reiki, and his advice was to make sure people do the symbols carefully and correctly, and not get sloppy or lazy. He went on to point out a couple of common mistakes people make when using them.

He told us that even when we "air draw" the symbols, we still need to do them carefully and correctly, because after all, they are sacred, and it is God or Source Energy we're working with, and so It should be respected. The Zetas are always very respectful of such things. I'm reminded of Ian's Mandala initiation, when all the Zeta Teachers stood around us in a circle with their hands joined in *Gassho* to show respect for the ceremony being conducted. Oris is also insistent that we must do the aura cleanses "mindfully," as with Tai Chi, for maximum energy flow. As the saying goes — energy flows where the mind goes — so any energy work needs to be done mindfully and with total focus.

He explained to us that when we do Reiki, if our hands feel hot then the recipient is drawing yang energy; if our hands feel cold then it's yin energy they need. This makes a lot of sense, and is in accordance with what was taught in the course on Eastern medical philosophy that was part of my Tai Chi instructor training. These natural-energy healing techniques are all about balancing the recipient's energy system, and lack of balance can be brought about by either a deficiency or excess of yin or yang (negative or positive) energy. During a Reiki treatment, the recipient's own energy system will draw whatever is needed. The concept of Yin and Yang isn't always taught in Western Reiki schools, because of the link with Japan being lost when Reiki was first brought to the West. Reiki is not faith healing or "magic." It is firmly based on the higher science of energy as understood in Eastern healing philosophy.

20

ZETA FIRST AID

December 4, 2001.
During the last week of school, the students were enjoying some outdoor activities on the sports oval. Kira's group was learning a Spanish dance, so of course who should appear but Oris? The steps were rather difficult to learn, but Kira felt somehow she knew the dance already (not surprising), and she picked it up very quickly, despite the fact that dancing is not one of her strong points. Oris stayed to watch for about 15 minutes then disappeared, but as Kira soon found out, he must have just shifted his vibrational frequency up a few notches so that she couldn't see him, even though he was still there.

When they finished dancing, everybody sat down for a rest and a drink of water, as it was a very hot day. Some of the boys had been playing football, so they too came over for a rest. One of them came over to Kira to compliment her on her dancing, and they sat chatting together for a few minutes.

Suddenly the boy complained of feeling strange. He said that his arms ached. Next he began to froth and vomit, falling backwards in an epileptic seizure. The teachers were on the other side of the field, so a couple of the boys ran to get help, but the situation quickly became potentially life-threatening, because the boy started to choke.

Oris must have intervened at this point, because Kira somehow knew what to do. Without hesitation she pulled the boy's legs apart, grabbed both his hands and pulled him up so that he was in a sitting position and leaning forward. Then, holding both his hands in one of hers, she jabbed the thumb of her other hand up under his chin and pressed very hard. As she did this, she felt a long, thin finger go up inside the boy's mouth to open his breathing passage. The seizure stopped immediately, and Kira saw several teachers running towards them. She was afraid of being questioned, so she ran off after seeing the boy was recovering.

It all happened quickly, but Oris had obviously saved the boy's life. Kira had neither first-aid training, nor any idea of what she was doing or why. What we found out later was that her technique was not standard first-aid procedure, but rather an *acupressure technique*. She has small hands, so there was no way she could have held the boy's two hands in one of hers, especially during a seizure. Also, she felt long Zeta fingers go up into his mouth to open his throat.

Another amazing aspect of this incident was that despite the boy being taken to the hospital by ambulance, no incident report was filled out, which was standard procedure at the school in such a situation. It worried us that Kira would be questioned. We invented a cover story just in case — that she'd once witnessed such a procedure being carried out on an epileptic in a shopping center. However, apart from the boy thanking her afterwards, nothing more was mentioned. Oris must have put a memory block on everyone involved to protect Kira from being questioned.

A few days after this incident, I had the opportunity to question one of my Tai Chi students who'd studied Chinese medicine, including acupressure. Sure enough, my student provided confirmation by explaining that *Kira's method most definitely is a standard acupressure technique to stop a seizure.* The pressure point Kira pressed is one that has the effect of *slowing down brain activity.*

My student then added that it is *a rather obscure, rarely used technique, because it is extremely difficult to apply to someone having a seizure.* This was incredible confirmation for us of what the ET friends can do. In all the ET contact cases I've ever heard of, this is the only instance I've come across of a human life being saved by a Zeta applying first aid.

21

DYING

Helene's mother-in-law Laura had long worked as housekeeper for a Catholic priest. Her only child, Helene's husband Gary, had been brought up in the Presbytery. When the priest retired, Laura took him to live with her, where she continued to look after him up until the time of her premature death from cancer. Needless to say, the months leading up to her death were very difficult for the family.

H: They certainly were sad and emotional times, as probably many of you can relate to. A lot of people die from cancer these days, and watching a loved one suffer in such a way is very stressful indeed. Grandma, as we called her, fought her illness for eight months. A month or so before Grandma died, Gary started seeing flashes from the corner of his eye, at first while visiting his mom in the hospital, and then, closer to the time of her death, he began seeing them in our home and occasionally while driving his car. He commented on how strange it was, and that he'd never seen anything like this before.

Towards the end, Grandma was in a drug-induced coma. We were all naturally very upset, but at the same time, we wanted her to let go, as it was dreadful to see her suffer in so much pain, especially knowing that she was at the stage of no return. I'd never experienced anything like this with family or friends, and my biggest worry was how to handle it with the children. I didn't want them growing up feeling scared or hating hospitals (as some people do), and I wanted them to learn to accept death as a natural process for all of us.

Three days before Grandma died, a nun visited while Gary and I were there. This nun was in her thirties, and she was a very pleasant, friendly, approachable woman. I was in the middle of giving Grandma some Reiki when the nun came in. She introduced herself and came straight over to me and asked: "Are you doing Reiki?" I couldn't believe my ears. This nun knew about Reiki! She then informed me that she'd learned Reiki too, and what a wonderful tool it is for easing the dying process. As she said, it helps a dying person find peace and assists them in crossing over more easily, as many people are still very fearful right up to the very end. It is very beautiful to give your love and Reiki energy to help a soul move closer to God.

I decided to ask her advice on how to handle the kids in this situation. I truly believe now that she was an angel in disguise, arriving as she did at the perfect moment to give me guidance. She explained that she'd been working in North Queensland with very sick children and had experienced much death and dying. I told her that I wanted my children to attend the funeral, but when Grandma dies, what should I do?

She said that it would be best if the children could visit her as soon as possible after she passes over. They'd be able to feel her energy/essence quite strongly then. It was important that they be made to feel part of it and experience the whole process with the rest of the family. She explained that the children had seen Grandma becoming sicker and frailer, and if we stopped them from experiencing the whole process, they might feel unimportant. She went on to say that adults think they're protecting children by keeping them away, but in actual fact kids tend to imagine a lot worse than the process really is.

I thought a lot about our conversation and discussed it with Gary. We decided to follow through on the wise words of the nun. We both agreed that we all must learn not only about life but about death as well. The day arrived — Grandma passed over at 8:00 a.m., so we picked the kids up and went back to the hospital to say our goodbyes. As we were driving along in the car, one of Grandma's favorite hymns, "Amazing Grace," came on the radio.

When we arrived, Gary went in first, and then he called us in. She looked so beautiful and at peace. Both Kira and Ben touched her on the arm and said: "Bye-bye, Grandma. We love you!" And you know, the kids never had one bad dream, and they handled it all so well. That evening we went outside and picked out a star to represent Grandma. After that the kids would sometimes go out into the garden at night and call out: "Hi, Grandma! We can see you watching over us! We love you!"

J: After Laura's death, the priest, whom the family simply referred to as "Father," stayed on in her house, for a minimal rent paid for by the Church. Laura had placed a condition in her will that Gary would not sell the property, but would allow Father to live out his remaining days there.

Father, a keen gambler, was very fond of scotch. Helene and Gary were concerned about his being in the house on his own because he would leave the stove on accidentally and do other silly things, but he refused to go into a home. He and Laura had become very close, almost like brother and sister, and he vowed that he would die in her house, close to where she lived. After Laura passed away, Helene and Gary continued to keep an eye on him, just to make sure he was okay.

Finances were extremely tight for Helene's family, with trying to get their camper-trailer business running while feeding and educating two children. A decent rental income from this property would have provided just the little extra each week they needed to get by. But the church continued to pay a ridiculously low rental for Laura's house and there was always the worry that Father would accidentally burn down the place, being both a smoker and a drinker.

The situation had gone on for a number of years, and one night Helene asked Oris if he could give them any idea of how much longer it would continue. His answer was that the old man would pass over before Christmas. During the next few months there was no change in circumstances, and Helene had almost forgotten Oris's prediction — until towards the end of the year when Father had an accident. He fell down the steps at the betting shop and broke his hip.

He was taken to the hospital, and despite a bout of pneumonia, seemed to be recovering. Helene and Gary were very relieved when he made the decision not to return to their house but rather to remain in an aged-care unit provided by the Church, and Gary decided to sell the house. With the poor state of the house, it was necessary to bring in a number of tradesmen to carry out repairs. Termites had made a meal of one section, and a new carpet and some fresh paint was needed before it could be put on the market.

At 8:00 a.m. December 11, the family stopped by the house to let the painter in. Ben flatly refused to enter the place, which was very strange behavior for him, since he was usually a very easy-going and generally obedient boy. Helene then tried to get Kira to come in to have a look at the new carpet in Father's room, but this time she was the one to refuse to enter, insisting she didn't like the energies inside the house.

When they arrived home later that day, there was a message on the answering machine informing them that Father had passed away at 7:00 a.m. Both Ben and Kira were probably sensing Father's presence there in spirit, as he would have returned to the house for sure after his death, looking for Laura. Oris's prediction had proved correct.

H: Father's funeral turned out to be the most amazing and symbolic ceremony I have ever attended. It felt like a wedding, and was such a wonderful celebration of life it almost took my breath away. It began with 30 priests entering the cathedral in pairs, with the coffin following behind them. Suddenly Kira whispered to me: "Mom, Grandma is here. She's standing against that pillar and is wearing a white robe." She described her as looking relaxed and beautiful. Grandma waved to Kira and kept staring in our direction. Then Kira started to cry. She could see Father, and he had his favorite pipe with him and his hat on. He stood next to Grandma and waved to us. The two of them then walked in different directions around the church until the end of the service.

Kira then proceeded to tell me, in between quiet giggles, that Grandma was pulling faces at a couple of people who were there. I asked her to point these people out to me. This gave me wonderful confirmation of what she was seeing, because I knew these folks and was aware that Grandma had had a few "issues" with them when she was alive, but Kira knew nothing of this.

Then a few Zetas and about six angels arrived. Oris was standing in the back, keeping an eye on things. Kira then told me that the whole inside of the church went dark and a bright light appeared. By this stage the church was filled with many angels and Zetas, the workers of the angels. As the service came to an end, Grandma and Father walked to the front towards the altar, as the priests sang in Latin. For a moment I really felt as if I were in heaven. The Latin hymn that the priests were chanting was the most wonderful, calming sound I have ever heard. Kira informed me that she could hear an angelic choir from "above" as well. The angels touched Grandma on the shoulder, one on each side of her, and they all rose up. Just before they left, she said to Kira,

See you around! Maybe in our next or future lives!

There was also an angel on either side of Father. They all rose up together and disappeared from sight.

I had heard from various people and more recently from Oris that one always visits his own funeral. To now experience it through Kira's eyes as confirmation really helped me to feel at peace. It brings so much comfort to understand that we are never alone, and are very well looked after both during and after the dying process.

When Grandma was alive, she was a very strict Catholic and never believed in reincarnation. So it was very interesting to hear her say to Kira that she "may see her in our next or future lives." To me this provided more evidence of reincarnation. It's not that I don't trust what Oris tells me, but it is wonderful to sometimes get independent confirmation.

22
UNDERSTANDING TRANCES

F*ebruary11, 2002.*
Oris arrived for a visit to answer some more questions for Helene. She'd given someone a Reiki treatment and felt pain at the base of her spine in the area where the client was having problems. She wanted to know why and what she could do to stop such a thing happening again.

Oris explained to her that she is an empath and has chosen (on a deeper level of her being) to experience what the client is feeling. He advised her to place the symbols directly into the area of her body where she feels the discomfort, and if possible to also place one of her hands there while giving the treatment.

It's common practice in Reiki to give three initial treatments all within a period of ten days, then subsequent treatments whenever necessary. Helene had given this client a chelation for her first treatment, then for the second session had given her a standard Reiki treatment. She asked Oris which type of treatment format would be best for the third session. His advice was that she did right to use the chelation for the first one. This has the effect of quickly clearing any blocks that are present in the energy system to prepare it for further Reiki. After that he advised that we use our intuition as to what other treatments are needed, depending upon what the problem is.

Helene was set to conduct her first seminar later that month, and she asked Oris if some of the Zeta family could please be there to provide support. He assured her that all she needed to do was ask.

Her second question was on my behalf, asking Oris if I should get back into doing channeling again. His answer was a firm — "*Yes*, as often as she can!" He added that it's good for me on an energy level.

She then asked a question on behalf of another friend who had a little honeyeater bird persistently hanging around near his home. He wanted to know what it meant and why.

Oris's answer was that birds represent family, and this person needs to learn more about trusting family. He then added:

Judy should channel for him! Good exercise for both of them!

His answer to Helene's next question provided more confirmation on the reality of his presence as well as the Zetas' deep understanding of energy. Helene wanted to check with him on the fourth attunement of level-one Reiki, so he went through it with her step by step. When they reached the end part, he explained how the recipient's hands should be closed into fists, with their arms crossed over their chest to signify that the attunement process has been sealed.

Helene was practicing on Kira, who was passing on what Oris was saying, and knowing absolutely nothing of Qi Gong, crossed her right arm over the left. Oris pulled her up immediately, telling her to change the arms to left over right. It didn't occur to her to question why at the time, but she mentioned it to me over the phone the next day.

As I explained to her, at the end of a Qi Gong practice, females always close left hand over right and males vice versa. I told her to go back and ask Oris if this was the reason for his correction — and sure enough it was. This was great proof of Oris's understanding and presence, because neither Helene nor Kira knew anything at all about Qi Gong. She also asked him when Reiki-type healing first came into being on Earth and his answer was — about 7,000 years ago in Egypt. Maris came back to us later on this with a correction, that Reiki was actually introduced to the planet about 8,000 years ago in India, but was taken to Egypt a thousand years later. Maris specializes in Zeta history, so he would know.

March 6, 2002.

Kira always had problems with schoolwork, and her teachers' suspicions were aroused when she suddenly began improving, especially in math. She'd jumped a year ahead of her grade 9 class, and had developed a passion for algebra, which was usually her worst subject. She'd arrived home from school feeling very worried about the day's events, and she told her mom how the math teacher had approached her that morning with a seemingly innocent query as to whether she'd been doing a lot of extra study over the Christmas holidays to catch up, which she had denied.

"Well then," he responded, "can you please explain why you are now level five proficient in math when you used to struggle so much?" He went on to say that he'd spoken to a few of her other teachers, and that they too had noticed a big improvement. Then came the inevitable: "You're not *cheating* by any chance, are you Kira?"

"*No way*!" she responded, hotly denying such an accusation.

"Well," he persisted, with a glare meant to strike fear in the heart of the bravest soul, "how can you explain this improvement?"

At this point in the conversation Helene's heart missed a few beats. "Well," she asked her daughter, "did you cheat?"

"*Truly,* Mom, *NO*!" came Kira's vehement response, then she went on to explain: "The Zetas taught me a new formula to help with algebra, and it all just fell into place. It's made it so much easier for me now."

"Okay darl', I understand." Helene reassured her. "I'm sorry, but I had to make sure; I didn't mean to doubt you. So what answer did you give the teacher?"

"I told him that I'd had trouble settling in last year — getting used to high school, trying to make new friends — and (lips quivering in an effort not to giggle) I also told him I had family problems."

"*What*!" came Helene's shocked response. "What family problems???"

"Sorry Mom," Kira giggled, "I really meant "upstairs" family, you know, going up on the disc and visiting my *other* family. And you know what?" she went on, "it's really weird, because often I learn the same subjects up there as I'm learning down here."

H: In some ways I felt relieved and happy that she was getting extra instruction during her nighttime activities, but on the other hand it was worrisome. What if the teachers questioned us further, thinking we had family problems! Still, it was better and safer than telling them what was really going on. They would never believe us! I could just see it — Kira's mother dressed in a straightjacket and being quietly escorted to the nearest psychiatric unit. Not to mention the gossip — "There's still hope for poor little Kira — she is young, after all. It's the mother who is the driving force behind all of this! It's so cruel the way she's actively encouraging the child's imagination to the point where the poor girl is totally convinced that it's all real! Honestly!" On the subject of "reality," I just wish people knew how the ETs are helping, guiding and educating our children for all our futures' sake.

J: Helene called to discuss the matter because she was really worried that the school would start making further enquiries on Kira's uncharacteristic and seemingly inexplicable progress. We knew she wasn't cheating, but deeper questioning would have made things very difficult. However, even as we spoke a message came through that she would be protected, just as she was with the boy who'd had the seizure. Needless to say the subject was never raised again, and Kira went on to receive an award at the end of the year — for application and improvement. Thank you, Zeta family!

It was quite amazing having Kira consciously aware of the pair of us attending these regular classes up on the disc. I usually only remember events from "upstairs" if something down here jogs my memory, which isn't very often. According to her recall, our classes on the disc take place in a normal classroom, with us sitting at desks taking notes and answering questions as a Teacher in front delivers a lecture.

Kira often reminded me of how I'm always getting myself into trouble with various Teachers. Whether this really happens, or whether it was just a screen memory placed to make her feel more at ease with the whole situation, I can't really say, because my memory is rather limited. On one occasion she gleefully informed me that I'd been fiddling with my laser pen* in class the night before and had accidentally flicked off the end of it, hitting somebody on the back of the head. Another time I was supposedly rocking my chair back and forth on the two back legs when Maris came up very quietly behind me and hissed suddenly in my ear — "Number 9756 (my worker number) — will you *sit still and behave yourself*!" I apparently got such a fright, the chair flew out from under me and I landed in a tangled heap on the floor under the desk. I truly have no recall whatsoever of any of this!

I do, however, remember attending classes "upstairs" on energy work, including Tai Chi and Qi Gong, where I've had moves

*Oris once told us that one of these laser pens was among the artifacts found in the Roswell Disc. He was highly amused, because according to him, the experts examining these artifacts were convinced that it was a weapon of some sort. We've been disbelieved when we've mentioned these pens to investigators, but Col. Philip Corso provided amazing confirmation in Paola Harris's *Connecting the Dots*, (*ibid.*) where she writes that Corso once gave her a long, black laser-pointer pen, saying it was just like the artifact in his Roswell "nut file," and that, like a stupid human, he thought it needed batteries.

corrected, and Oris once showed us a wonderful Qi Gong breathing exercise that I now include in advanced Reiki classes. The Zetas made me aware of the intrinsic links between Reiki and Qi Gong many years ago, which has only recently started coming to light in the West. As Kira told her mom, often what we learn "upstairs" parallels what we're learning down here. One morning I woke with a clear memory of attending a lesson about various plants. When I mentioned this to Helene, she told me Kira had also been learning this at school. Another time I was shown the correct way to sew the dance costumes.

April 6, 2002.

Helene was awakened at 10:30 p.m. by Ben screaming in terror, and she knew immediately that he was having one of his trances. She found him crying and pacing around his room, and his eyes looked glassy and strange. It was as if he knew she was there, but because she was not part of his trance/dream, he looked straight through her. Turning the light on made no difference. At one point he spoke to someone, and Helene asked him who it was. His reply was: "A man and a woman. They're on a bike, and they want to take me." Helene questioned him further as to what sort of bike it was, a motor or pushbike. It was a pushbike, and the man was wearing an orange and purple shirt.

Gary then came in and Ben gave him a quick hug. Ben looked very upset and worried, and he sat on the bed next to Gary. In tears again, he said: "Dad must think I'm *nuts*!" They both tried to calm him, reassuring him that his dad would never think such a thing. At one point during the trance Ben went to his night light and put his hands over it. There was obviously some significance in this, because during the "purple ball episode" of August 22, 2001, Oris had instructed Kira to take the purple ball and place it on top of the night light, where it disintegrated. My feeling is that the light has a cleansing and clearing effect where negative energy is present.

H: Ben's whole persona (or energy) felt somehow different to me this time. This is so hard to put into words. It was as if he were in a deeper trance than before, and as if a part of his consciousness had opened up a bit more, but at the same time there was still a struggle going on with his other fearful, not-knowing side. His eyes had a deeper look about them. At one stage he seemed to be okay, but he was not looking in my direction; he was answering someone invisible to me. He replied, "About five or six o'clock." I realize now that whoever it was probably asked him what time he normally woke up in the morning.

Also, when he said that he saw a man and woman on a bike, I believe that the Zetas were using a screen image to help him feel more comfortable with the situation. Ben loved riding his bike around home. I felt as if he knew what he was doing and was okay with it, but then the other part of his consciousness came through, making him worried as to how his dad would handle all of this. By this stage his heart was pounding, and there was a desperate plea in his voice. He wasn't sure if his dad would understand, but he wanted and needed his belief and understanding so much. You could feel the raw emotion coming up from the very depths of his soul. Thankfully, Gary is open-minded and compassionate and loves his children dearly.

J: Helene went to the kitchen to get Ben a glass of water, and she sent a message out to whoever was there: "Please, not yet — he's still too young in human years!" A couple of minutes later the trance stopped. She and Gary both gave him Reiki and tucked him into bed. Before falling back to sleep he said to her: "I'm glad you're my mom — thank you for helping me. I love you so much!" Ben really is a most beautiful soul — a Star Child if ever there was one.

The next morning Helene asked him if he remembered anything of his dream. She was surprised when he said yes, because usually he had no recall. He told her he'd had two dreams. In one of them the world was spinning — plants were upside down and everything was whirling around. He added that he'd had that dream a few times before.

Kira informed us that she often teaches Oris new words. He wasn't familiar with teenage slang, and he often had her repeat herself because he couldn't understand what she was saying. One of her favorite expressions at that time was: "Go take a chill pill."

She used it on Oris one night when he was fussing over something she'd done wrong "upstairs." He had no idea of what she meant, and proceeded to give her a lecture on the dangers of taking drugs. It went on and on before she could even get a word in to explain what she'd really meant.

When Helene told me about this, I had a good laugh. I wasn't familiar with this expression either, but having now heard it, was determined to try it out on someone "upstairs," preferably Maris. Whether the following scenario really happened or whether Kira's young teenage mind created it as a screen image to make her "upstairs" experience more compatible with her mind-set, I don't know. I have no recall of it at all.

According to her, I was amusing myself during a very boring lecture (probably one on Maris's favorite subject — Zeta history) by drawing faces on my notepad with the laser pen. I'd never told her, but this is exactly what I used to do as a child in school, drawing Zeta-like eyes and faces on my exercise books. Then I accidentally burned a hole in the desk. Maris came storming over to tell me off, so I used my newly acquired human teenage expression on him, suggesting that he "Take a chill pill!" Not a good move — he sent me outside to stand in the corridor. (What a shame! This means I would have missed the rest of the Zeta history lecture). But as I always say, why stand when you can sit? The disc provides what is needed, so I got myself a nice comfortable chair to sit on.

Serapis then came by and wanted to know what was going on and why I wasn't in class. When I told him, we both burst out laughing.

As we spoke, Kira came past, and she was highly amused to see that, when anyone approached we both acted very serious, with Serapis pretending to be telling me off and me pretending to be really upset, then when the passer-by left, we both started laughing again. Kira later commented to her mom, "What a good actress Judy is."

One evening Kira was telling her mom about implants. Some of these are actually "keys" to enable easier access onto the disc or into other dimensions. Others are biofeedback devices, or else are put in to re-balance the energy system to assist in curing or preventing illness. She went on to explain that they generally don't show up in X-rays. This confirmed something that Helene had read only that day.

Many physical implants are put into peoples' bodies by the MILABS operations we mentioned in Chapter 16 in order to make people fear the genuine ET presence. Implants that have been surgically removed from people are most likely the result of this interference.

The whole idea behind the MILABS brainwashing program is to convince people that the ET presence is evil and to be feared, which then allows "authorities" down here to develop Star Wars-type weapon development programs and to impose even more "Big Brother" controls over the inhabitants of this planet, with the full approval of a frightened and cowered populace. Many authors and ET/UFO researchers are playing right into their hands with their false horror stories of negative ET interference and abduction.

The Zetas have developed what could be called technology-assisted consciousness, and consciousness-assisted technology. The implants are inserted where there are chakra points in the body, so they operate via the energy system, which is the key to interdimensional travel. To shift to another dimension the vibrational frequency must be altered, and this is done through the chakras, where the adjustments need to be made. The Zetas have this technology, which has only been touched on down here with Eastern healing techniques such as acupuncture and Reiki.

April 14, 2002.

Ben had a trance in which he saw people in the house and a disc, which he described as "a big thing with colored lights." Then he again experienced everything being upside down and spinning, and his tongue felt like "wood." He was terrified, saying that "the people who were in the kitchen looked horrible and had come to get him." Ben suddenly called out: "I love you!" He then placed his hands on his chest, not crossed but with his left hand on the left side and right hand on the right side, then both arms went up in the air and he made a sort of bow. Eventually Helene and Gary got him settled back in bed, and the next morning he could only recall a little of the "dream."

H: Ben's trances were now becoming more complex, with his emotions going from one extreme to the other. In the beginning of the trance he didn't recognize his Visitors and was very frightened, but by the end of it he was experiencing total love and respect.

J: A few hours later that same night, he had another trance in which he complained of feeling "stretchy." He was worried about Kira and wanted to know where she was, and he was also frightened of being "stiff." Here I think he may have been referring to the state of paralysis that comes over us prior to our stepping out of the physical body to go on board the disc. Our physical body is placed into a state of almost suspended animation to protect it from injury while we're away from it, but if you're partly conscious when this happens, it feels very strange and potentially frightening, if you don't know what's happening.

When you're in this altered mind-state, your perception is expanded into astral level awareness, so you may be conscious of the presence of other beings. Sometimes you can see them, sometimes you can't, and this can be quite scary until you become accustomed to it, because you feel very vulnerable and helpless.

Ben then said: "Last night — pirates — ugly faces — wear special suits — looks like coat — everyone close to me." Helene asked him if the people in coats were tall (thinking of the Zeta Teachers in their long black capes). Ben replied: "No, but not shorter than Ben." (Sometimes when in trance he referred to himself in third person). Then he added: "Has hat like Captain Hook, with white feather." (According to Kira, the trainee teachers wear a white feather in their hatband). Ben went on to say that there were six pirates, all wearing hats and some with tattoos. Some of them had green or blue feathers.

Helene asked: "What did the pirates do?"

Ben answered: "Hide behind boxes."

Helene then said: "Maybe the pirates are scared of you or maybe sad because you don't remember them. Do they hurt you?"

Ben answered loudly: "NO!"

Helene then suggested that next time perhaps he should ask them if they are his friends, and what their names are. Then the trance ended, and Ben went back to sleep.

H: Ben told me he was very scared of "being stiff," but he was able to share a few more details on what he was experiencing. At the same time I was asking more questions. How interesting! We were both opening up our consciousness at the same time — as I developed more trust and faith with our Visitors from "upstairs," Ben did too. As I was helping him to move through his fear by questioning (and showing belief) in him, I could see he was really shocked when I suggested that maybe they were sad that he didn't remember them. Then when I asked if they'd hurt him, he answered with a very loud and definite "NO!" At this point I felt that there was a deeper connection that he was linking into. It just seems to take one step at a time.

April 24, 2002.

Around 9:15 p.m. — Ben had another trance, saying, "It says I need this thing. You don't understand — I'm very scared — thing following me. It *hurts*! I can't help it! Everything is upside down — something clicks in brain — count 1, 2, 3, 4, 5, 6."

Helene asked Ben about this the next morning, and he did remember the "dream." He explained that he had to count so many seconds. He had to count to 100 or 1,000, but couldn't remember which. He then said: "Something follows me and everything is spinning. There's a big screen."

He was aware of running around the house while in trance, and asked his mom not to stop him, but as she explained, he could get hurt. He told her that during these "dreams" he needed her to protect him, and then said: "I'm sorry — I love you!" Sometimes the fear was so intense he screamed in terror and his heart pounded.

During one of Ben's trances, Helene made a tape recording so I could hear what was going on. It disturbed me greatly to listen to the poor child screaming in such profound terror, and I really felt for both Ben and Helene. Things did ease off a bit after that, so perhaps Helene's allowing me to emotionally react to what was going on registered "upstairs" as well.

Helene played part of this tape at a local UFO conference in which we were part of an experiencers' panel. The feedback we received afterwards was that there was very little support for Helene — only criticism along the lines of, "How could a mother allow such a thing to happen to her child!" Experiencers frequently encounter this sort of total lack of understanding. No wonder so many choose not to come forward.

Playing this tape at the conference took a huge amount of courage on Helene's part. She was nervous enough about getting up and speaking in front of the public, and if the audience found this tape traumatic to listen to, surely it would have occurred to them how awful it was for Helene, the mother of the child involved. However, she decided to do this for two reasons: firstly, to let people hear what can potentially go on during a genuine encounter experience, and secondly, to let people know that no matter how terrifying the experiences were at the time, they'd all moved through this fear to find only love on the other side. Both children have benefited in the long run, and much healing has taken place on all levels — body, mind and spirit.

In answer to whoever made such an ignorant and ill-informed comment, Helene is one of the most caring, loving and protective mothers I have ever met, totally committed to the welfare of her children and family. She's always been a stay-at-home mom because to her way of thinking; motherhood is a sacred vocation. Her energy and patience was being tested to the limits, with not one but two children going through encounter experiences, but both of them have now come out the other side as better people for these experiences.

We really would have liked to invite the judgmental people into Helene's home when all of the "activity" was at its peak, to see how they would have done more to "stop such a thing happening to a child."

When Helene told Kira what Ben said during his trance about the counting and the spinning upside down, she was able to shed a little light on it from her own consciously remembered experiences. She explained that, when we approach the disc, we have a certain time-span in which to get ourselves on board. I feel it has something to do with synchronizing our vibrational frequency with that of the disc. Perhaps the disc can only be held at our lower frequency for a limited time. Kira also recalled counting to 100 for timing, because she only had that limited "window of opportunity" to board.

The upside–down, spinning feeling happens sometimes when you move through dimensions. Some years ago on the Internet, I read of someone else experiencing this feeling, a person who also had conscious understanding of being a Zeta below the surface. I remember this person particularly commenting upon what an unpleasant sensation this can potentially be, and how they dreaded it, but that it couldn't be avoided as it is just part of space/time travel. Maybe we should carry airsick bags with us. After all, even Zetas eat that jelly-paste stuff in tubes, and what goes down can also potentially come up —!

Concerning Ben's extreme terror during his trances, one might think that if he really is an ET, and a fairly evolved one at that given the wisdom that comes out of his mouth at times and his gentle, loving nature, then surely he would not experience so much fear. This, however, is not so, because our cosmic consciousness and our Earth-human consciousness don't always coincide.

A few years ago I read an account on ET/human contact about a man who woke one night from sleep and found himself in Zeta form.

He was quite amazed but felt okay with it, and he was thrilled to find he could levitate and float around the room.

He decided to float himself upstairs to his young son's room just to check on him, and found him awake and also in Zeta form. An incredible glow of love surrounded them as they played together, floating around the room and having great fun, experiencing a bond even stronger than the human relationship they shared as father and son. However, the next morning the son awoke with his head full of a "horrible, frightening dream" in which "an ugly, scary-looking alien" came into his room and flew around over his bed. He was, like Ben, almost hysterical with fear.

This account of what it feels like to be in Zeta form is quite accurate. The freedom, joy, connection and love are beyond words, but the almost unbridgeable gap between the two equally valid but vastly different realities is also accurately described, and sometimes it is very hard to cope with.

23

FOCUSING ON THE POSITIVE

April 29, 2002.

The Carmelite Convent in the next suburb to Kira's school was hosting the relics of St. Teresa of Lisieux, a Carmelite nun who died at age 24 in France. She is remembered for her writing, which has inspired millions of people throughout the world. All the ninth-grade students attended to form an honor guard for the relics.

Kira noticed a number of Zeta workers present, as well as a few Teachers (including Oris) whose heads towered over the humans. As the students formed the Honor Guard, all the little workers ran to join the end of the line. As the saint's relics were carried past her, Kira suddenly got a headache, which lasted for the rest of the day. It wasn't until later that the reason was revealed.

At some point during the proceedings a little worker tried to get closer to the relics, squeezing between Kira and a large woman. One of Kira's friends got the shock of his life when he noticed the woman's dress depress against her leg as if something was pushing on it. A day or so later Kira mentioned it to Oris, who responded, "Ah, so *that's* what the worker was apologizing for. I didn't know what he was going on about."

The students had to stand out in the sun for an hour and a half, and poor Kira felt as if she was going to faint with the heat and the headache. Suddenly she felt someone giving her Reiki and physically supporting her. It was Oris of course, bless his heart.

She asked him why the workers stayed so close to the saint's relics. He explained that, when a person's remains are preserved in this way, for example a saint's relics kept on show as an object of worship and adoration, or even somebody's ashes being kept in the home instead of being disposed of and returned to nature in the form of burial or scattering, part of their spiritual essence becomes trapped, and cannot go on to where it's supposed to be. With one such as St. Teresa, there's an even greater problem because of all the religious fervor and emotion that's directed towards the relics, which would really hold her back.

As Oris went on to explain, the risk is, that while she's trapped in this sort of limbo, and unable to move on naturally, she may become separated from her physical remains and get lost. It's therefore the job of specially appointed workers to keep her with her remains until such time as they crumble to dust or are disposed of properly, which will enable her proper release. It was the frustrated energies of this poor trapped spirit that caused Kira's headache. There's just so much about other-dimensional realities and the after-life that we don't know or understand about down here.

May 23, 2002.

H: Ben was having trances on a very regular basis (three in a row at the end of April). I was getting a strong feeling that I was being tested by "upstairs," and that they were watching to see not only how I was handling Ben's trances, but also other things that were happening in my day-to-day life. I was consciously aware of standing back and thinking more about my own reactions to people and situations. I mentioned to Oris that I could feel a change within myself. It was as if I could see things with more clarity, and my energies felt stronger somehow. I asked him if this was so.

He proceeded to tell me that he didn't like to use the word "tests"; he preferred to call it training, or simply "a learning experience," that is, learning more about one's self. I hate to admit this, but like lots of other people, I've always been caught up in day-to-day living without ever thinking about the bigger picture. Having learned so much from Oris in the last two years, I felt as if I had been asleep a long time. Oris responded,

> Oh no, Helene. You weren't asleep — you were just standing in the corner!

What a sweetie! He's always so respectful and has such a wonderful way with words. Judy and I still joke about this.

J: One evening Gary noticed a mark on Helene's brow chakra, and when he went to brush it off they were both zapped with static electricity. She later asked Oris about this, who explained that it was because they are true soul mates. He told them that they've been married in a number of lives, which according to him is a fairly rare occurrence, and then he went on to make a very profound and quite typical "Oris statement":

When you marry your soul mate, you do not complete each other – you complete yourself.

Although Oris didn't actually say so, I had to wonder if Helene had undergone the needle-and-crystal procedure on her third eye, which would explain the sudden clarity and strength of spirit she was experiencing and would also account for the mark on her brow chakra point. She couldn't recall the experience, but, being a busy wife and mother, she has to remain centered and grounded in human life down here, and therefore has very little personal recall of anything happening "upstairs." But this does not mean that she isn't involved in Zeta Work. In fact I'm sure she has responsibility for hybrid children up on the disc. She would be perfect in this role, embodying the very essence of motherhood.

If you are an experiencer who is aware of having given birth to hybrid children that are being raised elsewhere, *please* don't be concerned for your little ones. Don't believe the misinformed and totally inaccurate disinformation that some people spread around down here about the Zetas not properly looking after the hybrid babies and children on the disc. This is simply not true. They are loved and cared for, and their birth mothers are brought on board regularly to interact with them. Maris once explained to me that the Star Children down here are Earth humans with an increased amount of ET genetics in their makeup. The hybrids seen up on the discs are essentially ETs with added Earth human genetics.

On one occasion Oris spoke of the crop circles, explaining that these are like big "stamps" that contain important information for humans. They are rather like Reiki symbols in that they encapsulate energy. The crop circles link into consciousness, on a personal as well as a planetary level, invoking particular vibrational frequencies that aid in bringing about evolutionary changes to the human and planetary psyche. They act as a catalyst to awaken deeper levels of conscious awareness in humankind.

At the time Kira was learning about crop circles "upstairs," and was trying to work out the message being conveyed through one particular one. At first she could only work out the very last word, which was *peace*, but finally she managed to translate the rest of it, which said — *we are trying to help you find peace*.

She also remembered being taken to a laboratory/museum "upstairs." She'd gone there several times and always enjoyed it because visitors are allowed to touch things, unlike in Earth museums, where everything is behind glass. One clear memory she had was of an exhibit of a strange being known as a "Zaphien." They have a weird appearance, sort of like stick figures but with wings. The wings are not usually visible, but blue dye had been injected into the museum exhibit so the wings could be seen.

During one of his visits around that time, Helene asked Oris if we should be sending Reiki to America because of the terrorist threat, and how to word the sending. He said to put it this way — "I wish to send Reiki to the American heart. Please let this protect and heal us for our nation's good."

What worries the ETs very deeply is the very real possibility that the Powers That Be down here — the behind-the-scenes orchestrators of global terrorism, are planning to stage a "fake attack by evil aliens" as we approach 2012. This possibility has been put forward as the next planned step to give government and military leaders the excuse to develop even deadlier weapons and tighter controls over the entire population of the planet.

June 26, 2002.

Helene was on the phone talking to me and trying to print out pictures of crop circles from the Internet. Something was going wrong with the computer and stopping her from doing it, so she called on Oris to come and give her a hand, which he did, bless him. He then wandered off into the lounge room to sit and watch the football finals on TV with Kira. After all, what else would a Zeta Teacher do on his day off?

As we later joked, he really should have replaced his red feather with a maroon one — the team color for Queensland. My Teacher Maris wouldn't have been welcome, sporting a blue feather, which is the color of the opposing NSW team. These ET Visitors really should study up on such matters of diplomacy before coming to Planet Earth!

Around that time Kira commented upon the large number of discs she'd seen, and she wondered if another terrorist attack was being planned. Sure enough a week later such a report came out in the paper. She also had a feeling that the terrorists were planning an attack on a couple of big bridges in America. Again confirmation on this came a few weeks later in a newspaper report in the *Queensland Courier Mail* of August 14, 2002, specifically mentioning the threat posed to bridges in that country. Obviously the surveillance system on our disc was back in full operation.

July 15, 2002.

Kira woke feeling nervous and worried, having seen a warning "upstairs" of another potential attack. Oris too was very concerned about the situation, and told us that we were all needed to try to avert anything happening. He requested that we keep ourselves in a state of quiet meditation while going about our daily work, not wasting energy on idle chatter but rather staying focused on calming the human energies on Earth.

That day I asked my Tai Chi class to focus their energies on world peace and healing during practice. As I explained to them, the ultimate harmonizing and balancing of planetary energies starts with each and every one of us on a personal level. We as humans can only heal our world by healing ourselves first, which involves practicing mind discipline by not allowing ourselves to get too caught up in the lower emotions of fear and anger. Two negatives never do make a positive, so the answer is always love.

By evening Kira was depressed and tired. Helene tried to console her by telling her how helpful she'd been in getting information and confirmation through on Reiki, as well as all the other wonderful information Oris had been able to convey to us through her. Kira hadn't even realized this, and she shed a few tears. Helene suggested that because she was so tired after such a trying day perhaps she should get to bed early.

At this, Kira dug in her heels. She informed Helene that there was *no way* she was going to go to sleep. She insisted that she couldn't face another night of "upstairs work," as she knew she'd have to. She was just *too tired*! Helene tried to comfort and cheer her up, but nothing seemed to help, so in the end she let her be and went into the lounge to watch TV.

About five or ten minutes later Helene thought to herself how strangely quiet Kira was, and she went to check on her, but there was no sign of her in the kitchen where they'd been talking only minutes before. All that remained was Helene's dressing gown, which Kira had been wearing, now draped across the kitchen bench.

Helene had a feeling that Oris may have turned up and ordered her to bed, and sure enough there she was, in her bedroom sound asleep, lying on her back, hands in the peace sign position and totally out of her body. Helene could always tell when she was "away." It had all happened so fast, and it was very unusual behavior for Kira, who always took ages to get to sleep. It was obviously Oris's doing.

Sure enough, the next morning Kira came out of her room looking very subdued, and not her feisty "grumpy-teen" self. She told her mom how annoyed Oris had been with her for refusing to go to work. He'd turned up in the kitchen as soon as Helene had left, and had "really yelled" at her, telling her in no uncertain terms to:

> Get straight into bed and stop mucking about! There's important work to do!

Kira had never seen him so angry, and she'd run into the bedroom in tears. He didn't even wait for her to get to sleep, as was usual, but he just pulled her out of her body, and off they went, which wouldn't have been very pleasant for her at all.

H: As hard as this was for Kira, Oris was just trying to get her to appreciate the enormity of the task at hand for all of us, both ET Zetas and "human" Zetas. Each one had an important role to play as part of a team, and all were needed to help settle the very negative energies that were running rampant on Earth at that time. Oris's actions may have seemed rather harsh, but remember, he'd also shown her many wonderful things and given her a lot of love and protection, and a huge amount of knowledge.

J: Strangely enough, when Oris spoke to her in physical words he often used Spanish, because this was where he'd lived his last life in human form (as *Manolo*), so when he wants to use human speech, Spanish is probably the easiest language for him to remember, which finally answered my question of why Maris spoke to my friend Catherine's daughter all those years ago in Russian. His last human life was that of a Russian Gypsy.

The work being carried out "upstairs" still involved the ongoing terrorism threat, because I too had a strong memory from that night of a group discussion going on. Ideas were being exchanged on what the best course of action would be to disrupt any further attacks. Somebody put the suggestion forward of trying to cause dissension among the ranks of bin Laden's followers, and an attempt was also made to influence one of them who was rather anxiety prone, by causing him to believe that something was wrong with their plans or equipment, and that everything needed re-checking. Kira could recall one of the Zetas wrapping long, thin fingers around the throat of one of the leaders of the group (who wasn't aware of the ET presence), and the others chuckling grimly and commenting,

> If only it was that easy!

Although we weren't aware of it in our physical human consciousnesses, these events were of course leading up to the tragic attack on the night club in Bali, October 12, 2002, in which so many of our fellow Australians were killed, so naturally those Zetas resident here in human form would have been doing everything possible to intervene.

At that time, something was really puzzling me. We kept being given all these dire warnings of imminent terrorist attacks, with one friend even being told by a "mysterious stranger" not to visit Sydney on a certain date as there was going to be an attack there. Nothing happened, thank goodness, but I couldn't understand why "upstairs" was making such a fuss and giving out all of these ominous warnings when nothing ever actually happened. I thought to myself that surely they would know whether there really was a danger or not.

The same applied with all the psychic warnings of gloom and doom that have proliferated over the past 30 years or so. Okay, disasters have occurred, but nothing like predicted e.g., in 1998, when a well-known psychic predicted that World War III would erupt with a full-scale nuclear attack by Muslim countries on the U.S. and its supporters. Iraq would lead the Muslim world. Eight nuclear bombs would explode in eight American cities in one day. Not that you want such things to occur, but why were the warnings given out in the first place? Was it the negative forces working subtly through the minds of some psychics to create fear?

Yes, in some cases, but not always. As we teach in Reiki, everything that manifests in the physical body as symptoms of illness has its cause in the more subtle realms of the etheric or astral. In fact the way all natural healing modalities work is to address this cause — the imbalance or disharmony at the subtle level, before it can manifest on the gross physical level as an effect, or symptom of illness.

Just as Reiki energy ideally intervenes at the deeper-cause level, before the effect has the chance to manifest into physical reality, so the Zetas, as caretakers of energy, try to intervene in planetary affairs at deeper levels. By treating the cause as it were, in some instances they are able to restore balance and harmony to the otherwise negative energy that has been set in motion to manifest in the form of terrorist attacks, earthquakes, wars, tidal waves, etc., thus blocking the effect before it occurs. We can do this from down here, by sending love and prayers out for the healing of our planet, and also by *not focusing too much fear and emotion into the numerous predictions of gloom and doom.* This is the reason why the urgent message was given for all of us to *meditate upon peace and harmony* whenever the possibility of an attack is imminent. *It's a way of neutralizing the negativity before it can manifest into physical reality.*

For every physical effect expressed or manifested on Earth in what humans think of as "reality," there are many possibilities set in motion on the etheric and astral planes, which are the realms of ideas, thoughts, emotions and dreams, where cause is created, and on this subtler level the higher forces can more easily intervene, while the cause is still in the form of malleable energy that has not yet solidified into physical action or effect.

The thoughts, ideas and plans for the negative happenings we were being shown were certainly in place, but by showing us the imagery of possible outcomes, we were able to set off enough positive healing energy through our Reiki, meditation, Tai Chi, etc. (aided of course by many others the world over), to neutralize the negative thought forms, which is why many people taken up onto the discs have been shown possible scenarios of terrible disasters happening on Earth.

We are shown what possibilities lie ahead if we don't start making positive changes in how we think. The scary scenarios revealed to people during their experiences are not threats, but warnings. *And the point is we do have the power to change these future scenarios to something more positive.* When we receive these prior warnings, it is *most* important to detach from any sort of negative reaction such as fear, hatred or anger, and simply send love, peace, healing and harmony to wherever it's needed. This is where Reiki is so good. It's just pure unconditional love, with absolutely no emotion attached to it.

There are computers on board the big discs that continually monitor such possibilities and give prior warning of major disasters that have been set in motion. Sometimes the ETs are able to intervene, sometimes not. It was exactly three weeks to the day before the 9/11 attacks that these on-board computers were tampered with, and there are some humans who can do such things, which is why Oris was so frantic to get the equipment repaired.

A number of respected scientists on Earth have reported nuclear missiles being put out of action by UFOs, and there was an instance of Earth scientists sending a test missile to the moon, just to "try it out," and a UFO intervened, sending it off course. All the ETs are doing is trying to protect humans from themselves.

Kira remembered coming across a Zeta worker shedding tears of frustration. When asked what was wrong, he described the difficulty he was experiencing in trying to give healing to one of the humans he'd been assigned to work with. This person began screaming in terror every time the worker tried to approach. The poor Zeta didn't know how to handle the situation. As he said to Kira: "I just want to do my work!"

July 28, 2002.

Helene and Kira were coming to my place for a Reiki support group meeting. Just 14, Kira was prone to "hormone attacks" on a fairly regular basis. Helene often joked that she needed to be fitted with an alarm system which would alert the rest of the family to give them enough warning to escape in time. Just before leaving home they'd had an argument, but luckily Oris arrived on the scene to give Helene a helping hand. He travelled up to my place with them, sitting in the back seat of the car with Kira to keep an eye on her. He certainly didn't let her get away with too much!

He had some information to pass on to one of the others coming to the group, so they came early, about an hour or so before anyone else was due to arrive. Once this task had been taken care of, Helene took advantage of Oris's presence to extract more information. He knows her *so* well, and sometimes, when he turns up ready to answer questions and she assures him that she "only has one or two," he replies,

> Oh sure, Helene! Just one or two —Ha!

He'd mentioned a couple of times that he can be in two places at the same time, and Helene wanted to ask him more about this. He explained that he could actually be in *three* places. By allowing his physical body to sink into a deep state of meditation, he can project himself astrally to two different places at the same time.

Helene then asked him about people suffering from Down syndrome — why does this happen? His answer was that often they're old souls who've voluntarily chosen to take on the condition in order to help others work through karma.

August 13, 2002.

Helene was home alone with Kira, so she decided to take advantage of the situation to call Oris in to answer more questions. Apart from the brief session at my place on the 28th, it had been six weeks since they'd had a good talk, and she had *lots* more questions for him. Lucky Oris! He was tired when he arrived, and informed them that he hadn't had a proper sleep in 12 years. I really think he was just feeling sorry for himself that evening and exaggerating things a wee bit. After all, Zetas are "only human," so to speak, and they can get moody at times, although Kira did comment later that he had bags under his eyes, so maybe he was feeling out of sorts. With all the terrorist threats going on around that time, the Zetas were kept very busy trying to provide protection down here.

Helene's first question on the night of his visit dealt with a handbook on Reiki that had recently been brought to light, supposedly written by the founder of the system, Dr. Mikao Usui. She asked Oris if he knew of it. His answer was no.

Her next question concerned Sekhem (also known as Seichim). This is a healing method a little bit like Reiki that arrived on the scene in the late 1980s — early 1990s. It was said to have come out of the Sufi tradition and has its roots in ancient Egypt. It became entwined with Reiki in America, and one form of it makes use of symbols, some of them taken from Reiki. Helene, Ian and I had all been attuned to it, Ian and I had both gone to Teacher level and in fact Ian travelled to New Zealand to attend a Master training course with Patrick Ziegler, the one who "rediscovered" it during a trip to Egypt in which he spent a night in the Great Pyramid.

I'd really enjoyed using it for a while, finding it a very potent energy form, but there were a couple of points about it I wasn't so keen on. For a start, unlike Reiki, Sekhem can potentially be used in a more invasive and manipulative way. I got the feeling that it wasn't quite as gentle and "respectful" as Reiki, and it seemed to appeal too much to those with over-inflated egos. A few who were using it were very much into power and control, and this was extremely off-putting. One of these folk even went so far as to phone me one evening in a quite abusive way, insisting that what I was teaching wasn't "real Sekhem" but only a watered-down version, unlike the "authentic" method that *she* was teaching. This is the reason why, when I re-established my link with Oris through Kira and we received so much positive feedback and teaching on Reiki, I moved right away from the Sekhem, as did Helene.

Helene's question to Oris was — "What do you think of Sekhem?"

> It's a bit questionable. It taps into dark magic but can be used for good. Be very careful with it, particularly those you teach it to. I prefer Reiki.

I totally agree with Oris on this. He verbalized my suspicions very succinctly.

On a positive note however, on one occasion Ian gave a Sekhem treatment to a friend's daughter who'd been trying unsuccessfully for years to become pregnant. After one session she conceived and is now the proud mother of a healthy boy. As with so many of these things, it's not so much the tool at fault but rather the tradesman.

H: "Why are whales beaching themselves?"

> They are picking up on the negative energies of the planet in the water, which is a good conductor of energy. This interferes with them and they try to get away from it.

"What happens when you die?"

> You're helped out of your physical body by an angel, or sometimes also by a family member who has already passed over. You're taken up through various frequency levels, and at each one you receive guidance and assistance. Once you reach the appropriate level for your soul evolution, you're shown what you have or have not accomplished in the past life. You are first shown your failures, then your successes. Ideas and advice are then provided to assist you in your next life.

"Do we always attend our own funeral?"

> Yes, to say your goodbyes to everyone, then the angels come to fetch you, to help you to move on. If you are fearful, a family member or close friend who has already passed over is brought along to help you.

"What happens to the soul after death if the ashes are kept instead of being disposed of?"

The soul cannot move on — it stays near its remains. At a burial or cremation, once the coffin is covered or the ashes disposed of, the spirit is released.

Helene then asked some questions about Reiki. At that time a so-called Tibetan form of Reiki had appeared on the scene, with its own Master symbol. We'd learned this, but were beginning to feel rather confused by the whole thing. "New" forms of Reiki seemed to be appearing on a regular basis, and some Reiki Masters were charging large sums of money to teach all these different methods. Something just didn't feel right about it.

At that time both Maris and Oris had given us quite a lot of deeper information on traditional Reiki, a lot of which was confirmed several years later when a very good book* on Reiki was published by a couple who travelled to Japan to gather the correct information on how Reiki came to be developed. They carried out some very in-depth research, even managing to interview several of Mikao Usui's students who were still living at that time.

It was wonderful to receive this confirmation on material provided by the Zeta family. There'd been so much of it given that I'd managed to put a whole seminar together, which is now taught after level-two Reiki, either as preparation for those who wish to go on to Teacher level, or else to simply provide more depth and inner work for those who don't necessarily want to teach, but who feel the need for even deeper understanding of the traditional Eastern philosophies behind Reiki.

"Do we use the Tibetan master symbol in the (new) Reiki Three initiation?"

No! You should not mix cultures/lineages. You must use the traditional Japanese master symbol. I will give you an additional symbol to be used at this level. It is for bridging the dimensions and connecting back to the higher self.

"When we attune a pregnant woman to Reiki, is the unborn baby attuned as well?"

Yes, if the higher self so chooses.

---

*Stiene, Frans and Bronwen. *The Japanese Art of Reiki: A Practical Guide To Self-healing*, Berkeley, California: O Books, 2005.

"What is really going on when channelers and psychics claim to connect with 'ascended masters,' 'angelic beings,' etc.? Are they genuinely doing this?"

> In some cases yes, but many times they are simply tuning in to their own higher selves or else the planetary consciousness. Sometimes, however, it is an astral-plane entity playing tricks on them. This is always the case if any ego or manipulative behavior is involved on their part. In other cases it is one of us they are linking in to. In this way we are able to test them on whether they allow the contact to "go to their heads" or not. We also do this to see if they are using their supposed "powers" correctly. A truly spiritual psychic only ever offers teachings and advice for the highest good of all – never ever to control or manipulate situations or people. When we work in this way, we only allow the person to see what they are able to handle, thus we may appear quite angelic-looking, so that the message can be transmitted without fear clouding the issue.

Some weeks earlier Helene and I had been discussing the possibility of allowing Oris to step into my body to do some channeling. This was something I'd learned to do in Irene's circle in 1989, and I now know that he used to work with me then on a regular basis, under the past-life human guise of "Manolo." With Kira able to see him consciously, we agreed that this exercise would be most interesting to try, so we'd give it a go when they were visiting. The next time they came, however, Oris got in first and vetoed the idea, again complaining of feeling tired, and explaining that when he's in such a state, if he tried to step in to channel it would affect my digestive system. The fact that he brought the matter up was excellent proof that he's around us all the time, because Helene and I had only discussed it briefly between us over the phone. This often happens.

24

REINCARNATION AND NDES

August 19, 2002.

Helene and Kira came to my place for a visit so we could call Oris in to do some final polishing on the level-three Reiki information Maris had been giving me. We also wanted to clarify a few points on the attunement procedure. Oris went through it with us step by step, adding, deleting and explaining the finer points. I also wanted to allow him to step into my physical body to try some channeling, if he was agreeable of course, and not too tired (I didn't want digestive problems).

As it turned out, this time he also was anxious to try, both of us having learned so much by working together in this way previously. We were also both feeling a bit nervous, not having channeled in eight years, but I knew that with Kira present using her clairvoyant sight to guide us, it would be a very interesting experiment.

After Oris's earlier comment about causing digestive problems if he tried to step into my body when he was feeling tired, I suggested that he take a little nap while we went upstairs to have lunch. The whole afternoon could then be spent on our channeling session. God love him he took my advice and lay down on the bed under the house for a rest. He is *so* thoughtful that way!

After we'd eaten I settled myself down to get my energies calm, centered and receptive. I warned Helene and Kira that it could take a little time as it was years since I'd done it, and in Irene's circle it usually took at least half an hour of meditation before I could detect their approach. I really had lost a lot of faith in my own abilities, so I instructed Kira to only confirm Oris's presence in the room, but to allow me to indicate when I felt him stepping into my body. This was a good test of my sensing ability.

He must have been ready and waiting for me to settle, because only about five minutes had passed when I became aware of a tingling sensation just behind my right shoulder. Checking with Kira for confirmation, she explained that Oris was indeed standing exactly where I could feel him. As I became aware of his slow, careful movement, she then confirmed that yes, he was stepping into my body.

That first time wasn't easy for either of us. Oris was out of practice too and had to go very slowly. In fact it took him about ten minutes to get comfortable. He was being careful for my sake too, because if a spirit person comes in to a medium's body too fast, it becomes a very unpleasant sensation of nausea and dizziness. What didn't help matters is the fact that he is an almost eight-foot-tall Zeta and I'm in a 5' 3" human body, but he just took his time, not trying to rush things.

The process did seem to go on for quite a while before he was in properly, but what I didn't realize and in fact only found out later was that he came up against a bit of a problem at one point and had to stop and pull out. Kira was scared, and her fear was blocking him. He asked her what was wrong and why she was suddenly so fearful. She told him that she was worried that I would go all strange and jerky, and start gasping for breath like some medium she'd seen on TV.

Oris assured her that this wouldn't happen — that what she'd seen on TV was most likely just an act and not for real, or else spirit and channel were not as compatible as we were. He reassured her that I was perfectly safe, and that of *course* he wouldn't do anything to put me at risk. I'd been so nervous about channeling again that I hadn't even thought to discuss this with Kira or Helene, or to explain to them what was going to happen, and I had no idea that Kira would get scared or that her fear would block Oris.

This was a good lesson for me, because all previous channeling I'd ever done had been in the protected confines of a closed circle. I was however quite aware that there's always a potential risk present in opening up to spirit in such a way, and would not have attempted it without Oris there. It's only that I know him so well and we've worked together in this way before that I was willing to participate.

Once he'd calmed Kira's fear, he was able to proceed, and suddenly the old and familiar sensation of a spirit taking control came over me *very* strongly. I really didn't need to ask her if he was in, because his presence was very tangible, but she confirmed it for me anyway. Also, there was no doubt that it was Oris. His energy signature is quite distinctive and extremely strong, just as I remembered him from before.

This sensation of being overshadowed by a spirit person is hard to describe, but quite amazing. Physically it really does feel as if someone else is in your body with you. Sometimes a part of your body will move involuntarily, or you'll feel the other entity trying to work your muscles or voice box. I still clearly recall the weird sensations that occurred the first time one of the Zetas tried to work in this way with me. Not being accustomed to the workings of the human speaking mechanism, it took some practice before they were able to manage it, and I could clearly feel them struggling to master the technique of using the throat muscles to get physical words out.

As Oris settled in, I felt his four long, thin fingers sliding down into my fingers as if my hands were gloves he was putting on. He went slowly, quietly and gently, making the whole process very pleasant but strange as well. As we both adjusted our energies to accommodate each other I felt tingly all over, and found myself quite involuntarily placing my hands in the peace sign position which, as Kira explained later, is how Oris always holds his hands when he's meditating or teaching. There was also a strong need to sit up very straight and tall. I could recall from previous channeling sessions that another Zeta Teacher used to always place his hands in prayer position in front of our chest while he was speaking, and would sometimes bring his fingertips up to his lips with a slight bow of the head. On a couple of occasions I tried to resist, but I had great difficulty. It was an ingrained habit with him so eventually the hands would come up anyway.

Emotionally and spiritually the experience of channeling is nothing short of amazing. The feeling that accompanies such a Teacher is total love, non-attachment and compassion — a glorious sensation to experience down here in the gross physical plane. In fact it's the sheer bliss of "Nirvana." They also fill you up with a huge amount of energy, so between that and the love, you're on a high for several days after.

The beauty of our Zeta family is that they never take complete control, so part of me stays present to enjoy the experience. Helene asked Oris about this during the session, and he explained that, as a Zeta, he wouldn't be able to operate the human container (body) on his own. They always have problems with physical human speech because they communicate so differently — generally telepathically — but if they do converse in a physical language it's more like a dolphin sound.

Also as he told Helene and Kira, ethically he wouldn't take over complete control anyway. After all, it is my body, and out of respect he wouldn't do this. As he explained — it's as if you stay in someone's home. You might use the stove or use the washing machine, but you don't put the hosts out of their own home. In fact you enjoy sharing it with them. That's the whole point of staying with a friend! He also explained that in cases where spirit and channel aren't quite compatible on the energy level, the consciousness of the channel has to step aside completely, but Oris and I share quite happily, and in fact I wouldn't want to leave when he's there because it feels so *good*!

I found working with him this time around to be much more enjoyable than before. In the circle it had to be harder because back then the whole ET thing was a bit of a mystery to me. I knew very little about the Zetas, so I never quite understood who or what I was linking in to and channeling. And, since then I've done a lot more healing, clearing and opening up deeper levels of consciousness, both through the Reiki Mandala initiations and through contact with the Zeta family.

A couple of comments made by Oris over the years have caused me to look at channeling from a rather different angle. In psychic development groups, the spirit person's point of view is not really considered. All the safety measures for example are more for the benefit of the medium, as in never touching them when they're channeling, and never leaving the circle suddenly or without permission, because a negative entity can enter through the vacated place. These precautions are excellent and necessary, but many are unaware that if any of these things occur while a spirit person is with the channel, the spirit person is affected too. If the circle is broken, or someone touches the medium, the spirit person receives an unpleasant jolt, like an electric shock.

Another thing I understand more clearly now is the need for anyone undertaking channeling to keep their energy frequency as high as possible through regular spiritual practice of some sort. If there is any negativity at all in the way of fear, anger, depression, ego, jealousy, etc., then this is the spirit energy that will be attracted to the medium because like attracts like.

Cleansing rituals, candles, incense, prayer and the wearing of such protective talismans as crosses, crystals and pentagrams may help to clear the energies to a certain extent, but the bottom line is self and what is truly in your heart — love or fear. This is like the ancient Egyptian test of worthiness for entering Paradise by weighing the heart of a deceased person against a feather.

Oris has always advised us to use Reiki when working with energy. Developed out of Eastern philosophy, Reiki teaches non-attachment to emotion. No matter what the circumstances or situation you send Reiki to, no emotion is involved. Reiki is simply pure non-polarized energy and therefore very safe. This is where things can go awry with some other magical-type practices where emotion is required to energize the process. Spells, for example, need emotion to energize them, but if a spell is cast with any emotion other than pure unconditional love, a negative thought form may be created, either knowingly or unknowingly.

During our session with Oris, Helene asked some questions, including one on near-death experiences:

"What happens in a near-death experience?"

> You come to the threshold of the astral plane. Humans think of the astral plane as "heaven," but really it is comprised of many layers, some of higher and some of lower vibrational frequencies. We create our own astral-plane experience with our mind, however, this does not lessen the reality of the experience – all of reality is created through the mind. Humans of Earth mistakenly think of their mind as a closed room. In actual fact the mind is a doorway – a portal through to other dimensions. In a near-death experience it is as if you approach the doorway, open it and look through, maybe even place one foot through, but do not completely step inside.

"Are there more colors to work through than the seven colors of the spectrum that we can physically see down here?"

> Many more – even more than we are able to perceive at our level.

"Do you have any advice for Jude?"

> Tell her not to worry - all is being taken care of. She will be given strong and clear guidance, as we trust her actions. She must just tune in to the bigger picture and trust her own ability. Everything will happen in its own timing. Things have to be put in place that she is not yet consciously aware of.

"Why don't Jude and I like using crystals?"

In a past life you were both hurt with crystal energy. Crystals are safe as long as they are used with pure intention and clarity of vision, but they can be used in a negative way to cause harm.

"Is there a real being known as Satan?"

Satan is the energy of fear, as opposed to the God energy of love within the heart of man. In the greater reality there is no Satan or hell – these are illusions created out of the energy of fear.

"How will peace come about in 2012?"

Through the transmutation of the Satan, or fear, element to the higher frequency of God, Christ or love element within the hearts of increasing numbers of humans on Earth, which you can see happening now. Hopefully, by the end of year 2012, a "critical mass" will have been reached. Free will, however, does play a part in this, and such a major step cannot be forced or rushed.

The number 13 represents transformation, so 2013 is the appropriate year for such a shift in consciousness to begin making itself felt. Numerologically, 2013 adds up to 6. When the number 6 arises, it is time to consider changes in life and to decide what action needs to be taken to bring them about. It is time for reflection and for greater clarity on your path.

August 22, 2002.

Ben had lost a tooth, so this called for a visit from the Tooth Fairy in the form of Helene, along with Assistant Tooth Fairy Kira. Once he was asleep, they entered his room to deliver his two dollars plus fairy dust. Talk about economic inflation! It used to be sixpence when I was his age, and no fairy dust whatsoever. With money and dust duly delivered, Kira announced to Helene that Ben was off "upstairs." She explained that she could see a Zeta face overshadowing his human features. Also, he lay very straight and still on his back with hands crossed in front.

Later that night Helene lay in bed unable to sleep. She wasn't really worried about Ben, but she wondered what he was doing. After all, in human years he was still only a young child. At around midnight he came in to her and announced: "Mom, my bones feel all stiff. When I go...." Then he stopped talking.

"When you go where?"

"Can you take me back to bed?" Helene tucked him in and everything was fine. She had the distinct feeling that he'd come in just to let her know that he was back home safe and sound so she could get to sleep.

August 26, 2002.

A mutual friend phoned Helene to get her to ask Kira to ask Oris for information on a past life. Helene explained that it would be better for her to do it for herself while giving herself a Reiki treatment. In this way she'd get practice in using her own intuition, as Oris has always told us to do. The Zetas do *not* like "spoon-feeding" us information and answers. They much prefer us to work things out for ourselves.

I was pleased that Helene gave her this advice because the feeling was very strong while I'd been channeling Oris that he really does not like answering personal questions. Giving information on spiritual matters and the universe is not a problem — he's happy to do it, but not personal information and *definitely* not future predictions — that's a real no-no.

Kira told her mom about how the disc is actually a living, sentient being. The walls feel moist, warm and soft to touch. She also spoke of how it provides whatever is required, for example if you want to sit down a chair appears. If you wish to enter a room a doorway manifests in front of you. She'd also seen suits hanging up, some green and some silver. What is worn depends upon the work being carried out at the time.

She's spoken on several occasions of the "magical chairs" that are made of a plastic-like material, but can mold themselves comfortably to the shape of whoever sits in them. They also provide healing and relaxation. The beds used for sleeping are the same, and I remember using one during work at night.

The mother ship, known affectionately as the "Workshop," is absolutely *huge*, with many levels and encompassing a number of dimensions, that is, it is an interdimensional portal, so once you're on board, you can potentially visit other dimensions quite easily, *providing you have the necessary level of spiritual evolution, or else the appropriate implant(s) to enable you to access the different vibrational frequencies*. This is a protective measure, so that lower-frequency beings cannot enter higher frequency dimensions, unless they've been fitted with an enabling implant. A higher Teacher can descend to a lower frequency to work, but a younger soul can't rise into a higher frequency band to cause trouble, which is why the negative interference being experienced by Earth humans is not coming from an outside ET presence, but rather from Earth's own astral plane.

The small mini-discs, or scout ships, are stored in the bottom part of the big disc. There's also a completely see-through room made out of a glasslike material that appears to have no walls. Kira nicknamed it the "sun room," and being in it is just like free-floating in space.

One night up on the disc, Kira was telling everyone she was looking forward to an up-coming birthday. Oris and Serapis asked her why she was so happy and excited to be born an Earth human. Serapis remarked that really we shouldn't be wishing each other a Happy Birthday but rather a Happy Hellday — Hmm.

September 9, 2002.

Helene had some more questions for Oris. Some of them concerned my writing.

"With all the information you've given us, is there a reason other than Judy's book?"

> Yes, one reason – preparing you. This life we prepare you for battle, for the war [between Love and Fear] is yet to come.

"When Judy channels you, would you like me to give you an aura cleanse?"

> Oh yes, please!

Helene then asked him who should be there the next time we have a channeling session. We'd tried a session with a couple of others present who were open to such things and eager to ask questions, but both Oris and I had found it rather hard going. One had been a bit scared, which tended to block the energy flow, and another kept starting up whispered conversations with the one sitting next to her, which was really distracting, particularly for Oris, who has trouble hearing and understanding human speech anyway. Even picking up telepathically on many humans is hard because their thought patterns are so jumbled. He explained to Helene that he simply couldn't hear what was going on. A couple of other suggestions were countered with:

> No, he/she is too negative. Please, let it be just us three.

"You mean just us four, don't you, Oris?"

No, only three — I'm inside of Judy!

"Smarty pants!"

Oris is obviously very aware of the need for caution when we're working together in this way. Negative energy is not good to have around during channeling, and safety is most important so both spirit and channel can relax and feel comfortable.

That evening Helene asked Oris if she and Kira had ever been Native Americans, as that particular culture really appeals to both of them. He answered in the affirmative, and explained that we were all there as part of a "family." As in the Spanish life, the parents were killed or died fairly young, and "Helene," as the elder sister, took on the role of mother. Helene then asked an interesting question on reincarnation, which elicited deeper teachings on the difference between soul and spirit, and yes, there is a difference, even though we tend to interchange both terms.

Helene, prompted by Oris's saying that she and Kira had been sisters, asked,

"Does the soul remain either male or female all the way through?"

Yes.

When she told me about this the next day I questioned it, because I personally recall mostly male past lives, and Helene agreed. After all, you need to experience life from both sides to gain deeper understanding and balance.

We discussed the matter, wondering if Kira had perhaps allowed her own mind-set to color Oris's answer, which can certainly happen in channeling, but Kira wasn't actually channeling. She was acting more as an interpreter, simply listening to his answers then conveying his words to Helene, who generally couldn't hear him herself, apart from once when he'd corrected her aura-cleansing technique.

Remembering Kira's confusion and misunderstanding in October, 2001, when she was so sure that Oris was asking her to choose between an Earth human or Zeta life, I decided to investigate further, just in case she'd misinterpreted his words. The Zetas are not the easiest folks to communicate with, and in a way I can understand why a fearful and confused "abductee" may not be able to pick up clearly on their communication. You have to be on the correct brain wavelength. Their communication is very gentle and subtle, and they aren't "wordy" at all. In fact, if a channeled message goes on and on, as some of them do, you can be fairly certain it's not a Zeta on the other end of the line. What anyone else might take 20 minutes to say, a Zeta will say in less than five minutes. Usually they use no words, but rather flash an idea or image in your mind, which takes time and practice to interpret.

A reminder the Zeta Teachers have given us on several occasions is to *always keep things simple.* As they've explained, overly complex messages/teachings are often a cunning way of disguising disinformation, and I've often found this to be true. It's not always the case, but certainly something to be aware of and is more common than most realize. Such messages always carry basic grains of truth to draw you in and to provide credibility, but cleverly mixed in among them are many untruths as well.

I asked Maris about reincarnating as male or female.

> To understand this properly, you must grasp the difference between spirit and soul. Spirit is more about the emotional/personality part of the mind. It is at the spirit level of the psyche that reincarnation through the various levels of the Human Ladder occurs, and where the balance is struck between male and female. One may reincarnate as either.
>
> The soul on the other hand is higher/whole mind and may be referred to as the Monad. This tends towards positive (yang) or negative (yin) polarity, and remains the same for one whole cycle of the Human Ladder. It is not really "male" or "female" in the human sense of these terms, but that is the way it is interpreted on a level-one planet such as Earth. The Monad (soul) does alternate or fluctuate between positive and negative polarity, but over a much longer span than spirit, which may change with each life lived.

This is a really good example of how you have to be very precise when asking questions of the Zetas. In her question Helene used the term *soul.* If she'd said *spirit* the answer would've been the opposite.

Maris then said that the real concept behind Christianity's Holy Trinity also refers to the three levels of self. The "Father" is the soul/Monad part of our being; the "Son" is our physical self; and the "Holy Ghost" is the spirit part that reincarnates from life to life on its journey back home to the Monad — the God-part. At the end of a full cycle of the Human Ladder, the soul itself will reincarnate, embarking upon yet another cycle of a higher vibrational frequency. Thus nothing remains static — not even God.

That evening everyone was feeling very relaxed, and with Oris present, there was a real sense of family. According to Oris, each family member has a role — Helene is to work through feeling (clairsentience), Kira through seeing (clairvoyance), and I through hearing (clairaudience). Oris was tired that night, so Helene didn't pressure him with too many questions, but she wanted to test her alleged clairsentient ability by getting Oris to touch her, and then to have Kira give her confirmation through her clairvoyant ability, as we'd done in our channeling session.

Helene immediately felt a sharp sensation of coldness between the top of her head and her right shoulder, and Kira verified this, explaining that Oris had one hand on her head and the other on her shoulder. Helene asked him if he'd enjoyed feeling the energies when he'd stepped into my body for the channeling session.

Yes, very much, but it does feel different.

October 10, 2002.

Ben had a most interesting trance session that, as we've since discovered, conveyed a most important message to us. He had come home from school with a bad cold, and, not feeling very well, he decided to retire at 7:00 p.m. At 8:00 p.m. he called out to Helene, who immediately knew he was "off." He was agitated but not as terrified as usual, and Helene reassured him gently, as always, telling him he was safe and to try to feel the love. She did some Reiki symbols over him to help as well.

He got up and walked through the house, and then he came back to the bedroom saying something about a door. He was getting more agitated, so Helene questioned him carefully to find out what was bothering him. It turned out to be this door that he was worried about. Helene suggested he try to go through it and perhaps he would find love on the other side. She assumed that this door represented a fear barrier in his mind. His reply was: "I can't — I'm scared!" Helene then asked him if he would like to hold her hand and they could then go through the doorway together. He agreed to this and grabbed her hand. About 30 seconds later he woke up, telling her he'd just had some bad dreams. He went on to describe how he'd felt "energies" as he'd walked around the house. Helene asked him how they'd felt, and his answer was, "Weird and good." She then asked where the door was.

B: "It was a door at the back of a church."

H: "Do you remember holding my hand? Did we walk through together?"

"Yes."

"What was on the other side of the door?"

"Lots of people fighting, but when we walked in they stopped."

"Could you feel the love?"

"Yes."

By this stage I was getting more used to Ben's trances. I was learning to stay calmer and to think more clearly — after all, practice makes perfect, as they say. This time there was a big difference, too. While Ben could see and experience things in his "other" dimension, he could also communicate better with me in our shared third-dimensional reality. It seemed like we were both opening up and consciously linking into each other more within the same "extended reality."

Although it was starting to feel like Alice in Wonderland in that we never knew where we would turn up, I had this inner knowing and confidence that somehow, even though we were both operating in two different dimensions, I could still tune in to help him. Ben just needed a bit of reassurance and support from me, which seemed to be enough to enable him to walk through that door.

This is very complex when you think about it — parts of Ben and me were consciously in one dimension/reality, while other parts of us, including my reassuring hand, was in another. He was also relaying back to me everything he was experiencing. Wow — Reality sure is multidimensional!

J: As I understand it, and Helene totally agrees, this "dream" of Ben's sums up exactly what the Zetas' presence is all about down here. Coming in quietly through the "back door," their job is to assist humans in gaining a deeper understanding of love and Oneness, which in turn will hopefully lead to a much more integrated and peaceful society on Planet Earth. When humankind finally reaches this point of deeper understanding, the shallow and transitory differences of religion, color and race will cease to be such issues and points of contention. Earth humans will become much more attuned to Oneness, respect and acceptance of each other, which is what the ET presence is all about.

The timing of Ben's trance was interesting because I was coming to visit them the next day. He still wasn't well and he had a day off school, so the three of us gave each other Reiki. I've felt a real connection with young Ben right from the start, and I do feel strongly that we work together "upstairs." A hint of this was given that very day when Ben took me into his room to show me his pet goldfish. Walking back down the hallway towards the family room, Ben was behind me. For no reason at all (in fact I don't think he was even consciously aware of doing it), he placed his left hand on my right shoulder, just as the Zeta Teachers often do. He's a very tall boy for his age, and he towers over my five-foot-three-inch frame, and just for a fleeting moment I was aware of an interdimensional shift — the two of us were walking down a corridor on the disc.

October 13, 2002.

Kira came home at lunchtime from her friend Kate's place, and a birthday sleepover. One of the girls had brought along a Ouija board, so luckily Oris also turned up to keep an eye on things. Remembering his words of caution from an earlier episode at school, Kira insisted that if they really had to play with the board then they should do it outside rather than inside the house.

That evening (October 12), their first apparent contact was "Tom," an American boy who'd died from a drug overdose. They asked him how to help stop all the terrible things that are going on in the world.

Be all One.

"Will the terrorists attack again?"

Yes, soon!

The next contact seemed negative, and one of the girls got really scared. The glass planchette kept going in her direction, even following her when she changed places with someone else. Kira, feeling confident because she knew Oris was close by, ordered it in a firm voice to *go now* — and it did. This little fright had the effect of dampening their enthusiasm and sending them off to bed.

There's no doubt in my mind that "Tom" was really Oris, playing games with them and keeping an eye on things. He then pretended to be the "bad spirit" that scared them, deliberately aiming his "attack" on the one in the group most easily frightened. With Oris present, no genuine negative entity would have been able to approach, and the way the whole thing was done is very typical of the way Oris operates. It had the desired effect of scaring them into stopping and hopefully teaching them a lesson at the same time. That night he must have stayed close, because one of the girls with whom Kira shared a room told her the next morning that Kira had been speaking Spanish in her sleep.

The next day, teenage silliness overrode caution, and they decided to give the board another go. This time Kira felt Oris's presence and active intervention. He told them, via the board, that his name was "Alice" and that "she" was a 17-year-old girl. "Alice" then went on to lecture them on the dangers of playing around with a Ouija board. One of the girls, "Sally," was a very angry and rebellious teenager into drugs, witchcraft, etc., who had attached herself to Kira. Helene and Oris were concerned about this, but Kira felt that she was helping this girl when in fact Sally was doing her best to pull Kira into her own negativity.

Sally became annoyed about these cautionary messages coming through the board. She didn't like being lectured and told what to do, even by a spirit person, so she told "Alice" in no uncertain terms that what she was saying was "just a load of crap," and that "no f___ing spirit" was going to tell her what to do. With that she got up and flounced off. Kira saw how this sudden breaking of the energy circle that had built up around them caused Oris a very unpleasant electric shocklike effect.

Still determined to continue with his lesson and give them all a fright that they wouldn't forget in a hurry, he took a few minutes to recover. With their circle broken in such a dramatic way, the girls put the board aside. The glass they'd been using as a planchette was turned upside down next to the board, which was a few feet away from where they were now sitting and talking. Suddenly there was a loud crack, and to their complete amazement, the glass was now right side up, in the middle of the board and partly broken, with bits of glass lying nearby. Good one, Oris! (Although Kira silently teased him that he could've done better than *that*!)

Tom's prediction of an imminent terrorist attack proved chillingly correct. A newsflash at lunchtime the following day announced the bombing of a night club in Bali, five hours after Tom's prediction.

25

PACT OF THREE

December 15, 2002.

Through Kira, Oris explained the difference between soul mates and twin souls. In the case of soul mates, two different souls share a bit of the essence of each other. Twin souls are simply the dual aspect, the yin and yang polarities of the same soul.

I love the way Kira interpreted this concept in her 14-year-old mind, likening the process to making rum balls, one of the family's favorite Christmas treats.

K: "To make a brand new soul — you have the bowl of rum-ball mix, and the Archangel takes a handful and divides it in two. These then are twin souls, which everyone has somewhere, but not necessarily here on Earth. If the Archangel has two different handfuls, then he takes a raisin out of each and swaps them over. That is how soul mates are created.

"This is all done in what I call the soul factory. Oris has taken me there, and it's like a big black room that goes on for eternity. An old Archangel calls your name, and you go into like a big 'bowl,' and your memory goes into a deep sleep, then you wake up as a new person." She then added: "There is God, and 12 others who run the universe."

J: We asked Oris for clarification on this only recently, and his explanation was that these 12 beings have a closer link to God (are higher up on the Human Ladder), guiding consciousness for humanity. When he said this, a pyramid shape came to mind as a way of visualizing the universe, with God Source as the apex, and consciousness gradually expanding outwards and downwards towards the bottom.

January 30, 2003.

The evening before Helene was to begin teaching her first Reiki Two Seminar was a hectic time for her, being a mother of two school-age children. With family dinner to prepare, school homework and lunches to organize for the next day, as well as getting ready for the seminar, who should turn up on her doorstep for a friendly visit but a pair of passing Zeta Teachers, all dressed up with nowhere to go and time to kill — Oris and Serapis,

Just passing, thought we'd drop in!

and they had teachings to impart — lucky, lucky Helene!

She was sitting out in the pergola with Kira, and Serapis wanted to tell them about "The Pact of Three." But he wanted candlelight, not electric light, so Helene had trouble taking notes. She commented to Kira on how soft, gentle and loving his energies are, and unbeknown to her, Oris was there as well, listening in, and he chimed in.

Hey, what about me? Don't you like my energies!

Several moments of awful embarrassed back-pedaling by Helene passed before she realized that he was only teasing her. Oris can be a real stirrer at times, most especially when Serapis is around. The two of them seem to feed off each other, which is really funny. If only people would relax more and open up with the Zetas, they'd come to realize that this is how they are — very human in many ways, with a great sense of humor and quite individual characters. We feel extremely privileged that they're comfortable enough with us to act like this.

I recall reading in John Mack's *Abduction — Human Encounters with Aliens*,* of a woman experiencer named Anne, who woke up immediately after being returned to her bed by a Zeta worker. The worker didn't realize Anne was awake and watching him out of half-closed eyes, and he was caught unawares just standing there looking at her with eyes so full of fondness and love, like a doting parent watching a beloved child sleeping. When he realized that his depth of feeling was being openly observed, he became embarrassed and made a hasty retreat. This is exactly how they are.

The Pact of Three

Serapis — I bring Truth to those who do not wish to see.

*Mack, ibid., p. 416.

> Maris — I bring Understanding to those who do not wish to know.
>
> Oris — I bring Emotion to those who do not wish to feel.
>
> We bring Love to those who do not wish to experience.
>
> Thus we work as Tryers and Testers of Souls

This dislike of strong light on Serapis's part provided great evidence of the reality of his presence during a channeling session in early 2008. Fully expecting Maris to step in, I was surprised to feel a different energy signature coming in prior to the session. It felt much warmer, and the others present were quite amazed to encounter a patch of very warm air, which remained for several minutes in a normally breezy doorway where I'd been standing. Then as we were about to start, and knowing nothing of Serapis's dislike of bright light, I commented to Helene that I hoped she'd be okay taking down notes in the half light, as whoever was with me didn't want the overhead fluorescent light on. I'd actually started moving towards the switch to turn it on when a clear message came through: "Please no, leave the light off." Helene then burst out laughing and informed me of Serapis's dislike of electric light.

February 20, 2003.

Kira was sick with bronchitis and having trouble breathing, so she slept with Helene, who asked her if Oris and Serapis were there, because they'd been visiting a lot during the past fortnight, but at that point only a worker was present. Helene started sending Reiki to Kira and asked the worker if he could see and feel her energy. He said yes, he could see all the energy swirling around, and it felt good. Then the other pair arrived. (Helene nicknamed them Huey and Dewey, but never to their faces).

Oris asked Helene to give Kira an aura cleanse. Poor Helene was very tired, having had her husband sick as well that week, so she asked him to do it for her.

> I already have, but now I need you to do it, and you can just visualize it if you want.

Despite her tiredness, Helene responded:

No, no, it's all right. I'll get up and do it if it will help."

No Helene – you can visualize it. It's just as good.

She followed Oris's advice, and Kira could clearly feel it being done, which was good confirmation that visualization works in such cases.

Helene asked Oris why they'd both had to do the cleanse on Kira, and his answer was that he'd worked on the spiritual side, but it also needed to be done on the physical side. He added that there are many reasons why we do an aura cleanse. Helene's physical visualization helped ground the energy on that lower level and served to balance out the whole process.

With two Zeta Teachers present in the room, Helene, exhausted from her long day, was feeling quite "out of it." She asked Oris why he always chose to discuss deep subjects with her when she was feeling so tired.

That is when you are more relaxed and open. During the day you are running around and stressed at times, but when you're tired you are quieter and more accessible.

This does make sense, but Helene joked that he probably turned up at those times when she had less energy to ply him with a million questions, as she does.

True to form, tired or not, more questions followed. She asked for more details on the "many reasons" for doing the aura cleanse. His answer was that it brings negative energy blocks up to the surface so that a better healing can take place. When we work together with the Zetas, a more intense healing is achieved. They work spiritually while we work physically, which brings in greater balance. He later provided us with a detailed step-by-step explanation of each movement involved in the cleanse.

While they all worked on Kira, Helene asked Oris if there was another name for the Human Ladder, which she felt didn't sound quite right. A typical Zeta answer was given.

Think about it – you already know!

An "amazing coincidence" occurred the next morning when Helene called me about the previous night's events. Before she could mention her comment to Oris, I told her that I'd thought of a more suitable name for the Human Ladder — Universal Cycle.

Helene of course had more questions for Oris, but he must have read her mind and told her to be quiet before she had a chance to open her mouth. Kira intervened, asking Helene what her question had been. Helene explained that she'd just wanted to ask him about something she'd read, of a tectonic plate that was going to shift in May 2003 and create a lot of damage.

> Don't worry about it. That's months away.

The ETs have done a lot of work to minimize these expected geophysical events, so maybe they intervened on that one too, as I don't recall anything major happening at that time. Some of these predictions of gloom and doom are also the result of fear mongering on the part of certain ones down here who either claim false connections to "Higher Sources," or else impinge upon the minds of psychics to do it for them.

Serapis then interrupted with a message for me concerning my writing. His advice:

> Lighten up on the teachings and don't be boring like Maris can be; add in a bit about the Human Ladder, and good luck with it all.

God love him.

By midnight everyone had left to get on with other work, but Helene could see a light flashing through the kitchen skylight. She was tempted to go outside to see if it was a disc, but she decided she was just too tired. After all, who really cares about "lights in the sky" when you have them visiting your home on such a regular basis!

February 24, 2003.

Ben had a trance while Helene was out retrieving Kira from her baby-sitting job. Gary had to deal with it on his own. The next morning Ben couldn't recall any of it.

The day before, Ben had been tired in the morning and he hadn't wanted to go to school. Helene had the feeling he'd been "upstairs" working, and she asked Kira, who said that she thought he worked with animals and other creatures, but she wasn't sure, because they go on different ships.

Maybe he's being trained in a number of jobs, because she once asked Oris about Ben's trances and was told that "upstairs" he sometimes does work helping lost or trapped souls to move on to where they're supposed to be. As Oris explained, some people who are very scared of the idea of dying get stuck in this way, and help must be provided to free them.

If this is the case, it's no wonder that Ben's human child's mind goes through so much fear, because this type of work is not pleasant. Some of these souls are trapped in horrible places. Around the time Oris told this to Kira, I'd been having recall of doing this work alongside someone who was "in training." There was a worry in my mind about taking them with me and exposing them to a situation that was going to be unpleasant. After hearing what Kira had found out about Ben, I wondered if it was he.

Helene once asked Oris about the so-called animal mutilations supposedly carried out by ETs. She'd seen a program on TV about this, and she wanted to know. Oris knew absolutely nothing about such things being done on their part.

> Yes, we do take animals on board for monitoring and testing purposes, but they are always released alive and unharmed back to where we picked them up.

More and more evidence is now coming to light that the killing and mutilation of animals is being carried out by humans right here on Earth. They try to make it look like the work of ETs to cause maximum fear and panic. The so-called Men in Black are a similar phenomenon. All I can say is that in my *many* years of association with the Zetas, I've *never ever* seen any animals killed or injured. Unlike most Earth humans, the Zetas are totally vegetarian, so they don't even kill animals for food.

Since opening up to my own link with the Zetas, I've become extremely sensitive to cruelty in any form. I can barely stand to watch the news broadcast on TV with its graphic depictions of cruelty and violence; and to see an animal hurt or badly treated affects me to my core and disgusts me beyond words. Humans at their best can be almost angelic and a very beautiful race of beings, but at their worst they are worse than beastly. No wonder the Zetas find them one of the hardest life-forms in the universe to work with! This, by the way, is what the "devil's number" of 666 means, that is referred to in Revelations. It is indeed the "mark of the beast," which is a numerical representation of those humans who have hardly evolved past the Animal Kingdom.

26

Star Children

It was a Sunday afternoon, and Helene was tired and a bit down. With so much going on in their home, between "downstairs" family matters and "upstairs" family matters (or Grey matters as we jokingly refer to such things), I sometimes wondered how she coped with it all. She was trying to recall all that had happened over the past week or so, but couldn't think because of sheer tiredness, and she was feeling sorry for herself and a bit depressed.

Oris must have been around and picked up on her mood because the next moment he turned up in the office where Kira was working on the computer. He told her to go into her mom and read her three poems that had been posted on the net. "Oh, what a lovely gesture!" thought Helene when they came in to her with their offer, and settled herself down in a comfortable chair to listen, anticipating something pleasant and spiritually uplifting, perhaps with a message of encouragement to help her through.

Instead, the poems were *really* depressing, one of a little boy abused by his mother, the second about a lover who never returned from the war, and the third about a girl losing her young brother in a car accident. "How *delightful*!" said Helene when Kira and Oris had finished reading them out to her. "Do you want me to slit my throat right here and now? Maybe you could both give me a hand!"

Kira of course placed full responsibility on Oris, protesting that *he* was the one who *found* the poems on the net, so Helene turned on him with: "Oris, what *are* you anyway — some sort of twisted, demented alien?"

"Well — no," he stammered, (now it was his turn for embarrassed back-pedaling). "I was just trying to help you to see how good your life really is — you know — trying to make you feel *better*!"

H: Needless to say, this got us all laughing! I do remember the pressure I was under at the time, and feeling like I was being watched all the time. By this stage I was getting used to Oris, and on that day with his little poems he really reminded me of an annoying brother in a cute, "family" sort of way. I vividly remember sitting there attempting to write down some notes on the latest happenings, but I just couldn't get going. I had a brain freeze. That was when Oris turned up and told Kira to give me these three horribly depressing poems.

I mean to say, how weird giving them to me, but you know what — they worked! It made me realize what a great life I have compared to some others, and what have I really got to worry about! The psychology he used was very clever indeed, and it was great to have some fun with each other, but typical of Oris, there was a meaning behind it as well. Talk about multi-layers! Once the pair of them went out of the room and left me in peace the light turned back on in my head and I started writing.

J: One night Helene went to Kira's bedroom to say good night, and while she was standing in the doorway she felt a burst of energy. It was a strong shivering sensation as when "somebody walks over your grave," as the saying goes. She asked Kira who was there, and it turned out to be a little worker. This is what triggers the sensation of a sudden shiver. It's just somebody from another dimension passing through and touching your energy field. After all, every dimension is right here and now, but with our limited third-dimensional conscious awareness we usually can't perceive them.

On the subject of workers, according to Kira she and I, along with a third worker (living out a human life in America) were doing a lot of healing work on children. She could recall us working on a young girl aged about 10 or 11, rather solidly built and with long black hair. She was very frightened at first, so we sat on the floor to make it less intimidating for her. We talked to her and tried to explain that we were not there to harm but rather to heal, and placed our hands on her to allow her to experience feeling the energy.

On another occasion we visited a young boy who was absolutely terrified and began screaming when we appeared in his room. The next thing his father came running in. He too could see "those terrible Greys," so picked his son up with one hand and started swinging a baseball bat around with the other (must've been in the USA), all the while yelling and swearing at us, and vowing that we were "not going to get them." It was so sad. We apparently make it our practice to allow people to see us leave so they won't be lying awake scared and nervous for the rest of the night wondering where we're hiding.

Most children born now have a higher percentage of ET genetics in their makeup. This is necessary, as the human species as it was has gone way out of balance and is wrecking the planet. Hopefully a higher infusion of ET genetics will introduce deeper sensitivity and a respect for the environment, and also for the other creatures that have to share our world.

March 8, 2003.

Helene lay down to give herself a Reiki treatment. She hadn't been feeling well for several days, with pleurisy-like pains in her chest. She had a rare opportunity to relax completely, because for once the rest of the family was occupied elsewhere.

She placed her hands in the peace sign position on her sacral chakra and began sending Reiki to herself. Suddenly she became aware of moving out of her body but remaining fully conscious. She felt one of the Zetas working on her chest area, and then a sharp sensation of highly concentrated energy passed into the base chakra. After that, somebody was working on her crown chakra. She knew exactly what was going on and was strongly aware of the family presence, thoroughly enjoying the energies and the sensations, and eventually returning to her body with a big gasp of breath.

She was tingling all over and still paralyzed from head to toe, as happens when work is being done on the etheric or astral levels, so she just lay quietly to allow everything to settle back into place. Luckily I'd described the sensation to her previously, so she wasn't scared at all. Finally, still feeling stiff and a bit out of it she was able to move, and was astonished to find an hour and a half had passed. Her chest was now feeling much better, thanks to some concentrated Zeta healing.

Gary was away overnight working, so Helene was home alone with the two children when Ben had one of his trances. He started walking around the house very quickly, and then went to curl up in a ball on his bed, looking so scared. Next he tried to go out the front door, but Kira managed to talk him into lying down again, explaining that things would stop if he could just lie down and relax.

He complained of a huge amount of pressure on his body, and that he was really scared. They asked him what he could see, and he tried to describe something that looked like a string with a ball on each end. Helene said later that she got the impression that it was in the shape of the letter Y, and that the two balls were on the top parts, but she wasn't sure.

At one point he got up, ran into the bathroom *en suite* and crouched under the wash basin, still complaining about the pressure on his body. Kira figured out that his astral body was on the disc, and that he'd somehow found his way into the "engine room," (to use Kira's term for the area that is the power center on the big disc). She remarked that the energies there are very strong — hence the weight and pressure he could feel. This is quite correct, as I know from the experience of feeling powerful energy. It seemed that he was scared because he wasn't supposed to be there, but had been wandering around investigating, and was now worried that he'd get into trouble.

According to Kira, he was trying to get out the front door because the disc was about to land, and the physical part of him was trying to link up with the spirit (astral) part that was preparing to exit the disc to return home. In other words, he was trying to "get himself together," literally. I too used to do this as a child — sleepwalking in search of something — and when questioned, I answered, "I can't *find* the darned thing!"

Once they managed to get him lying down again, the spirit was able to re-enter more easily, and he settled down straight away and fell asleep. This happened again a few weeks later when he made another attempt to escape outside to join his astral self. Often when these trance episodes occurred, he'd experience fear of both his mother and sister, as if he didn't recognize them.

Late December 2003.

Ben had another trance and was again trying to get outside to join his astral self. He seemed very "busy," and on a "mission" of some sort.

January 1, 2004.

Another escape attempt, and Helene tried asking him where he was. He answered: "Door."

Not hearing him properly, she asked: "Did you say 'store'?"

He corrected her by saying: "Entrance," which was a word he would never use normally.

Helene then asked: "Is it the entrance to the ship?"

"Yes!" came his reply. He was shaking all over and seemed really scared, so Helene suggested they hold hands and go through the door together. She then asked whom he could see, and he replied:

"Just you, Mom." She told him to try to feel the energies — did they feel loving? He answered yes. Like his mom, Ben is very sensitive to the energies around people and places. He then fell asleep.

October 1, 2004.

Ben started running around the house again, and it was becoming a real worry. He was a big, strong boy for 11, and Helene sometimes had to physically restrain him from going out through the front door. It was okay if Gary was there, but he was often away from home with his work, leaving Helene to manage the potentially dangerous situation on her own. It was definitely time for "upstairs" to intervene. As it turned out, they were becoming increasingly worried and frustrated as well.

Helene and Kira both tried to help him, and it turned out he could see someone standing in the doorway to his bedroom, which was what had frightened him. Kira confirmed that it was a female Zeta Teacher by the name of Anabis, and she was dressed in the usual long black nun-like garment and with a hood pulled forward to cover her face.

Ben was partly aware of who she was, and tried to communicate, but couldn't hear her. This is a problem so many people experience with the Zetas, and it applies both ways — they often can't hear us either. Kira could see that Anabis was having a communication problem and, not sure of how to get around it, was looking very stressed and upset.

Helene suggested to Ben that he put his hand out to let Anabis touch him so he could feel her. This he proceeded to do, and described the sensation as "warm and tingly." Helene looked to Kira for confirmation and she nodded, indicating that yes, Anabis was touching him as he could feel. Ben suddenly became very drowsy, came out of the trance and went back to sleep almost instantaneously.

H: I'd become very concerned handling Ben's trances, especially since he'd been trying to get out the front door. He was so strong and tall for his age, and when he was in trance and seemingly "on a mission" it was becoming extremely hard to stop him. During that period I used to sleep very lightly as I was worried that he would escape outside.

I don't know what made me think of getting him to touch Anabis. The idea just dropped into my mind out of nowhere, but I somehow knew he had to feel her energies. In his waking state Ben is so sensitive to other peoples' energies, and for him to consciously link in to her on this level made it more real for him, and also more connected, especially with having my understanding and support as well. This in turn gave him the confidence to move forward in trust and faith.

J: Once he was settled, Helene was able to discuss the situation with Kira, who explained that Ben's Teacher, Anabis, had arrived with Oris to take both of them to the disc. It was while Oris was assisting Kira out of her body that Ben suddenly cried out in terror. Oris called out to Anabis, asking her what was going on, and she was really upset and not sure what to do. It was at that point that Helene and Kira both went in to Ben, leaving Oris waiting out in the hallway.

The next morning Helene asked Ben if he remembered anything of the night before, and he did. In fact he even recalled touching Anabis's hand. Helene asked him what it had felt like, and his answer was: "All tingly and 'gooey' — like you Mom." In his 11-year-old way he was trying to describe the soft, gentle, loving maternal energy felt in the presence of a mother figure. By "gooey" he meant it made him feel warm, safe and happy inside.

He went on to tell his mom that he kept having the same dream in which he had to count to one hundred before he reached the edge of a cliff. Someone then tried to push him off, and sometimes they succeeded. When this happened he would land on a big bed of nails, which pierced his body, hurting him.

Helene explained to him about love and fear, and to have faith that in a dream you can do anything you want, even fly. She told him that it was important for him to trust in himself and that the magical key is to know and have faith that love always wins out over fear. She suggested to him that the next time he has the dream and is scared of being pushed over the cliff, to try to fly like Peter Pan. (They'd recently watched the movie). Ben really liked this idea, and promised to try it the next time the dream occurred.

Not long after connecting with Anabis, Ben wrote a lovely little story titled "Touched by an Angel," describing in his own words how it felt. It is not included here as it's special and private to him, but the last line says: "So if you ever have a bad dream like that, try to feel your angel's energies."

Once this conscious contact was made, Ben's trances stopped completely. It was as if an inner connection was finally established.

It didn't mean that his life was perfect from then on. Ben is most definitely a Star Child if ever there was one, and this in itself causes some difficulties for him, but he really is a very special soul with an incredible depth of sensitivity, love and insight way beyond his years.

Here are two good examples of his inner knowing which occurred around this time. On one occasion Helene was having a hard time with somebody close to her who was a very difficult person to deal with. She had reached a point where she felt she just couldn't take any more. Ben sensed there was something wrong and asked her. "Come on Mom," he said, "you need to talk about it. It's okay to talk to me. I want to know." As Helene told him, she burst into tears. Ben sat quietly listening to her, gave her a hug, and in a firm but gentle voice said: "I *know* she is very hard to deal with Mom, but you just have to *dig deeper*. I know you can do it. It will all work out!" Remember, this was from an 11-year-old child.

On another occasion Helene was giving Ben a Reiki treatment and they were having a quiet chat about life. Helene started explaining to him that if we find that something in life is particularly easy for us to learn or to do, chances are that we have learned or done it all before in a past life. She asked him if he understood what she was saying. He replied: "Oh yes, Mom. You mean it's *soul knowledge*!"

A few weeks after establishing conscious contact with Anabis, Ben complained of feeling "homesick," but couldn't understand why because he was at home. Helene asked if anything was worrying or upsetting him and his answer was: "No Mom, nothing is upsetting me here. All I can say is that I feel homesick, which doesn't make sense because I am at home." Helene gave him a cuddle and he settled down to sleep. This happened three nights in a row.

A little mother and son talk a day or so later revealed that he wasn't happy at school. Ben has an auditory processing problem, and the teacher he had at the time was not an understanding type. She was inclined to yelling and impatience, which was the last thing poor Ben needed. He also hated the way many of the other children at school had a habit of swearing. He just can't stand being around angry, aggressive or noisy people. This is very typical of Star Children.

Helene asked him to write a list of all his fears, and what he felt people didn't understand about him. The fears he listed were: spiders, the dark, and the really scary dreams he had. He also wrote: "People don't understand me. I have hearing problems, and I'm not like any other person in this world. They don't know what I can't do (here he means that people don't understand his difficulty with auditory processing). No one knows who I am properly — not even my mom or dad or anyone. I can't really explain in words — to know me you would have to live with me for like fifty years or more, but it's very hard to understand who I am. I don't think I'm like any average person. I am different."

After he'd finished the list Helene discussed it with him, asking him how he felt about feeling different. Was it good, bad or what? His answer was that he felt good, and would be helping people later. Helene then suggested that maybe he just needed to learn to understand others more now, so that he could help them in the future. She gave him a cuddle and assured him that she was there for him whenever he wanted to talk. She asked him if he'd had any more bad dreams and he said no, not since touching Anabis's hand.

Several researchers of ET/human contact have specialized in "Star Children," a generation of children being born on Earth since the 1980s who carry a higher percentage of ET genetics in their makeup. "Star Seeds" are adults born during the "baby boomer" years after WWII who also carry a higher percentage of ET genetics. These souls came here ahead of time to prepare the way and to be parents and mentors for the Star Children to come.

The criteria that are usually cited for parents to look out for in order to recognize a potential Star Child are strong psychic/clairvoyant abilities and very high IQ. The problem here is that if these are the only factors used as a benchmark, then many Star Children are going to fall through the net, which is a real worry. Some may certainly display these tendencies, but definitely not all.

Star Children are different, but often seemingly in the other direction, appearing not quite as smart as normal because of problems like Ben's inadequate auditory processing. I totally understand this, having difficulties myself, both in hearing and also in oral communication, most especially when operating in "Zeta mode." Perhaps this is a problem more common with us, because when Zetas communicate it's generally not through words but rather through very profound telepathically communicated imagery. The old saying of "a picture paints a thousand words" is very apt in Zeta communication, because trying to translate this imagery into the spoken word is, for me, one of the hardest and most frustrating tasks imaginable, which is why I much prefer to communicate the Zeta teachings through the *written* word, which allows me the time and space to process the content of the imagery more fully and to go back and add to it as it filters through the workings of my limited human brain.

If I try to speak it out directly in real time, much gets lost in translation, making it extremely tiring and frustrating. Often I can't express the appropriate words or phrases immediately, and my mind goes blank with overload. I have trouble trying to mesh the two realities that I experience simultaneously. If I link totally into Zeta reality, I can't express what needs to be said in human speech, but if I link too much into Earth human reality, I lose the gist of what is being conveyed. Sometimes my head feels as if it's going to explode, which would not be pretty!

I can fully understand where Ben is coming from in his difficulties with school. The school recess was refined torture, as far as I was concerned, and hiding in the toilet or escaping back into the classroom was an excellent option. The noise and mayhem used to make me physically ill, and I just couldn't cope with bad-tempered, impatient teachers. "Upstairs" it's all so *very* different. Up there I am "in tune." Down here I am not.

Thinking back on it, hardly a week went by that I didn't stay away from school at least a day and preferably more. How I ever managed to still pass all the exams and even get reasonable grades was nothing short of a miracle. I must have more "Star Seed" brains than I give myself credit for!

27
FREE WILL

January 17, 2004.
Helene had a clearly remembered out-of-body experience. Visitors were due to arrive late in the afternoon and she had a bad headache, so she decided to lie down after lunch to give herself a Reiki treatment.

The experience began with the momentary appearance of a male face, and then she felt the presence of one of the Zeta family, along with the sensation of a needle being inserted into her navel. "I don't mind what you're doing guys," she told whoever it was, "but it *is* hurting!" (We tell them if something they're doing is painful, and they always stop. It's simply that they don't realize how sensitive human bodies are to pain). This sensation seemed to last for about thirty seconds before moving upwards to the heart chakra. When this happened the pain eased. Her spirit self then left the body through the crown chakra.

There was absolutely no fear involved whatsoever, despite a sensation of great speed. She was then instructed to lean forward at a forty-five degree angle. She felt perfectly safe and was happy to do this, trusting her companion totally. As she moved into the required position, someone behind her took hold of her hands, which were placed close to her body near hip level and towards the back. Then they took off at great speed. She tried to open her eyes but couldn't.

The next moment she found herself walking through a room where lots of babies were floating around, seemingly suspended in mid-air. The umbilical cords were still attached, and they were all wearing different, brightly colored diapers. Afterwards she could recall seeing one in red and another in yellow. This reminded her of the different chakra colors. The sight of these babies made her feel emotional and excited.

The scene then changed and she found herself in a room with some people. There was one woman standing to her left, quite a few feet away and just looking, who then moved away. To her right she saw a man and a woman standing hand in hand, and near them was a beautiful young woman in her late teens or early twenties, with olive skin and long, black, straight hair. The older woman who was holding the man's hand moved away from him and walked past where Helene was standing, giving her a nasty look. She seemed to be in her fifties, with dark, frizzy, shoulder-length hair and not particularly attractive.

The next moment she found herself face to face with the man, who appeared to know her very well. She felt embarrassed and sorry because she couldn't remember who he was, although he did remind her of her deceased uncle. He spoke to her, saying: "I miss our larrikin* songs," and gave her a hug. The feeling was of total love, respect, friendship and closeness. The next words he spoke were something to the effect of: "Everything went wrong because someone died and we couldn't be together." Helene then started to walk away, but turned around to look back and saw him move off with the older woman (who'd given her a nasty look).

She then became aware of the feeling of holding onto a hand, and she realized that it belonged to the one who was taking her on the "tour." It felt like a male hand, and it was slippery, soft and warm. She was surprised by that, expecting it to be cold (but then that's how Zeta hands are — quite warm and human-feeling in a way, unless the Zeta is making use of an artificial body).

They flew over a city, holding hands and positioned as they had been before, with her in front leaning forward and her "guide" behind. The sensation of flying was quite amazing, and it was so beautiful. All the buildings were rounded on top, with round windows and arched doorways, and they were all different sizes and of a brown color. There was such a sense of beauty, wonder and awe, and it felt very familiar — like home. She sent a message of heartfelt thanks to her companion for taking her there to see it all.

The next moment found them heading straight for a river near the city. She wondered if they were going to dive straight in, and thought to herself: "How cool! Maybe he's going to show me some nice sea creatures;" but instead she found herself back in the bedroom, returned safely to her physical body. It was quite some time before she could move or open her eyes, and nearly two hours had passed. She felt relaxed and happy, and the headache was completely gone.

---

*Australian slang word meaning cheeky and fun loving.

H: What an amazing experience, and I felt so safe the whole time. Time also ran completely differently. It was as if the "tour" lasted for hours and hours when in actual fact it only went on for one hour and forty minutes. When I arrived back in my room I didn't want to return to my body straight away. I really wanted to keep flying and floating around. It was such a euphoric sensation and just incredible to feel so safe, at peace and without a care in the world. If dying is like this, it must be the most amazing, freeing and uplifting experience!

February 23, 2004.

While I was giving Helene a Reiki treatment she had a vision of being in a smallish disc. It was round in shape, with the controls set in a central console, which was constructed around a sort of "sky-light" in the floor. Six people were sitting in a circle, each with their hands on the controls and able to see out through the opening in the center.

She asked Kira about it that evening and she confirmed it as correct, and then went on to describe another type of disc that has been developed only recently. It looks like glass and can be safely landed in broad daylight and yet not be seen. Even when you're inside it seems not to have any walls, because they're completely see-through. Sounds a bit unnerving!

Kira then went on to tell her mom about a boy she'd met "upstairs" who came from a sort of parallel world. She described him as being about seven feet tall, with dark skin. His hair was rather curly, and brown in color. His fingers were longer than ours, and his eyes were larger than ours, but not as large as Zeta eyes. He attends school and lives a life very similar to ours, and they're right into studying astronomy. She was told that their "teenage fashion" is to have their hair dyed all one color, as opposed to the streaks that Earth teenagers go for. The feeling was that they live very much like we do, only their world is a lot kinder, and more peaceful and loving.

This boy Kira met seems to me to be a cross between Earth human and Zeta, maybe a product of the genetic program being carried out by the Zetas. I rather suspect that she was being shown a glimpse of Planet Earth in the future, and maybe the boy was a future life of her own.

After three years of very full-on contact Kira's conscious experiences gradually stopped. She was still aware of Oris being around, but his influence became much less. She was 15 and needed to start putting more thought and energy into getting on with learning and experiencing life on the physical human level, so Oris backed off as he'd tried to do earlier on, but this time he withdrew slowly and gradually so as not to upset her. Funnily enough, I was fifteen when contact became stronger and more conscious, so in a way hers ended when mine began, only a generation apart.

Kira is now busy working through her own very normal human/soul issues and lessons, and is very grateful for the teaching and knowledge she has received from Oris. For the time being she feels she needs to follow her own path, and experience what it's like to move through from being a teenager to a young woman. This is her free-will choice, which we all, including Oris, respect and understand entirely. He will always have a special place in her heart, and will be there quietly in the background to guide her whenever she needs him.

Free will is a very important aspect of ET/human contact that needs to be clearly understood. *The genuine ET Visitors — and this includes the Greys, Zetas or whatever you choose to call the Visitors — never force themselves onto unwilling humans. If you ask them to back off, they will. In cases where this respect is not shown, the "contact" is coming from down here and is not genuine, no matter how "alien" it appears.* (See Chapter 16.)

The conscious contact Kira experienced between the years 2001 and 2004 was highly successful in that it achieved the 3 objectives that it was supposed to. Firstly, it brought me back online with the Zeta family and restored my belief in myself. Secondly, it brought Helene online and linked us back together on a conscious level in order to get on with work that we've carried out through many past lives. Thirdly, it initiated Zeta/human communication through the writing of this book, which continues to grow stronger and clearer with ongoing help and encouragement being provided by our beloved Grey family.

The descriptions given of those three years of conscious and almost nightly contact really don't tell the whole story. In addition, a multitude of quite complex and very personal past life issues came bubbling up to the surface, needing to be dealt with and released. Accompanying all of this was a deepening realization of the work both Helene and I have been carrying out on other levels past and present. Part of the Zetas' work down here is to help us heal our past by bringing it up to the surface of our consciousness. This process is not always pleasant, but it is *most* important if we wish to progress spiritually, because our past creates our future. This has been made very clear to us.

We still have our ups and downs of course, living as we are down here as Earth humans with all the responsibilities of family, home and work to keep us busy and well-grounded, but we are both profoundly aware of the Zeta family close by to give us a boost and a helping hand when needed.

H: Through everything we have experienced as a family, we are all still close and have a very strong bond. All that we went through between the years 2001 to 2004 served to open up our minds and our hearts, and we are eternally grateful for this. What I love most about the Zetas is how important family is to them. Their love has no bounds, and they are so patient, understanding and forgiving. I feel both honored and blessed to have this extended family in our lives.

J: The ending of Kira's conscious experiences did not mean the end of our contacts. Mine are still ongoing, as are Helene's and Ben's. Following are some more recent excerpts from Helene's notes, as well as an experience of mine and another shared with Helene and a friend. I've also included some teachings from the Zeta family.

January 5, 2005.

H: Ben was sick with the flu, and by evening he had a temperature, a headache and a sore ear. He went to bed at 7:00 p.m. At 8 he called out "Mom!" and it sounded quieter than normal. I ran into his room and he called out to me again. He didn't realize I was there — he was still asleep. Then he woke and asked me why I was still up. I explained to him that it was only 8 p.m.

He was very hot, and Gary suggested he have a shower to bring his temperature down, which he did. As I was putting him back to bed he said: "Mom, I can't get to sleep. I can see these very small boxes, and I have to count the gaps between them. I can't do it — it's too hard and it makes me feel giddy." I told him to just roll over and try to get some sleep.

About ten minutes later he called out again, so I came and sat on the bed next to him and he started to cry. He was feeling so miserable with the flu. Again he complained of seeing the boxes, and I thought and thought, trying to work out what these boxes were all about. "What do you have to do with the boxes?" I asked him. His answer was that a voice in his head was telling him to make them bigger, but he couldn't. I suggested he just try to really concentrate and have a go. "I can't do it. I'm scared!" he replied.

"Why are you scared of the boxes?" I asked.

His answer: "Their energies feel awful. My head gets giddy."

I then suggested he try again, but said to him: "Remember this time you have the power. Remember that dream you kept having about falling off a cliff onto those big nails, and I said to you that in dreams you can be whoever you want to be. You can even be like Peter Pan, and fly." He nodded. "Well," I went on, "I want you to know that you have the power at all times, and I know you can make the boxes bigger. I'll be right here with you. Just give it another go and really concentrate, and know that you have the power to do it. Who knows what will happen! Maybe it could even be fun!"

"Okay;" he replied rather reluctantly, "I'll try."

At first his eyes were slightly open, and he moved his hand upwards to point at them. He then lowered his hand and closed his eyes, and I could see he was really concentrating. I asked if he could see the boxes, and he answered yes, so I then asked him what they looked like and what color they were.

His answer: "They look like little TVs, and they're all blue." Then "Mom, I am making them bigger!"

"Good boy:" I replied, "I knew you could do it! What's happening now?"

"I can see through them."

"What can you see?"

"My room," he answered, then "Now they've all disappeared."

"Well done," I said, "now maybe you can get to sleep." I gave him a hug and left the room.

Ten minutes later he called out again: "Mom, the boxes are back. It's like looking into a TV!"

"Okay," I said, wracking my brains on what to say next. "Have they told you what they want you to do with these boxes this time?"

"No, I don't know. They're everywhere in the room!"

"Okay then, what if you try to turn them into flowers, or teddies or gold fish — something that you like."

"No, *I can't do that Mom!"*

"Hmmm, okay then, how about you try to walk inside one and see what's in there. And don't worry — you'll be safe. I am here!"

"No, I'm just me. I can't walk into them."

"Okay, what I mean is, you are magical and you can walk in there. You might be able to see ahead what's there. Maybe there's a magic garden, or something special. Just try! This could be a great adventure for you. And remember, I'm here with you, all the way." His eyes closed and he started to concentrate.

"Where are you now, Ben?"

"I'm in a dark room and I feel scared."

"Why are you scared?"

"There are bad spirits here. I can see them in my mind."

"Okay, now do you remember what I told you before?"

"Yes Mom — Love conquers all!"

"Yes, that's right! Love is your power — you are stronger than them. They can't hurt you! They like fear — that's what they feed off, but when they see that you are full of love they will go. They know they can't hurt you because you are stronger than them. What can you see now?"

"A bad spirit in front of me."

"Maybe he needs a hug. What do you think?"

"I don't know."

"Do you think you could give him a hug? He's probably not a bad spirit, just a sad spirit, and your love might be good for him. Do you want to give it a try?"

"Yeah, okay."

"Now remember, Ben, your love is your power, and you have a lot *of trust and faith in yourself. I* know *that you can do this. Are you ready to give it a try?"*

"Yes!"

"What's he doing now?"

"He's trying to run away from me. He's running around like this." Ben held his hands up to his sides with arms bent and loose wrists. I don't know why, but I thought of how a penguin runs.

"Now he's turning around and coming towards me."

"Give him a hug now Ben. Remember you are full of love and power. What's happening now?"

"He hugged back."

"Where are you now Ben?"

"Back in my room Mom. It's all gone."

"Oh I am so *proud of you! You did* so *well! I* knew *you could do it — well done! Now it's time for sleep, hey! Good night my little man."*

> *"I love you Mom. I* really *mean it!"*
> *"Good night darling."*
> *Ten minutes later: "Mommm!"*
> *"Yes darling?"*
> *"My energies feel yucky and I can't get to sleep."*
> *"How about I give you an aura cleanse?"*
> *"Oh yes, please." And so finally we all got some sleep.*

The night before, Ben had complained of a sore throat, and I had been writing some notes up on my feelings from a mother's point of view when our first contact experiences began, and Judy had a dream about Maris trying to pull a baby chick out of her throat.

J: Discussing this episode afterwards, we came to the conclusion that the "little boxes" that looked like TV sets symbolize the way our human minds are so limited and compartmentalized, with everything separate, divided and closed off in its own little box. We often find it hard to see the bigger picture, particularly if it involves looking at something from another person's point of view. In fact many people find this extremely confronting. The ETs on the other hand take more of an overview, and in this way are able to tap in to a truer perception of reality, and what is really going on.

The fear Ben experienced stems from the fact that it is fear that causes us to tie everything up in neat little boxes, because in order to see the bigger picture of any given situation, we need to look more deeply within our own self, which requires a giant leap of faith and trust. Many people simply cannot do this. It's too confronting, and causes them to feel as if they're spinning out of control.

It was the act of focusing on the spaces between the boxes that caused Ben to feel scared and giddy. He was being asked to focus upon this hidden aspect of his psyche, because it is this very thing, these "spaces between the boxes" that represents the almost unconscious state of mind in which we, as humans, operate. Having to focus on this brought about a sense of unease and off-centeredness.

For Ben, as for all Star Children, this act of having to look at the bigger picture in a more unified, less fragmented way, and being made to confront any issues connected to it, is a major part of accepting and melding into the ET aspect of their psyche. For some Earth humans this can be almost impossible, but it is something the Star Children must learn to cope with. Some find it easier than others, but it's all about starting to tap into another tenth of their potential conscious awareness. This is "the whole new world, if we can take it" that Col. Philip Corso's ET contact referred to.

What parents need to be aware of is that it's not only your child's journey but also your own as well. It's learning to "tune in" and ask the appropriate questions in order to guide the child past their fear and out the other side into empowerment and love. Getting scared or angry with "those terrible aliens," or else pushing it all away as being "just too hard," or "nothing more than my child's over-active imagination" will not solve anything, and can potentially be very damaging for your child as well as for you.

The "bad spirit" was Ben's own inner fear being externalized. The way he described how it ran from him, arms close to its sides and waddling like a penguin rather than running freely is symbolic of how the fear was "tying him up" in his progress and blocking his freedom of movement on the soul level. It was also symbolic of the fear wanting to be healed, and so only making a token attempt to escape. The love was beginning to over-ride the fear, and that is *exactly* what it is all about. It is the ultimate triumph of love and trust over fear, which in the end will bring about a state of Oneness and wholeness. All the Zeta tests are directed towards this end

Helene emailed a description of Ben's trance, the way she handled it and the conclusions we arrived at regarding it to the psychologist Dr. Janet Colli, an associate of the late Dr. John Mack. Helene and I had been in contact with Dr. Colli previously, to congratulate and thank her for her wonderful book *Sacred Encounters*, which deals with the ET contact experience from the consciousness angle. This scholarly and beautifully written book confirmed everything we ourselves had come to understand from our own encounter experiences — that ET contact is all about expansion of consciousness and evolution of humanity.

Dr. Colli put the time aside to email back, congratulating Helene on the way she handled the situation, which gave a huge and much-needed boost to her confidence, and also agreed entirely with our interpretation of the meanings behind the trance. Coming from such a respected mental health professional this meant a great deal to both of us.

April 2007.

H: I'd been thinking a lot about Ben during the last few weeks, and wondered if I'd done everything I could for him. Have I explained enough to him? Will he be okay in the future? Will he come out of all this sane and happy? Is there anything else I should be doing? I sent a prayer out to ask for guidance. That night I had a "dream," but it was so real, and took place in our house just as it is in waking reality.

Ben came into my room (in the dream) to tell me that two people were in his room. We both went in and these two people were standing on his bed holding a sheet up in front of them covering their faces. They then lowered the sheet and one of them put his hand out to greet me. I asked why they were here, and the answer given was: "Just to tell you to keep on doing what you are doing with Ben. You and Gary are doing a good job with him." It was so *real, and afterwards I felt much more assured and confident.*

Mid-April 2007.

As I was falling asleep I heard the sound of three knocks in my bedroom. I was so excited! I've read about people hearing these in connection with the Zetas, but have never experienced them myself. I was so excited in fact that I started singing the song "Knock three times on the ceiling if you want me," and gave myself the giggles. Boy I've come a long way! I felt totally safe and happy, and looked forward to whatever was going to happen next. It took me a while to get to sleep, but once I did, found myself walking through a children's ward. Everyone was saying hello to me, as if they knew me very well. There were many cots there, and the children looked to be about six to twelve months old. I clearly remember saying: "It's so *good to be back here!"*

J: Helene's job up on the disc is caring for the little hybrid babies. She epitomizes the term mother, so if any of you reading this are consciously aware of being the parent of one of these little ones in the care of the Zetas, have no fear. They are loved, cherished and cared for completely.

H: Ben had a dream that I died. On the same night the young daughter of a friend of mine dreamed that I was pregnant. Also on the same night I had a dream that I was a doctor in a hospital and that I healed a girl child. In my dream Gary arrived to join in a celebration that the child was healed, and watched me hand her back to her relieved and happy parents.

April 30, 2007.

I wasn't feeling well, with a bad pain in my neck and shoulder and dizziness. In the morning I went to have some acupuncture done, and was told my neck might need adjusting. This worried me, as I hate the thought of such things. When I arrived home I decided to give myself a Reiki treatment. As I began, coldness spread over my whole body, and I went into a very relaxed altered state.

Next minute one of the Zetas was there manipulating my neck and moving my head from side to side, then quickly jerked my head and I felt a click, click sound in the upper part of my neck at the base of the skull, where it had been sore. As I woke up I heard a bird chirp three times, and knew it was a sign from them. My neck was healed. Thanks guys! I'd rather have them do it any time — they're so efficient and focused.

September 30, 2007.

Ben had a "dream" in which he was standing at the back of his classroom at school. He had two friends standing either side of him that he knew very well, but not in his waking life. They were taking children from the room and putting them into carts to be taken underground down a tunnel for protection. Ben and his two friends suddenly had to escape as "bad" people were chasing after them. A car turned up and the three of them climbed in. The "door" of this car opened up in the middle section, and there were two seats in the back on either side, leaving them plenty of room to stretch out, and one driver's seat in the middle at the front. There was no steering wheel. One of Ben's friends gave a telepathic order to go, *and the car moved off. They got away safely.* (J: This is a very good description of the "mini-discs" that the Zetas use.)

October 1, 2007.

Ben dreamed that he was in a cave and there was an underground tunnel. He was walking in front and children were following behind him in a line. He would think something in his mind, for example rain, *and it would rain, or* wind, *and a wind would start blowing. If any of the children became frightened, they would have to go back to the beginning and start again. The rest followed Ben right to the end.*

(Wow, is this Star Kid stuff or what! And speak about the baddies trying to stop our progress with these special kids gosh!)

March, 2008.

Ben had a dream of walking into houses and bars in America and Europe to compare people and their energies.

J: One morning a year or so ago while driving to work, I started thinking about things and feeling a bit sorry for myself, caught as I am between two worlds. It was just one of those days occasionally experienced when I don't quite know where I fit in to all of this. There I was sitting in my car at the traffic lights, just one of many other perfectly normal humans on their way to work in the morning, but with a head-full of Zeta business, and a class of Tai Chi students waiting for me. I thought of how this whole situation has been the direct result of the very open, fully conscious and clearly remembered Zeta intervention that pushed me into taking up Tai Chi in the first place — the encounter experience of 1983.

As I sat there waiting for the lights to change, thinking about that encounter which had changed my whole life so profoundly, my mind went back over the past few years, then all the way back to my childhood. Other strange happenings came to mind, and also the ongoing problems I'd had of simply trying to fit in, and how hard it's been at times. Then I thought of how this deep connection with the Zetas even went back to past lives — so what the hell am I? At times I feel totally Zeta, at other times very Earth human, so where do I fit in and *what am I — really*? This was the question that was foremost in my mind and bringing tears to my eyes as the lights changed and I turned onto the main road.

Driving along in the outside lane and still trying to figure out where I really stand in all of this, a strange sound began filtering into my consciousness. The next moment one of the oddest little cars I've ever seen passed me in the inside lane. It was round and squat, almost looking like a wind-up toy, and for some reason my attention was drawn to the number plate. It was one of those fancy personalized ones that are available, and my eyes almost fell out of my head and into my lap as I read it — *Zeta*. My first reaction was to go cold all over, and then I burst out laughing. "Okay, fair enough guys!" I said to myself and to whomever else was in the car with me. "You win — I'll go along with that!"

January 13, 2008.

Our local UFO research association conducts night Watches on a fairly regular basis, which involves a group of members travelling to a quiet location away from the city to see if they can spot any UFO activity. We've never attended one of these, but on this date Helene and I, along with a member of our own little group who is a regular and highly successful "— spotter," drove to one of his favorite locations to try to get a sighting. His parents spend about six months of the year doing gem fossicking[†] out west, and have had numerous sightings, as well as a fully conscious experience of an ET Visitor in their caravan one night. The father of the family is a retired police officer, and therefore a reliable and credible observer.

It was a very dark night because of a heavy cloud cover, and we arrived about 8:00 p.m. so were the only ones present at the location, and were treated to an amazing display. A series of lights, some flashing so incredibly bright at times that we had to look away, appeared spread out over a distance of many miles in the dense bush land. We could see the lights of a town further away, but our lights were closer, where there are no houses or roads. Sometimes they blinked out then came on again, then began forming themselves into specific geometric shapes, executed to absolute perfection, moving slowly but very clearly and deliberately into position.

Nine of them started out as three triangles, spread out over many miles, then we tried communicating with them telepathically, asking for different geometric shapes, and they obliged immediately. When we asked for a square, a fourth light drifted in slowly to join the equilateral triangle to meet our request. We then asked for a rectangle, so they elongated two sides of the square. The next request was for a cross, which required a fifth light to enter the scene, and then a perfect rainbow shape was produced for our pleasure. They seemed to move slowly, but considering the distances involved must actually have been travelling reasonably fast. This went on for hours, until about 11:00 p.m. when we decided to call it a night.

It truly was an amazing and very beautiful experience, and by the way they were moving and the distances involved there was no way they could have been house or car lights. They were far too bright and spread out over too great a distance to simply be somebody in the Bush with a torch. And there were also the patterns

[†] Australian for seeking fossils in the Outback.

— perfect geometric shapes formed in answer to our telepathic requests, not once or twice, but over and over again, way beyond the realm of "sheer coincidence."

I would like to finish this account on a reassuring and positive note, to illustrate the Zetas' human-ness and also their wonderful sense of humor, and with a reminder that yes, they do dress in black, but up until a few years ago so did priests and nuns.

One day as I sat at the computer with Maris standing by to answer questions posed by members of our little ET information group, some very deep and profound ones had come up. We'd been at it for some time and the task was almost completed when we were faced with a *really* heavy question. "Oh God!" I groaned to myself. "This one's a bit of a worry!"

The whole atmosphere suddenly changed to lightness as a telepathic question popped into my mind from my companion:

> Yes, maybe, but do you know what is a real worry?

"I don't know, Maris," I answered, sensing a joke in the air. "What is a real worry?"

His answer came back quick as a flash:

> Being abducted on board an alien spaceship and finding a copy *of An Idiot's Guide to the Universe* open on the control console.

Needless to say I burst out laughing, and repeated it to myself several times so I'd remember it, at the same time having a go at him for using the terms "abducted" and "alien," neither of which the Zetas like much. Trying to be more politically correct I suggested changing it to "being taken on board an ET disc," but the answer came back: "No, leave it as it is. It sounds funnier. Besides, it's time we lightened up a bit, don't you think?"

Some Zeta Teachings

Throughout our many years of ongoing contact with the Zetas, many wonderful teachings have been received, some only a line or two in length and some up to several pages.

Oris: Some Advice

Accomplish many small tasks that become one big one.

Conquering fear is the biggest. In human life, keep things simple.

Learn to live like a peasant – frugally rather than wastefully, and to be grateful for what you have.

Help yourself while helping others.

2012 will be the end of hatred – 2013 will bring peace.

Kira is a great fan of the Harry Potter series, and she found some parallels in the story with life up on the disc with the Zetas, which she once pointed out to Oris. Not being much of a reader, she asked him if she'd been led to the Harry Potter books to help her remember her time "upstairs." He answered her through this channeled message given to me:

Oris: The Spiritual Meaning of Harry Potter

May 11, 2002.

My dear Kira,

The information you have been given through the Harry Potter books is certainly to assist your memory, both of the time you spend with us, and also of the magical creatures of other levels of reality. These are the outer teachings, but now I want you to look more deeply to the inner teachings, for these are lessons you have come here to learn in the present life.

These teachings have been brought to Earth as a way of reaching the young people of this planet – to try to teach them spiritual values as a counter to the greed, selfishness and materialism that so many down here are caught up in. These very special spiritual values of compassion, kindness, humility, honor and respect for all, are embodied in both Harry and his headmaster, Professor Dumbledore.

Here we have two of the most powerful people in the world of magic – one an old man who has fully mastered the most incredible power and knowledge, and the other a young boy who is also in possession of extraordinary gifts, even though he still does not quite realize the potential of what he has. However, what truly marks them as masters is not so much these magical powers they possess, but rather the humility, kindness and respect they show to all those around them. In fact, if you recall from the stories, it is to those "beneath" him, the young ones in his care, that Professor Dumbledore shows the most kindness and respect, rather than to those who are his equals, and Harry follows this example by always showing compassion and kindness to those weaker than himself.

This is the inner message that is meant to be understood through these books, both for you and others. The lesson you have come here to learn in the present life is that it doesn't matter how powerful, or clever, or gifted, or wealthy, or even how much magical ability you have, or how high up the Human Ladder you are as a Zeta, a human, an angel or whatever. You must always show compassion, kindness, humility and respect towards others around you. This, my dear one is true spiritual mastery.

Maris: Karma, Butterflies, and Jesus

In order to grow, learn and purify yourselves spiritually, you must return many times to the Earth plane, and other places as well, to be exposed to a variety of situations and experiences. For example, in one life you may be born to be a king or president of a country, to have the opportunity to learn to handle responsibility and power, hopefully tempered with wisdom and kindness. In the next life you may come as a beggar, to master humility and poverty. One life may bless you with great riches; another may bring pain and loss.

In one round of existence you may murder or rape a fellow human. In a subsequent life you will either find yourself the unwilling victim of such a crime, or will perhaps give your own life to save that of your former victim. Even if you think you are very clever and smart because you have gotten away with your crime and avoided the long arm of the law on Earth, there will be no escaping Karmic Law. We must all pay in the end for our sins, be they large or small. Everything must balance up in the end.

Karma may be likened to a cloak that you must put on in order to return again and again to physical life, until your tasks are completed and your lessons learned. It will then be cast aside, and you will emerge, fresh and shining, like a butterfly casting aside its protective but confining cocoon and emerging in all its true color and beauty.

Strong karmic ties connecting you to your past lives and also to others you have shared those lives with, are like anchors holding you down to the physical plane. At first this anchoring down is very necessary, because you must remain upon the physical plane for many lives in order to learn, grow and evolve spiritually. You must experience sensations and emotions such as pain, comfort, joy, sadness, fear and fulfillment before true understanding, compassion and wisdom can be attained. Many human emotions, particularly the negative ones, cannot be experienced in higher realms; therefore you must spend time in physical form to be able to perceive them. Unfortunately it is these negative, painful emotions that are so necessary for your growth.

As a soul nears the end of its physical lives, the karmic ties begin to unravel and the anchor is gradually pulled free. The vibrational frequency of the entity becomes increasingly higher and more refined, as the need and desire to return to the physical plane decreases. The last life of a soul upon the physical plane is often very hard, because all remaining karma must be resolved and balanced. All the outstanding debts must be paid, as they cannot be carried over to the higher planes for which the soul is now destined.

If a highly evolved soul wishes voluntarily to descend to the physical plane to carry out work as a guide or teacher, then that soul must take on some karmic ties in order to remain in physical form until their work is completed, otherwise their presence would not be possible. They must place a karmic cloak upon their shoulders. Often they will take some of the karmic burden off the shoulders of other less-evolved souls and place it upon their own, as did the one you know on Earth as "Jesus." This is an ultimate act of love, selflessness and sacrifice.

MARIS: NON-ATTACHMENT TO THE 2012 ENERGY SHIFT

November 21, 2006.

We have sent this message to our channel to assist her with certain difficulties manifesting in her life at this time. It has occurred to us that this applies to others on Earth also, as so many of you are being tested in one way or another. As you know, your planet is fast approaching an energy shift due to take place at the end of the year 2012. The number 13 represents transformation, and so certain preparations must be made now and up until December of 2012.

The past six years have brought a number of people on your planet to crossroads in their lives. The next six years will bring an increase in this, with major decisions and the need for radical change being presented to many. Those of you who have already made a clear choice to walk in the light may very well be experiencing a sense of frustration, as change and revelation do not seem to be taking place as quickly as perhaps you would like or have anticipated. To many of you it seems that the old and outmoded values of materialism, survival of the fittest and the mighty dollar still relentlessly hold sway, causing you to despair for the fate of your poor Mother Earth and her people.

Zetas and others are helping where we can, but Planet Earth is still governed by third-dimensional time, and so we also must respect this. We who have moved beyond the concept of past, present and future do not experience impatience, and as your planet evolves to higher frequencies, you too will come to this point.

The lesson we are trying to impart to you is non-attachment. Certain scenarios both personal and on governmental levels must be allowed to play out on Earth over the next six years. We cannot change this any more than you can. Evolution in the Human Kingdom is all about choice – choosing right over wrong, positive over negative – or vice versa. You as an individual person on Earth must be given the time and space to make these choices – nobody can make them for you. This is what free will is all about. But choices must be made. You cannot "cop out" as the saying goes. The time is now.

All of you are facing challenges on multi-levels, and the next six years will determine whether you sink or swim. Those of you who are on Earth as light workers must respect the choices made by younger souls. It is up to you as older souls to practice compassionate non-attachment. This is your learning experience for now. Two negatives never do make a positive, so take great care not to be drawn in to the lower emotions and dramas being played out.

This may be difficult for you as you are forced to stand by and watch someone you love spiral downward into destruction. You may try to throw them a lifeline, but you cannot force them to grasp it – the choice is theirs and theirs alone. Put your energy into protecting yourself, so that you do not get dragged down with them.

If such a soul is blocking your path at the moment, or other difficulties are holding you back from your chosen work, simply lie low and gather your strength for the future. Those who are not prepared to walk in the light will not be permitted to interfere with your work, but for now lessons in compassion and non-attachment are being given, karma is being balanced, and the "sheep" are being separated from the "goats," as your Bible states. Time still remains, however, for these choices to be made.

Once the sorting is done, your work will begin in earnest to heal and rebuild your planet and those who dwell thereon, for those who remain will have ears to hear and hearts that are open to truth. Be patient just a little longer, and all will be well.

Soul Evolution, Chakra Balancing and Healing

May 20, 2005.

J: The following teaching was received on the same night in two parts, one half received by Helene and the other half by me. When we tried putting them together they dovetailed very neatly. They explain what soul evolution is all about, and the chakra balancing and healing that is part of the process. This is also about ET/human contact, and how human evolution has been guided and assisted throughout the ages. What follows is our integration of these teachings.

As we evolve through what the Zetas refer to as galactic levels, which are actually levels of conscious awareness, our consciousness deepens and broadens. The only way this soul evolution can happen is through breaking down the limitations and boundaries set up on the subconscious level of our mind. These limitations and boundaries are created out of fear, which is the opposite of love. Fear expresses itself through lack of trust, duality, divisiveness and limitation. Love is Oneness (with self and others), openness, trust and limitless freedom to just "be."

As we gradually break through the boundaries/limitations/barriers of fear, we begin to perceive our purpose for existence and to understand more clearly why we are here. To do this we *must* open up, broaden and deepen our consciousness. This is the only path to enlightenment. Enlightenment is *not* a measure of how intellectual we are, or even how psychic/clairvoyant we may be. It is *all* about getting to *know, love and trust self.* It is when we learn to trust our feelings, be totally honest with and love our self, and learn from our experiences, whether we perceive them as being positive *or* negative, is when our consciousness moves past the limitations of fear and opens up to the energy of love, Oneness, family and universe — in other words, God/Source.

In order to open up our consciousness in this way, we first must move through our fear barriers. Once we learn to trust and love ourselves and others, the barriers that our fear has created through *lack* of love and trust will start to dissolve, and our conscious awareness will then become wider, stronger and deeper. This is what soul evolution is all about.

The reason we fear is that we lack understanding about self and others around us, but before we can begin to understand the bigger picture, we must start by understanding self. It is said in the Bible: "Man, know thy*self.*" It is God's nature to grow and expand, and since we are made of His essence (in His image), it is *our* nature as well, for we are all One — we are all energy and we are all love.

Soul and consciousness are one and the same. We are multidimensional beings, and soul consciousness has three parts:

1. *Lower physical self, which is of a lower and slower vibrational frequency. This is our body.*
2. *Higher mind self, of a higher and finer frequency. This is our mind/spirit.*
3. *Soul, of an even higher and finer frequency — of unconditional love, trust and awareness.*

Everything is created out of God (life-force) energy — plants, animals, people (including ETs) and planets. The soul is an expression of this energy, which is love. This love energy always has balance, is always moving and evolving, and is never static. Evolution is energy in motion and is a perpetual state of becoming and unfolding. The "tools" needed to give us a "smoother ride," so to speak, are awareness (opening up), trust (in yourself), and love (feelings, reactions and connection towards others as well as self).

Bearing in mind that evolution is energy in motion and is never static, it is important to understand that some belief systems can potentially hold us back and block our soul growth. These belief systems feed off our fears, and are expressed through greed, judgment, bigotry, ego, and jealousy. They create limitations and barriers to soul evolvement by "stroking our egos" and providing us with cozy comfort zones in which to hide. Thus they are very desirable, and we are tempted to stay put and not move forward. Soul evolution is *not easy,* because it is all about bringing our fears to the surface of our psyche to enable us to face up to them on the conscious level. It is only by doing this that we can ever move past them. In fact, breaking down the limitations and barriers of fear is the hardest thing that we have to do in life, but the bottom line is, this is what soul growth and evolution is all about. It is moving out of and beyond our comfort zone in order to become and unfold to greater levels of knowing, understanding and awareness. *This is what the ET contact experience is all about.*

The following words were given by Oris to be used as part of a Qi Gong breathing exercise, but even on their own they are very beautiful.

Oris: Benediction

Be one with yourselves,

Be one with your world,

Be one with your universe.

When you reach out to the universe

You receive love,

And when you share your love within the world

You shall be One.

EPILOG

The Zetas' main role here on Earth at this time is to help expand humankind's mind/awareness from level-one to level-two consciousness, where evolution is taking us as a species. A major part of this mind expansion process involves breaking down the very limited concept we have of reality; hence the answer given to Col. Philip Corso's question put to the ET: "What can you offer?"

A whole new world, if you can take it!

Evolution and spiritual growth is never easy or pleasant, for it inevitably requires a stepping out of comfort zones and venturing into the unknown. Whether the process involves crawling out of the ocean to adapt to existence on dry land, or opening your mind up from the limited and rigid "reality" of third-dimensional awareness in order to perceive higher and more expansive realities, it is all simply part of our ongoing evolution as humans.

Evolution in the Human Kingdom is all about breaking down barriers and expanding/opening the mind to these other greater realities. Children are born with a built-in natural tendency to do this. They are "hard-wired" for mind expansion, and do it brilliantly in their games of make-believe and imagination. Unfortunately, as children grow to adulthood, imagination becomes something to be put down and dismissed as time wasting and fanciful. Derogatory comments such as "Get real," and "It's just your imagination" gradually break down and destroy this most necessary component of human nature, to produce yet another carbon copy trapped within the limitations of a cultural, religious, scientific or family mind-set.

What many fail to realize is that imagination is the key that opens the closed door of the human mind to endless possibilities and realities. "It's all in the mind" should be an expanding rather than a limiting concept. The Bible says we must become again as little children in order to enter Heaven. If only people could grasp the fact that the "Gates of Heaven" are the doors to their own mind.

I will finish with the words of a song that has always resonated deeply within my psyche, just as it resonated with Roy Neary, the main character in Steven Spielberg's wonderful story, *Close Encounters of the Third Kind.* This song is from the Walt Disney adaptation of *Pinocchio.*

When You Wish Upon a Star

When you wish upon a star,
Makes no difference who you are,
Anything your heart desires
Will come to you.

If your heart is in your dream
No request is too extreme,
When you wish upon a star
As dreamers do.

Like a bolt out of the blue,
Fate steps in and sees you through,
When you wish upon a star
Your dreams come true.

Author Biographies

Judy Carroll was born in Queensland, Australia in 1952 into a Creole, English and Romany (Gypsy) family background. After school she pursued a career as a professional flamenco dancer, following in the footsteps of her grandmother. She feels strongly that this cultural background has helped her to assimilate her ET encounters into her daily life.

Carroll's lifelong encounters have always been with the off-planet visitors known as the Greys, or Zetas, which has given her deep insight into the field of ET/Human contact. At age 30 she had a fully conscious daytime encounter in which she recognized the visitors as "family." In 1995, during an encounter at a sacred site in England, the visitors asked her to start writing books about contact from the extraterrestrial perspective.

In 2000 she "coincidentally" met Helene Kaye and was a vital part in helping her family through their ET contact experiences. Through their joint efforts they co-authored their non-fiction book, *The Zeta Message*.

Carroll completed three levels of Reiki and spent several years as a practitioner before completing the master level, which qualified her to teach. She also teaches classes in Tai Chi and Qi Gong.

Helene Kaye was born in Brisbane, Australia. She attended business college, and after saving enough money, she went on a six-month trip to Europe, ending with a camping trip in Scandinavia, where she met her future husband, who was also from Brisbane — one of many coincidences that would occur in Helene's life. Kaye had two children and chose to be a stay-at-home mom. In 1996, when both children began suffering from asthma, she learned Reiki and achieved master level in 2001. Not being into "New Age stuff" initially, Kaye proceeded in learning levels I and II of Brain Gym, studied Feng Shui, and completed a course in Australian bush flower essences.

In 1999 Kaye and her husband started a business designing and manufacturing camper trailers. During this time her whole family began experiencing strange happenings in their home. They were well aware that at best doctors and psychologists would think they had great imaginations and at worst they would think they were all crazy, so they just hoped it would all eventually stop. However, it got worse after the rest of the family was attuned to Reiki I. They were finally led to Judy Carroll, when their whole life took a new turn and proceeded down a very interesting path.

After selling their business in 2005, Kaye became a practitioner and teacher of Reiki. She and Carroll teach seminars and do joint conferences to help others in similar experiences move forward from a place of fear, and into Oneness. The diary she kept during the height of her children's contact is a model for any mother, whether their children are experiencing visitations from ETs or just going through some difficult sleep patterns. Her techniques are perfect for allowing a child to work through their fears and/or inner terrors without losing their imagination or self-empowerment.

Notes on the Companion Volume

Human by Day, Zeta by Night is a reflection of *The Zeta Message*, but told in a semi-fictional story format to enable readers to step inside the Zeta mind. It provides a "virtual reality" experience of what it's like to actually "be a Zeta", and is the story of an ET by the name of Alarca (which is my Zeta name), who meets her untimely death in a crashed disc. As a result of this she decides to return to Earth to complete her mission, but reincarnated as an Earth human known as Ali to her family and friends.

At first Ali has only a very vague recall of her true identity, but this all changes on the night of her thirteenth birthday when a tall, black-clad Zeta Elder appears in her room. With the restoration of her soul consciousness, from that point on she must learn to lead a double life, as an Earth human by day, then at night as her human body sleeps, she boards the disc to carry out her Zeta work.

The description of Alarca's awakening process is taken directly from both my own and Kira's experiences in our early teens, as well as from the periodic upgrades I've undergone over many years as described in *The Zeta Message*. *Human by Day, Zeta by Night* approaches the subject of human/ET contact solely from the ET perspective, giving them a chance to tell their side of the story, which has never before been explained in such depth and detail. It is autobiographical and therefore based totally on fact and very real experiences, but I have made use of the traditional Romany art of storytelling, as taught to me by my much-loved mentor Kate, who, along with another respected Romany elder/teacher, is the model for the old Gypsy woman Mara in the story.

Paco, Mara's grandson who grows up to become a priest, is a combination of several people including my own brother, as well as the priest friend from the past life who went by that name, and also a very close family friend from the present life who was a spiritual brother to me during my childhood and who is now a priest. I've introduced a priest character into the story line because human/ET contact is primarily a spiritual experience. It is about the awakening of human consciousness to a higher and more expanded level of awareness, which is a natural part of our evolution as a human-type species. At the same time, it is so much more than the purely physical process of evolution as recognized by science. It is evolution of mind and spirit, with the whole process being governed by soul, making it an intrinsic part of spiritual growth. Introducing a priest into the story enables this aspect to be emphasized and given the importance it deserves. Many parallels are drawn between Earth human and ET spirituality, and the reality behind human beliefs and concepts such as God, Heaven, Hell, angels, soul, etc. is explained. All the Zeta teachings conveyed throughout the story deal with this deeper spiritual aspect.

As told in *The Zeta Message*, I grew up surrounded by the Spanish Gypsy culture, just as Ali does in *Human by Day, Zeta by Night*. Like me she too takes up dancing as a career, but after connecting back to her Zeta family, is encouraged to study natural healing techniques such as Tai Chi and Reiki, both of which she eventually teaches. This path enables her to work with Earth humans on a physical level, to provide them with a means of balancing and harmonizing themselves on an energy level, in order to assist in their process of accessing deeper levels of conscious soul awareness.

Ali also receives teachings on the ancient Lemurian culture from Mara, as I was given teachings from a Romany Elder who

could recall a life lived back then. Her feline friend Greypuss was a much-loved part of my own childhood. She of course is now reincarnated as the cat Woody referred to in this book, who sleeps curled on the end on my bed as I write these words. At 19 no doubt she will soon return again "to her own dear people in the Sirius System", to borrow a comment from Ali's Greypuss, but of course we'll continue to meet "upstairs" on the disc.

Alarca's Zeta friend Ashka, known as Kaz in her Earth human form, is Helene. In the story, Kaz, Paco and Ali join forces to provide assistance for a family going through seemingly frightening contact experiences which parallel Helene's real-life family's experiences. The mother of the family, Maddie, and her daughter

Kate, are modeled on Helene and Kira, with their emotional issues and questions paralleling those which came up for Helene's family during the early days of their full-on contact. Kaz, like Helene, is the mother of two "star children," and therefore she is fully empathic with the situation in which Maddie and her daughter find themselves.

An instruction given to me by the Zeta family on writing the fiction book was to "keep it light," and also to "please show the Earth people that we do have a sense of humor!" Sense of humor is understood by all sentient beings throughout the universe, and is an important yardstick by which true spirituality is measured, not just here on Earth but in all ET cultures as well. The instruction of "needing to become again as a little child in order to enter the Kingdom of Heaven" is universal. All spiritually evolved beings and cultures are blessed with a highly developed sense of lightness and fun.

Such beings are never pompous — they have the ability to laugh at themselves, and do *not* take life too seriously. After all, in the greater reality, all the temporary "roles" we play in the course of a physical life such as race, creed, political persuasion, skin color and language are nothing more than illusions that will pass away at the end of that life. They are there to provide us with a variety of learning experiences, but at the same time we should not allow ourselves to get too caught up, weighed down and serious about such matters. After all, none of these things are *us*, for in reality we are pure spiritual essence, without race, creed or color.

This clearer understanding of true reality automatically endows a soul with a sense of lightness and fun. This is a natural part of spiritual growth, and occurs as a direct result of opening up to deeper and more profound levels of one's own being. This in fact is an important component of what the Zetas are about, but it is an aspect that not too many down here have picked up on, hence their request for it to be conveyed through my writing.

The vehicle of storytelling has enabled me to bring a lifetime of varied experiences, understanding and knowledge together in a more coherent and condensed way for ease of reading. It has also been a way to convey concepts that otherwise would lose much in the translation from Zeta to Earth human reality.

Most problems that arise in inter-cultural relations are born out of ignorance and lack of understanding. My books are an attempt by the Zetas to overcome this barrier. They are a means of offering a hand of friendship and reassurance — that they do understand, they do not mean harm, and they are *not* the "alien monsters and invaders' that some down here have painted them. In fact, when you read *Human by Day, Zeta by Night* you will come to understand just how necessary their presence is on Earth, and the vast amount of help they are offering to counteract a very real Force of Negativity the like of which most Earth humans are blissfully unaware.

Ever since starting to access other researcher's material on the ET visitors, I've never felt comfortable with the term "Zetas." I've used it myself and continue to use it for convenience, and admittedly a few of them may have had physical lives in that particular star system, but it is not what they are. They are not physical beings from any physical planet in the universe. This is the reason why at times I use the term "Greys," but even this is not accurate, for it tends to conjure up a negative, racist image in the minds of some humans. Perhaps "Guardians" would be a better name to use, for their role in this universe is that of Guardians or Caretakers of Energy, this being creative life-force energy of which they have an incredibly profound understanding.

It is the Guardians' job to restore this lost heritage to humanity — to re-awaken the God Within through any means possible. The ways they are doing this, the reasons why and the myriad difficulties and blocks they come up against in their mission is told in great detail and under the guise of "fiction" by the Guardian Alarca and her friends in *Human by Day, Zeta By Night.*

INDEX

Human by Day, Zeta by Night
A Dramatic Account of Greys Incarnating as Humans

By Judy Carroll

ISBN 978-0-926524-71-2

Wild Flower Press, an imprint of
Granite Publishing, L.L.C. POB 1429
Columbus, NC 28722
828-894-8444

http://www.GranitePublishing.us
http://Granite-Planet.net
http://NotMadeByHands.com
http://www.TheZetaMessage.com
http://www.UFOGreyInfo.com

The not-to-be-missed companion volume to
The Zeta Message: Connecting All Beings in Oneness

Made in the USA
Coppell, TX
01 August 2020

32245721R00174